ECHOES OF THE PAST

German and European Studies

General Editor: James Retallack

DOUGLAS CARLTON MCKNIGHT

Echoes of the Past

Carinthian Slovene Memories
of the Second World War

UNIVERSITY OF TORONTO PRESS
Toronto Buffalo London

© University of Toronto Press 2026
Toronto Buffalo London
utppublishing.com
Printed in the USA

ISBN 978-1-4875-6504-6 (cloth)   ISBN 978-1-4875-6506-0 (EPUB)
                                   ISBN 978-1-4875-6505-3 (UPDF)

Library and Archives Canada Cataloguing in Publication

Title: Echoes of the past : Carinthian Slovene memories of the Second World War /
    Douglas McKnight.
Other titles: Carinthian Slovene memories of the Second World War
Names: McKnight, Douglas, author
Series: German and European studies ; 60.
Description: Series statement: German and European studies ; 60 |
    Includes bibliographical references and index.
Identifiers: Canadiana (print) 2025030726X | Canadiana (ebook) 20250307316 |
    ISBN 9781487565046 (cloth) | ISBN 9781487565053 (PDF) |
    ISBN 9781487565060 (EPUB)
Subjects: LCSH: World War, 1939-1945—Austria—Carinthia. | LCSH: Slovenes—
    Austria—Carinthia. | LCSH: Memory—Social aspects—Austria—Carinthia. |
    LCSH: Memorialization—Austria—Carinthia. | LCSH: Collective memory—
    Austria—Carinthia.
Classification: LCC DB299 .M45 2026 | DDC 943.6/60522—dc23

Cover design: Alexa Love
Cover image: Monument to the International Struggle against Fascism. Author's photograph.

The manufacturer's authorised representative in the EU for product safety is Mare
Nostrum Group B.V., Mauritskade 21D, 1091 GC Amsterdam, The Netherlands. Email:
gpsr@mare-nostrum.co.uk

The German and European Studies series is funded by the DAAD with funds from the
German Federal Foreign Office.

We wish to acknowledge the land on which the University of Toronto Press
operates. This land is the traditional territory of the Wendat, the Anishnaabeg, the
Haudenosaunee, the Métis, and the Mississaugas of the Credit First Nation.

University of Toronto Press acknowledges the financial support of the Government of
Canada, the Canada Council for the Arts, and the Ontario Arts Council, an agency of
the Government of Ontario, for its publishing activities.

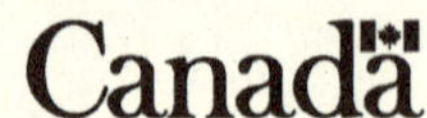

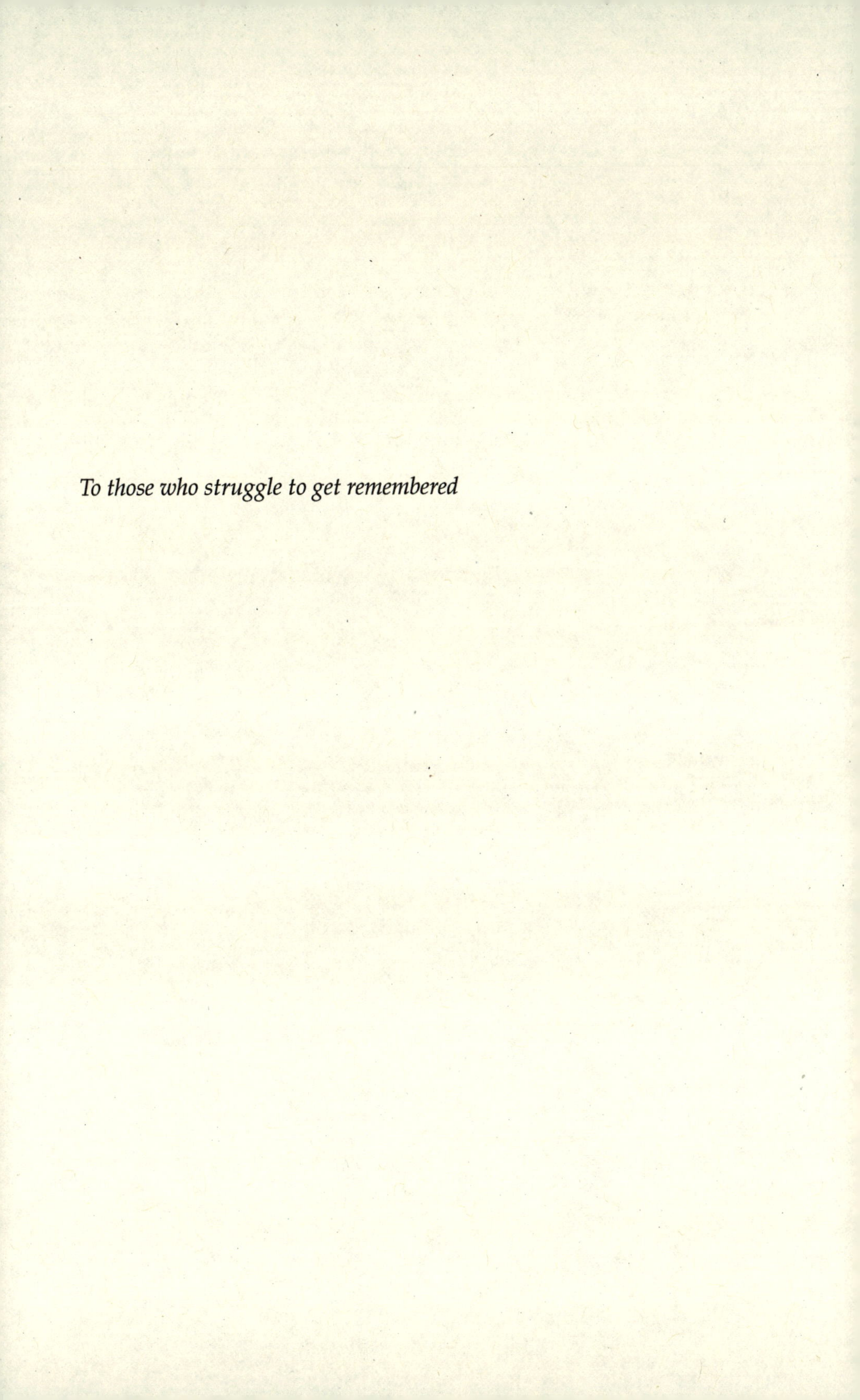

To those who struggle to get remembered

Contents

Figures

Acknowledgments

This book, the basis of which formed my dissertation at Georgetown University, is the result of over five years of research and writing. Katrin Sieg, my academic mentor and PhD advisor, spent countless hours reading chapter manuscripts and helping me fine-tine my argument. From introducing me to the field of memory studies almost a decade ago to advising my master's project, my dissertation, and now a book, she has had a tremendous positive influence on my ability to think like a scholar.

Multiple institutions provided funding for this project. At the beginning of my research, a grant from the Mandel Centre for Advanced Holocaust Studies at the United States Holocaust Museum (Washington, D.C.) provided me the time required to delve into the topic in the summer of 2018. Generous funding from Fulbright Austria and the Austrian Federal Ministry of Education, Science and Research let me conduct the necessary fieldwork in Austria for this back in 2019–20.

I want to also express my gratitude to Valentin Sima for guidance during my time in Austria, particularly in Klagenfurt/Celovec. I want to thank Andrej Mohar, Gudrun Blohberger, Hans Haider, Alexandra Schmidt, and Zdravko Haderlap for taking the time to participate in interviews with me.

I want to express my deepest thanks to my parents, Beverly and Leo McKnight. Ever since I was a child, they supported my interests in history and literature. When I wanted to study history and German in college, they never once questioned this. Without your support, the work that went into this book would never have been possible

This project has followed me through a large chunk of my life, and I would never have been able to finish it without my wife, Edvina. Her critical eye, willingness to accompany me to the places described throughout the book, and her much-needed support and patience during the rewriting process after our son was born helped me finish this project. One day, I hope my son, Edwin, will enjoy reading it.

A very special thank-you is in order to the three anonymous reviewers who helped make this book what it is today, as well as Stephen Shapiro, my editor from the University of Toronto Press. Without his guidance, this book would never have made it across the finish line.

ECHOES OF THE PAST

Introduction

On 14 and 15 April 1942, German police went door to door in southern Carinthia, the southernmost region of the ever-expanding German Reich. Lists were distributed, families were woken, and individuals were arrested. Katja Sturm-Schnabl remembers armed soldiers entering her home in the early hours of that morning, yelling orders in every direction and forcing her family outside. As the family was led up the street, her aunt began to cry, and her mother's face glazed over. Katja, who was only six years old at the time, looked up at her father, unable to recognize him. His face, usually a reflection of the seriousness with which he ran the household, had changed. It had turned grey, which gave her an apocalyptic feeling for what was coming next.

By foot, the soldiers led them from their farm through the village to a bus two kilometres away. Forced onto a bus, they were then taken to a collection camp in Ebenthal/Žrelec, a town just outside of Klagenfurt/Celovec, the capital of Carinthia. The camp was filled with people from southern Carinthia, including her 84-year-old grandmother and eight-month-old cousin, both of whom were lying on a pile of straw in a barracks. Her grandmother, once a happy, lively woman, had broken down. "Nemci nas nekam vlečej," she said. "The Germans are taking us away." The next day, Katja and her family were brought to the train station and packed into cattle cars. Day after day, night after night, they sat in complete darkness as the train rattled on before it arrived in a town outside of Stettin, Poland. No food, no water, no heat. From Stettin, they were taken to a camp in Rehnitz and from Rehnitz to Eichstätt in Bavaria.

In Eichstätt, her mother was forced to work at a factory for shoes, her father toiled at one for beer. The adults, so filled with fear, helplessness, and confusion, almost disappeared from her world. In such a place, Katja remembers, parents could not raise their children. Completely disoriented from the life around them – ripped from their homes, packed into trains, sent to various camps, forced to work – her parents turned inwards. Discipline came from the children themselves. They learned the rules of camp life from the brutal yelling and screaming of their German guards. Although left in the dark as to what her future held, Katja, even as a child, understood what was happening around her. She knew what the word *Ravensbrück* meant, and she knew what it meant when the camp commander yelled that he would gas them all. Sickness soon swept the camp. A friend of hers, Zvonko, soon died. Veronika, her eight-year-old sister who had protected her from a German guard when they had been separated from their parents, died as well.

But there was also good news in the camp, and it travelled at lightning speeds. Listening in, she overheard the adults speak of the war in Yugoslavia and partisans, of German defeats and US bombing raids. For Katja, Tito, the leader of the Yugoslav partisans, became a hero from a fairy tale, a mythical figure that knew exactly where she was and was on his way to save her. Through the eyes of a child, the US bombing raids that targeted cities near the camp were nothing to fear because how could one of these bombs land near a child that was not supposed to be there in the first place?[1]

By the summer of 1942, the Slovene Liberation Front (Osvobodilna fronta slovenskega naroda; OF) began sending partisans across the Karawank mountain range from Axis-occupied Yugoslavia into southern Carinthia. The OF was the main Slovene antifascist political and resistance organization, founded in the spring of 1941 in Ljubljana, Slovenia, as a response to the Axis invasion of Yugoslavia. It found widespread support among the Slovene-speaking community in Carinthia. In early 1943, almost a year after Katja had been deported and the first partisans had entered the region, Lipej Kolenik awoke to the sound of knocking on his bedroom window. The voice from outside startled him: "Wake up, the partisans are here. We are the Slovene army." At this point, Lipej remembers, he had not yet seen a "partisan," he had only heard of them from the Germans, who had made clear that anyone caught helping the "criminals" would be executed. Although everyone was scared, his mother, alone at home with her two boys, let the partisans, who had a female commander, inside. The night was filled with food and song, and Lipej's fear soon dissipated. The next morning, he brought their breakfast to them in the forest. From that point on, the partisans visited the various houses in the area nightly, and it was decided that when Lipej received his conscription orders for the Wehrmacht, he would join the partisans beforehand.

But by August 1943, the situation on the ground had shifted. The partisan groups in his area had been destroyed. He was soon conscripted by the Wehrmacht and went to Klagenfurt/Celovec with the idea of getting basic weapons training before he would then desert. Before he knew it, however, he had been shipped to the Italian front, wounded, and sent back to Klagenfurt/Celovec to recover. Once back in Carinthia, he deserted and joined the partisans. Terrible food. Cold and wet winters. Snow and ice-filled mountains. No medicine for the wounded. Hiding from the Germans, ambushing the Germans, and hiding from them again. That was the life of the partisan, a life that around 1,000 Carinthian Slovenes lived between 1942 and 1945.[2]

One night, he and six others went to visit a farmer who was known to help the partisans. Unbeknownst to them, the Germans had surrounded the house beforehand. Upon leaving, Lipej heard something in the distance, and then the Germans opened fire. Unable to shoot back since they knew if they did, the Germans would completely destroy the house and farm, Lipej's group ran in every direction looking for cover. One of them was severely wounded, shot seven times in the legs, but managed to crawl down a ridge, evade capture through the night, and survive until a woman and her daughter found him and saved him. For Lipej, the fear of being wounded was constant. With no medicine and limited options for doctors or hospitals, the partisans had to rely on themselves and the support of locals, which is what happened when he was wounded in the leg in February 1944 on a patrol outside of Dravograd, Slovenia. With the help of a woman who brought food and milk, he slowly recovered over the course of a month and survived the war.[3]

Born in the south of the Austrian province of Carinthia in the years between the World Wars, Katja and Lipej were thrust into a world of violence and brutality that swept through Europe in the 1930s and 1940s. As Carinthian Slovenes – as members of a Slovene-speaking minority who had lived in this region of Austria for almost a millennium – they were targets of Nazi racial policy. Unlike the more than 500 Carinthian Slovenes who were killed by the Nazis in various ways up until 1945, both Katja and Lipej managed to survive the war.[4] But it affected them for the rest of their lives. Because he could not have his leg operated on until after the war ended six months after he had been wounded, Lipej struggled to walk and could barely move his foot. Katja, like other survivors, carried the camp with her through the rest of her life and was unable to enter a government office or speak to someone in uniform without breaking down emotionally.

In the years following the war, stories like Katja's and Lipej's were largely ignored in Austria outside of the Slovene-speaking communities of southern Carinthia.[5] While numerous firsthand accounts of persecution, deportation, and resistance were published in various regional Slovene-language newspapers and magazines immediately after the war – which is a topic I explore in more detail in chapter 4 – it was not until 1979 that the first German-language history of the partisan war in southern Carinthia was published.[6] Since then, aside from a handful of historians whose work I rely on extensively in this book, these events have received marginal attention from scholars interested in resistance during the Second World War.[7] Those historians who have written about the Slovene-led resistance inside Carinthia consider it to be the most effective resistance to have been put up against the Nazis from within the Reich, which makes this gap in the field surprising.[8] When Katja's and Lipej's stories are put in the context of how the National Socialist era, the Second World War, and the Holocaust has been officially remembered in Austria since 1945, however, this gap is perhaps less surprising.

The "victim myth" (Opfermythos), or the idea that Austria had actually been a victim of aggressive German policy and not an active participant in the Nazi project, dominated post-war Austrian politics and society.[9] March 1938, when the Germans entered Austria in what became known as the "Anschluss" (annexation), was cast as a violent incursion. The years between 1938 and 1945 were repackaged through government policies and cultural productions as seven years of a German-imported dictatorship, with Austrians either heroically resisting Nazi tyranny or dramatically falling victim to it.[10] Although the victim myth had its origins in the 1943 Moscow Declaration, a document that outlined Allied policy goals for the post-war period and referred to Austria as the first free country to fall to Nazi aggression, Austrian politicians immediately incorporated the language of victimhood into Austria's formal Declaration of Independence from Germany on 27 April 1945.[11] In August 1945, just three months after the Nazis had surrendered, Leopold Figl, Austria's first post-war chancellor, painted an early picture of how the Austrian government would approach its recent past:

> For seven years, the Austrian people languished under Hitler's barbarism. For seven years, the Austrian people were subjugated and oppressed. No free word of opinion, no confession of an idea was possible. Brutal terror and violence forced the people to blind servitude.[12]

In Austria's first post-war parliamentary elections held at the end of 1945, a Grand Coalition was formed, and the victim myth became the "foundation stone for independent Austrian statehood"[13] that all political parties cultivated during the Allied occupation period (1945–55). It became the "principal pillar" of Austria's identity over the ensuing decades.[14] From 1955 until the mid-1980s, the victim myth was not only remarkably stable in the official realm, but it also successfully marginalized competing narratives of Austria's role in the Second World War.[15]

Almost 80 years after the collapse of the Third Reich, this interpretation of Austria's role in the Second World War – one of "the most imaginative constructions of the past in the twentieth century" as Alon Confino describes it – is no longer considered a tenable political or academic position.[16] Over the last three decades, a broad, interdisciplinary and international consensus has developed,[17] which, while acknowledging that Austria was indeed invaded by Nazi Germany on 12 March 1938 firmly asserts that the Austrian post-war emphasis on victimhood let scholars overlook Austrian mass support for the Anschluss, the absence of an Austrian-wide resistance movement, and the "overrepresentation of Austrians among SS officers and death camp personnel."[18] Indeed, as Matti Bunzl concludes, "the majority of the Austrian population never perceived the National Socialist state as a foreign regime and that the end of war was seen predominantly as a defeat rather than liberation from a foreign yoke."[19]

For a country that was long hostile to acknowledging its active role in National Socialism, however, much has changed in Austria since the late 1980s, the decade in which the victim myth began to crack under both international and domestic pressure. Since the Waldheim Affair – the international controversy that erupted in 1986 when it was revealed that the then-Austrian presidential candidate Kurt Waldheim had served as an intelligence officer for the Wehrmacht in the Balkans during the Second World War – there has been a significant shift in how Austria engages with its National Socialist past and how it commemorates victims from that era.[20] Since chancellor Franz Vranitzky's speech to the Austrian parliament in 1991, in which he officially acknowledged Austria's role in the war, a whole host of policies have been enacted aimed at reconciliation and restitution, including the establishment of the National Fund of the Republic of Austria for the Victims of National Socialism in 1995, the Historical Commission in 1998, and, more recently, the easing of the process for the descendants of those who fled Austria to become naturalized Austrian citizens.[21] Since 2000, there has even been a prominent memorial to the Austrian Jews murdered in the Holocaust on Vienna's historic Jewish Square, and the Stones of Memory organization has laid "stumbling stone" memorials throughout Vienna since 2005 with the support of the city government.[22]

But however much has changed over the last few decades regarding Austria's official stance towards remembering the Second World War and the Holocaust at the national political level and in its cosmopolitan capital of Vienna, the memory of Carinthian Slovene persecution and resistance – the stories of those like Katja and Lipej – has still not been incorporated into Austria's official memory culture, particularly its variant that is found in the state of Carinthia. Here, in the south of Austria, both of these phenomena have been recast to marginalize Carinthian Slovenes' role in defeating Nazism, downplay Carinthians' active participation in the Nazi project, deflect Carinthian Slovene postwar claims for redress and justice, disregard the rights that are guaranteed to the Carinthian Slovenes by the 1955 Austrian State Treaty, and absolve the Austrian government of particular duties explicitly defined in that same treaty such as caring for graves of Allied soldiers and promoting the use of the Slovene language (Figure 0.1).[23] Far from including memories of persecution and resistance, Carinthia's official memory culture has long marginalized them. Travelling through Klagenfurt/Celovec, Bleiburg/Pliberk, or Völkermarkt/Velikovec, the economic and population centres of southern Carinthia (Figure 0.2), you are hard-pressed to see symbolic traces of Slovene resistance and persecution from the war. It is not until you leave these towns and head farther south towards the villages near the Austrian–Slovenian border that you notice a shift. Here, in the ravines and steep gorges of the Karawank mountains, where Slovene-language signs become as prevalent as German ones, these twin historical experiences occupy a central space in the local commemorative culture.

This specific Carinthian Slovene commemorative culture is the main theme of this book, in which I explore Carinthian Slovene twenty-first century efforts to create a "vernacular" memory culture of the Second World War that is at odds with its "official" counterpart in Carinthia.[24] Although I began this book with the stories of Katja and Lipej – two stories from a larger oral history project that collected the stories of Carinthian Slovenes from the National Socialist era and was initiated by the Documentation Centre of the Austrian Resistance – and I rely on historical scholarship throughout, mine is not a work of history. I am not attempting to place the Carinthian Slovene resistance from the Second World War or the Nazi's racial policies against the Carinthian Slovenes into a larger historiographical context, nor am I trying to add a new historical perspective to these phenomena. Rather, I am analysing memory practices in the early twenty-first century to investigate what happens to a minority's vernacular memory culture when it is in an unsupportive official memory environment, two terms that will be described in

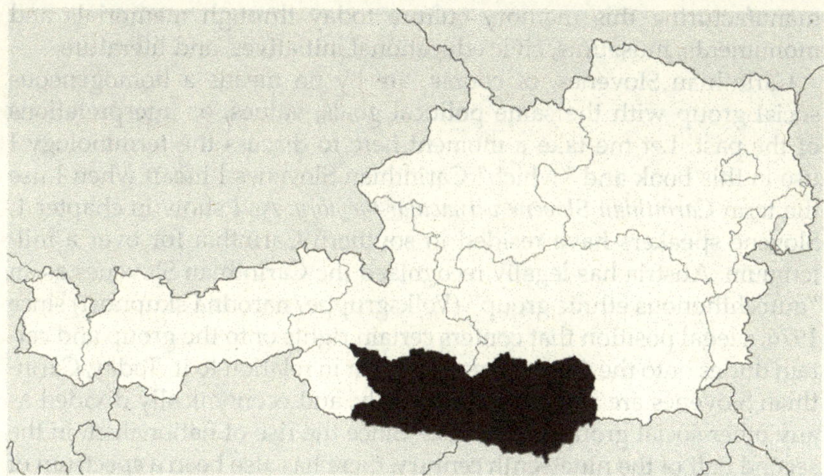

Figure 0.1: A map of present-day Austria, with the province of Carinthia shaded. Adapted from "Kärnten in Austria" by TUBS. Used under CC BY-SA 3.0 license via Wikimedia Commons.

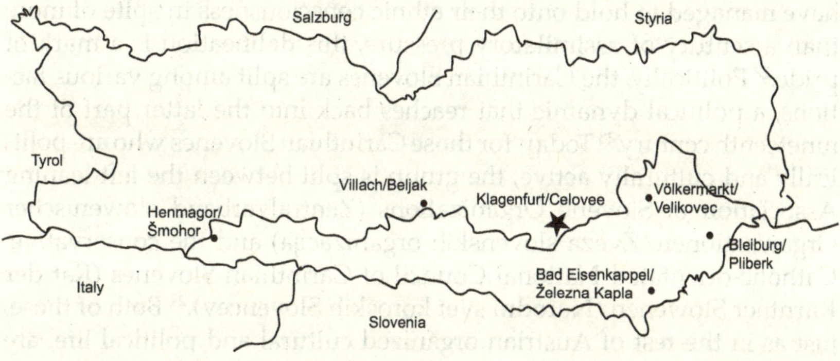

Figure 0.2: A map of the Austrian province of Carinthia. The region known as "southern Carinthia" is considered the region in the lower part of the state.

more detail in chapter 1. When a small group wants to commemorate a past that the official political environment would rather not emphasize in public, how does this group navigate the commemorative terrain available to them? What commemorative strategies are at its disposal? From artists and memory entrepreneurs to writers and museum curators, I investigate how Carinthian Slovenes and their supporters are manufacturing this memory culture today through memorials and monuments, museums, civic educational initiatives, and literature.

Carinthian Slovenes, of course, are by no means a homogeneous social group with the same political goals, values, or interpretations of the past. Let me take a moment here to discuss the terminology I use in this book and "which" Carinthian Slovenes I mean when I use the term *Carinthian Slovene vernacular memory*. As I show in chapter 1, Slovene speakers have resided in southern Carinthia for over a millennium. Austria has legally recognized the Carinthian Slovenes as an "autochthonous ethnic group" (Volksgruppe/narodna skupnost) since 1976, a legal position that confers certain rights onto the group and certain duties onto the Austrian government in relation to it. Today, Carinthian Slovenes are as politically, socially, and economically divided as any other social group in Austria.[25] Since the rise of nationalism in the second half of the nineteenth century, there has also been a spectrum of Slovene identity in Carinthia that ranges from politically active "conscious Slovenes" (bewusste Slowenen/zavedni Slovenci) to those who have actively assimilated, some more willingly than others, into the German-speaking culture of the region and are considered "German Carinthians" (Deutschkärntner).[26] For those Carinthian Slovenes who have managed to hold onto their ethnic consciousness in spite of more than a century of assimilatory pressure, this delineation is a mark of pride.[27] Politically, the Carinthian Slovenes are split among various factions, a political dynamic that reaches back into the latter part of the nineteenth century.[28] Today, for those Carinthian Slovenes who are politically and culturally active, the group is split between the left-leaning Association of Slovene Organizations (Zentralverband slowenischer Organisationen/Zveza slovenskih organizacija) and the conservative, Catholic-orientated National Council of Carinthian Slovenes (Rat der Kärntner Slowenen/Narodni svet koroških Slovencev).[29] Both of these, just as in the rest of Austrian organized cultural and political life, are umbrella organizations with several smaller affiliated organizations within it.[30] This split became more pronounced in the post-war period in light of the former's consisting of former partisan resistance fighters (and their descendants) and the latter's containing many Slovene Catholic emigres who left communist Yugoslavia at the end of the war.[31] Particular media of the Carinthian Slovene vernacular memory I explore in this book – for example, the memorials that I examine in chapter 2 – are held in higher esteem by certain factions more than other ones, while other media – for instance, the memory literature that I analyse in chapter 4 – cross these political boundaries more easily. But the persecution and resistance of Carinthian Slovenes during the Second World War is a key component of Carinthian Slovene narratives of the past regardless of political orientation.[32] Moreover, since having been victims of National Socialism is a prominent way Carinthian Slovenes distinguish themselves from the majority culture in Austria and is still a core aspect of Carinthian Slovene identity in the twenty-first century, bundling these differences under "Carinthian Slovene vernacular memory" is appropriate for this study.[33]

I remember my first encounter with this commemorative culture. After two years of graduate school, I moved to Carinthia to teach English in a small town outside of Klagenfurt/Celovec. One day, I came across what someone told me was a "partisan memorial." Confused, I looked closely at the memorial, not much more than a large stone slab with an inscription on it. Carved into the stone in two languages – German and what I soon found out was Slovene – was a simple and direct message: "Here rest partisans who fell in the struggle against fascism, 1941–1945." As someone who had always been interested in the Second World War, I was surprised that I could not connect the context of the memorial to any historical event or university seminar. I had heard of the partisans from the Second World War. But I had not heard of them being in Austria.

A few weeks later, I was walking around the town's small bookstore. Going through some of the aisles, I made it to the Austrian literature section and picked up Maja Haderlap's novel, *Angel of Oblivion*. Published as *Engel des Vergessens* in German in 2011, the novel tells the story – part fiction, part autobiography – of the deportations and the partisan resistance through the eyes of a female narrator coming of age in post-war Carinthia. Haderlap, who had already made a name for herself in the Slovene literary scene as a lyricist, had a breakthrough in the German literary world with the novel, which, at least for a few years after the book was published, brought much-needed international attention to the plight of the Carinthian Slovenes during and after the war. Whether it was the fact that I was living in Carinthia while reading her novel or that I was starting to have a broader interest in the former Yugoslavia after having met my wife, *Angel of Oblivion* had a lasting impact on me. The novel, with its beautifully crafted, rhythmic sentences about war and remembrance, spurred my interest in literature and memory, an interest that would go on to form the core of this book.

Having written the introduction to this book, I cannot help but reflect on all the chance encounters I had with this history for me to get to this point. Ignorant of the people, the history, and the language, I never expected to write a book on this topic as my original interests when I started graduate school had much more to do with German and Soviet entanglements in the early post-war period than anything with Austria. Much like the "stumbling stone" memorials that you find in Germany and Austria – the small, golden square cobbles that tell the unsuspecting person who "stumbles" over them who lived in the building they are next to before having been deported to a concentration camp – I, too, stumbled my way into what, for the most part, had been a local commemorative culture, ignored or inaccessible to those from outside of southern Carinthia. And once I stumbled into it, leaving was difficult.

Book Outline

The structure of this book, as well as the mediums that I chose to explore, reflect the story of memory I want to tell. Because memory and history are interconnected – history, the scientific attempt to reconstruct the past, however imperfectly, through primary sources, sets the framework for how certain events are then remembered in the present – chapter 1 sets the scene for the rest of the book by providing a historical overview of Carinthian Slovenes in Carinthia that explains the content behind both Carinthia's official memory culture as well as the Carinthian Slovene vernacular one. In this chapter, I also lay out my theoretical framework.

In chapter 2, I explore the hidden, remote Carinthian Slovene sites of memory relating to the Second World War that dot the southern Carinthian countryside and examine several monuments and memorials as well as a museum. Along with being sites that mobilize public debates and carry "key symbolic value,"[34] monuments and memorials, as public manifestations of particular interpretations of the past, help construct, support, and maintain group identities, making them particularly significant as objects of analysis for memory studies scholars.[35] Reading these let me "see" the dominant interpretation of the past within a community.[36] Another important motivation for examining these monuments and memorials is that they effectively use aesthetic choices that are largely rejected by memory studies scholars as traditional, didactic, and even authoritarian. Particularly for sites of memory dedicated to victims of National Socialism in Germany and Austria, the keywords for "good" memory work since the late 1980s have been "self-reflexive, inclusive, participatory, and critical,"[37] all of which are adjectives that you would not use to describe Carinthian Slovene monuments and memorials in southern Carinthia. Analysing these offers a different perspective on what can be considered effective memory practices in the twenty-first century. The memorials, largely built by those with first-hand experience of the war in the early post-war period, communicate a vernacular memory of Carinthian Slovene heroism and martyrdom in the face of Carinthia's official hostility to it and thus affirm communal experiences of persecution and resistance. Originally, these aesthetically simple memorials were sites of mourning for the Carinthian Slovenes. Today, these support heroic memories of the past for survivors, descendants, and certain left-wing political organizations. Although a handful of historians have examined these memorials, they have concentrated on the politics, construction, and development of the individual memorial sites, and have not explored how this unique landscape of remembrance – through its symbolism, design, and framing strategies – creates a vernacular memory that is radically at odds with its official counterpart in Carinthia.[38]

Alongside these memorials and monuments, I also examine the Peršman Museum, a key site of memory within the Carinthian Slovene community, as a place of pedagogy and space of mourning for Carinthian Slovenes. My motivation for doing so is threefold. First and foremost, it is the only museum in Austria that has an exhibition on the Carinthian Slovene resistance. Second, museums, too, support the construction of collective memories for particular groups.[39] Finally, the Peršman Museum also adopts what museum studies scholars often consider "outdated" museum exhibition techniques. But, much like the memorials and monuments that fill this chapter, the Peršman Museum does this effectively. Taken together, then, not only does my analysis in chapter 2 offer a reading of an entire landscape of remembrance; it also offers counter-examples to what is often considered "good" memory work today.

But the Peršman Museum and the surrounding monuments and memorials – the tangible places and objects of the southern Carinthian landscape of remembrance – are not static sites of memory. To uncover how they are used, I shift my lens and my methodology in chapter 3 and present the results from semi-structured, expert interviews I conducted with "memory entrepreneurs," or the creative, passionate individuals involved in the hard work of "doing" memory on a day-to-day basis.[40] Through these interviews, I examine this other side of the landscape of remembrance to explore how local activist organizations use the landscape to activate the region's heritage as a political resource for today and demonstrate the more complicated nature of these sites of memory in the twenty-first century. From telling stories and offering tours of the past, to offering seminars and organizing lectures about the present, my interviews reveal that these groups use these sites in various ways. Although these memory entrepreneurs' approaches to cultivating a vernacular memory culture diverge from one another at times, they all see Carinthia's landscape of remembrance as still being fractured by ethnic group belonging and language, a phenomenon that complicates their work and makes it ever more important.

Finally, in chapter 4, I shift my lens to literature and analyse Maja Haderlap's 2011 novel, *Angel of Oblivion*, which shows it is indeed possible for Carinthian Slovene vernacular memories of the war to make inroads into one official landscape in Austria: the literary one. While Carinthian Slovenes' literary engagement with Nazism, the deportations, and the resistance has largely been ignored in Austria, Haderlap's highly acclaimed novel marks a significant shift between the vernacular and the official. Not only did she win various awards from the Austrian state, but she was also granted significant rhetorical space in the Carinthian public sphere to address issues of language, belonging, and memory in official settings. By integrating Slovene into her predominately German-language novel and crafting a complex, multigenerational story about the legacies of persecution and resistance in the region, Haderlap offers a narrative of the past that is not based exclusively on ethnicity or language and, in her own way, complements the work of the memory entrepreneurs presented in chapter 3.

Carinthia, the Carinthian Slovenes, and Memory of the Second World War

Although the Carinthian Slovenes are one of Austria's six legally protected autochthonous ethnic groups, meaning their home has always been Carinthia, their existence in the region has been contested over the last century and a half. Although a detailed history of how the Carinthian Slovenes ended up in the region is outside the scope of this book, a Slavic-speaking community has existed in what is now called Carinthia for over 1,500 years. Slavic tribes settled various valleys of the southern part of the region as early as the second half of the sixth century. By the turn of the seventh century, the region then known as Carantania was established with its administrative area centred in the Austrian region known today as Zollfeld/Gosposvetsko polje. This political entity is considered the oldest in the Slavic-speaking world. While the borders of Carantania shifted considerably over the centuries, the territory was large, spreading out of today's Carinthia into large chunks of central Europe. Until the middle of the eighth century, when Charlemagne gained control of the territory, Carantania remained an independent political entity. Afterwards, the region became a March in the Carolingian Empire. By the late ninth century, limited documentary sources refer to this area as the Duchy of Carinthia. From 1335 until 1918, Carinthia, along with Carniola, was a hereditary land of the Habsburgs.[1]

Since Germanic-speaking Bavarians arrived in the ninth century, the region has been bilingual. But power imbalances between the two language groups have always existed. Soon after the Bavarians came onto the scene, a pattern developed: Germanic speakers tended to occupy the main roads of the region and started new urban centres, while Slavic speakers lived in the more remote mountainous areas and worked the land.[2] This arrangement led to Germanic speakers dominating the upper levels of Carinthia's social hierarchy.[3] Over the centuries, this dynamic supported a form of "natural assimilation" on the part of the Slavic speakers in the region.[4] Particularly during the modernization and industrialization process of the nineteenth century, the region became more Germanized through economic development. "This was not the result of deliberate German national ambitions," argues Tom Gullberg, "but the natural consequences of a necessary adaptation to changing social circumstances. The crescendo in Slovene mobility, both social and geographic, fostered greater contact with the German, rather than the Slovene, cultural sphere."[5] This dynamic remained largely stable and peaceful throughout the next millennium until the rise of nationalist movements in the second half of the nineteenth century.[6]

With the arrival of the First World War, this delicate balance in Carinthia came under intense pressure, and by the last months of the war, the Austro-Hungarian Monarchy was in turmoil.[7] With the looming defeat of the Central Powers in 1918, the multi-ethnic Austro-Hungarian monarchy broke apart. In October 1918 in Vienna, German parliamentarians of the Imperial Council of the monarchy created a new body, the National Assembly of German-Austria. By the end of the month, they had declared their independence from the monarchy and established an independent state under the control of the State Council. By mid-November 1918, soon after Charles I had abdicated his throne, this group of parliamentarians declared that this new state, in a move that frightened the victorious Allied Powers, was to be an integral part of the new German Republic and would be called German-Austria.[8] The Allies, however, expressly forbid the joining of Austria with Germany at the Paris Peace Conference – something that German-speaking parties across the Austrian political spectrum had been clamouring for – and a provision in the Treaty of St. Germain, signed between the Allies and the new Austrian nation-state to officially end the war, expressly forbid a union with Germany. No longer would this new Austrian state be called German-Austria. From 1919 onwards, it would be known as the Republic of Austria.[9] Meanwhile, while these negotiations were occurring in Vienna and Paris over the redrawing of the map of central Europe, other independent states emerged from the former Habsburg lands, including one on Austria's new southern border: The Kingdom of Serbs, Croats, and Slovenes (referred to as the "SHS state," an abbreviation of its official Slovene name, the Kraljevina Srbov, Hrvatov in Slovencev).

Carinthia, a major part of the Habsburg lands since the fourteenth century, was now on the front line between two new states, and both Austria and the SHS state immediately laid territorial claims to southern Carinthia at the end of the First World War. Although both countries had agreed to let the "border question" be solved during negotiations at the Paris Peace Conference, militiamen and soldiers from the SHS state made their way into the Slovene-speaking areas of Carinthia and occupied large parts of it within weeks.[10] What happened in Carinthia, of course, was by no means unique after the First World War. Such border conflicts between the successor states of the European empires that had collapsed were prevalent around Europe.[11] Much of the new Austrian state was affected by such developments. In the country's east, Burgenland, a former part of the Kingdom of Hungary before the First World War, had been granted to Austria after it by the Allies, which sparked a border war between the two new countries that was not resolved until the Sopron plebiscite of 1921 granted a chunk of the region back to Hungary.[12] In the country's west, there was a movement to have Vorarlberg join Switzerland, a movement that, while peaceful, led to almost 80 per cent of the province voting in favour of it (the Allies, however, rejected this).[13] There was also tension on Austria's new southern border due to Italy's annexation, with the support of the Allies, of South Tyrol.[14] But by the spring of 1919, only a few months after its troops had entered Austria, the SHS state had largely achieved its military goals: It occupied Klagenfurt/Celovec and was demanding territorial concessions from Austria that amounted to about one-third of the province's population (about 200,000 people).[15]

The tide soon turned, however, and local Carinthian militias' counter-offensive brought the border conflict to a draw, with both sides occupying different pockets of the province. To somehow solve this dilemma, Austria, the SHS state, and the Supreme Council of the Paris Peace Conference (the French, British, US, and Italian heads of state) agreed, as part of the Treaty of St. Germain, to hold a plebiscite in southern Carinthia to let the local inhabitants decide to which state they wanted to belong. Articles 49–51 of the treaty, which went into effect 19 September 1919, laid out the terms of the plebiscite. The first vote would be held in Zone A (the SHS state's zone of occupation). If Zone A voted to join the SHS state, then a vote would be held in Zone B (which was considered the Austrian zone). The plebiscite was successfully held the following year on 10 October 1920, and 96 per cent of eligible voters participated.[16] Although there were twice as many Slovene speakers in Zone A of the plebiscite area, 22,025 people voted to remain a part of Austria, while only 15,279 voted to join the SHS state. In other words, about 60 per cent of the population voted to join Austria, which means that about 13,000 Slovene speakers opted for Austria instead of the SHS state.[17] In Figure 1.1, a map of these plebiscite zones can be found.

Why so many Slovene speakers voted to remain an ethnic minority in German-speaking Austria instead of joining the new SHS state has been

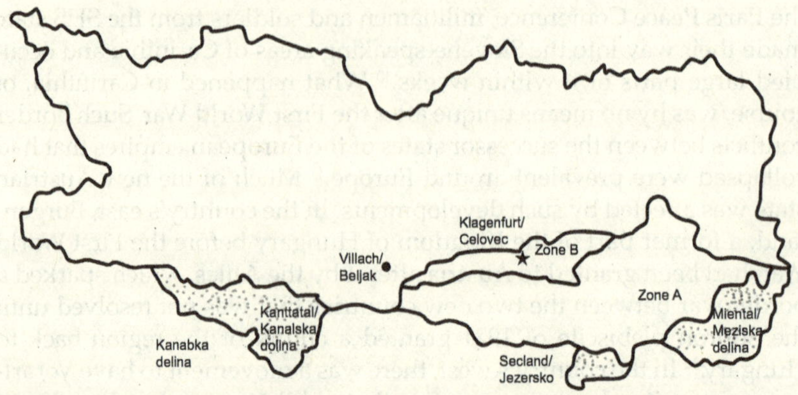

Figure 1.1: A map of the Carinthian plebiscite zones from 1920.

the subject of much scholarly debate. For one, the new kingdom, as a conservative, military monarchy, had a negative image in Carinthia, even among Slovenes.[18] Other reasons include the attractiveness of the new Austrian social welfare state (the early years of Austrian politics were dominated by social democrats), regional Carinthian patriotism, effective Austrian propaganda, and economics.[19] Those Slovenes who voted to stay in Austria "no doubt looked at the wall of the mountains towering to the south and the easy road to Klagenfurt/Celovec to the north, and pondered where they would sell their harvest in the future."[20]

In the weeks leading up to the plebiscite, Carinthia's political leadership promised the Slovenes that they would be able to retain their linguistic habits and rights in a newly unified Carinthia. But immediately after the votes were counted, Germanization of the region was given the green light. Although the Carinthian Slovenes had been under strong assimilatory pressures since at least the last third of the nineteenth century,[21] the discriminatory policies authorized in the decade after the plebiscite reached a legal level not seen before.[22] Instead of the slow, steady, economic assimilatory forces that often governed life in Carinthia in the latter half of the nineteenth and early part of the twentieth centuries, the Austrian government, hand-in-hand with German nationalist organizations in Carinthia, enacted policies that used legal measures to force assimilation of their Slovene minority. These policies influenced numerous areas of life in the state and affected financial administration, language use, and education policy.

Such issues were present throughout the new Austrian state. During the times of the Austro-Hungarian monarchy, Cisleithania – the

Austrian part of the monarchy – never had one official language. It had nine. In the later years of Habsburg rule, language policy was governed by the Austro-Hungarian Compromise of 1867, which protected minority rights in a wide range of activities, including in education.[23] At that time, German speakers were but one language group among many and were overwhelmingly outnumbered by Slavic speakers in the empire.[24] Once the first republic came into existence, however, this power dynamic shifted. German became the official language of the state while Slovene was relegated to a minority one on the country's southern periphery.[25] Of course, Slovenes – along with the rest of Austria's recognized ethnic minorities – had clear legal protections in their new state. Articles 63 and 66–69, Section V, of the Treaty of Saint-Germain laid out the obligations required of the new Austrian state regarding its minorities, including a right to be taught in a minority language. Article 149 of the 1920 Federal Constitutional Law offered similar protections.

Nonetheless, mass discrimination against Slovenes occurred in Carinthia throughout the 1920s, and these legal protections were only ever partially enacted.[26] Slovenes, particularly those who had voted to join the SHS state in the 1920 plebiscite, were denied jobs and harassed. Bilingual topographical signs were removed and the official language became German.[27] The state government had a new role as well: to teach those Slovenes who had voted to join the Kingdom of Serbs, Croats, and Slovenes how to become upstanding (German-speaking) Austrians.[28] The position of Arthur Lemisch, the provincial governor of Carinthia until 1921, perhaps best illustrates the active Germanization policies of the Austrian government towards its Slovene minority:

> We have only one generation to lead those that have been seduced back to Carinthianness [Kärntnertum]. This education process must be completed within a generation. … Home, school, and church must participate in the healing process. … Without pressure and without artifice, this Carinthian work must also be accomplished according to Carinthian custom. … The culture of the German people has made Carinthia the southern march. The culture of Central Europe, contrasted with southern hyper-culture, should and will succeed in helping Carinthia stay undivided. If school and church do their part, with German culture and Carinthian comfort [Gemütlichkeit], we want to have accomplished the work set before us in one generation.[29]

This had a major impact on the Slovenes in the region. In the immediate aftermath of the plebiscite, Slovene associations that organized cultural meetings and events were pressured into closing. Organizations, such as the Carinthian real estate brokerage company, purchased Slovene-owned farms in the area and provided funding for ethnic Germans to settle in their place, which incentivized a form of German homesteading of the region. By 1933, this had led to 196 Slovene-owned properties in the region being sold to German speakers.[30]

The Carinthian government's nationalization policies, of course, were by no means unique in the region. Similar policies were adopted throughout central and southeastern Europe after the end of the First World War. In the new SHS state, for example, German speakers who had lived in the region for centuries immediately came under immense assimilatory and exclusionary pressure there.[31] German was soon banned from public use, and German cultural associations and schools were closed, and German-speaking public servants were fired.[32] Minorities in the new Italy, including Croatians, Slovenes, and Germans, also came under intense assimilation pressure from the Italian government.[33]

But to understand why this pressure to assimilate increased so dramatically in Carinthia after the plebiscite, we have to consider how the armed conflict between Austria and the Kingdom of Serbs, Croats, and Slovenes – known in German historiography and popular memory as the Defence Struggle (Abwehrkampf) and in Slovene as the Fight for the Northern Border (Boj za severno mejo) – and the ensuing plebiscite of 1920 were remembered and interpreted in the following decade. For Germans in Carinthia, memory of the defence struggle was immediately recognized as playing a unifying role in a border province against the "Slavic threat" to the south.[34] This narrative focused on the heroism and courage of the Carinthian militia volunteers (270 of whom had lost their lives), while those Slovenes that fought for the SHS state or supported its goals were considered traitors to the new Austrian republic.[35] The plebiscite was also remembered in this fashion. The plebiscite itself was seen not just as a vote to remain an integral part of the new Austrian state but also as a vote for German culture (Deutschtum).[36] When seen in this light, then, a vote to join the Kingdom of Serbs, Croats, and Slovenes was deemed not just a vote to join a new country, but it was also a vote to be part of the Slavic cultural world. The day the plebiscite was held, 10 October, soon became the new Carinthian state holiday. Both currents – official discriminatory policies, hand in hand with popular perceptions of the defence struggle and the plebiscite – contributed to the immense pressure the Slovene minority was under in the 1920s.

Discriminatory policies continued into the 1930s. Although Carinthia had proved to be fertile ground for the early growth of Nazism in the country – the Nazis had already entered the Carinthian state parliament by 1921 – the persecution of the Slovenes did not occur immediately after Nazi Germany annexed Austria in March 1938 because the Nazis wanted to be sure of countrywide support for the annexation. In the lead-up to the referendum on the Anschluss – which occurred a month after the act itself, making what was de facto de jure – leaders of the Slovene community, including Franc Petak and Joško Tischler, not only supported the new National Socialist regime but also actively advocated for Slovenes to support the referendum for annexation. When the referendum was held in April 1938, Slovenes, in the end, supported it as ardently as any other group in Austria.[37] After the referendum was held, however, it became clear that Nazi racial policy, while not as hostile as it would be towards Austria's Jews, would nevertheless have little room for Slavs living within the new territories of the Reich. These policies, which slowly radicalized as the war progressed, can be divided into three phases.[38]

In the first phase (1938–41), policy in Carinthia was largely a continuation of the Germanization efforts that had been started in the 1920s.[39] Unlike the experience of Austrian Jews, the Slovenes were initially left with the small hope that they could survive through assimilation. During these three years, Nazi policy was generally directed at limiting the use of Slovene in public administration and in schools. As early as the fall of 1939, Slovene-language instruction in the dual-language schools of Carinthia was banned.[40] Moreover, the oldest Slovene-language publishing house, Hermagoras Verein/Mohorjeva družba (founded in 1852), which had (and still has) a branch in Klagenfurt/Celovec, was banned.[41] Although a limited number of leading Slovene priests and intellectuals were arrested during this time, German policy remained restrained in Carinthia largely for two reasons: Around 500,000 Germans lived in Yugoslavia during this time, and perhaps more importantly, Hitler, in the early stages of the war, was still trying to bring Yugoslavia into the war on the side of the Axis powers.[42]

On 6 April 1941, however, these international dynamics shifted. With the Axis invasion of Yugoslavia – the Germans invaded from the north, the Italians from the west, the Hungarians and Bulgarians from the east – these constraints were removed, and the second phase (1941–42) began.[43] During this time, the severity of the discriminatory policies against the Carinthian Slovenes increased dramatically. With the defeat of Yugoslavia, Nazi policy made less and less of a difference between the Carinthian Slovenes and those Slovenes living in the newly occupied northern regions of Yugoslavia of Lower Styria and Carniola.[44] Alongside the continued targeting of leading Slovene intellectuals, this phase was also characterized by its attempts to limit all public displays and use of Slovene in public.[45] The Slovene Cultural Association

(Slowenischer Kulturverband/Slovenska prosvetna zveza) was soon deemed illegal, and using Slovene in religious institutions was also banned. For those Slovenes who could not be Germanized (or refused to be), deportation became the solution. These deportations began in the spring of 1942, when Heinrich Himmler's directive to deport the Slovenes to make room for new German settlers from northern Italy was put into motion.

The third stage (1942–5) consisted of mass deportation and terror. On 14 and 15 April 1942, 221 Slovene families were rounded up by local police and taken to a collection camp outside of Klagenfurt/Celovec. Of these individuals, 917 would eventually be deported to various camps in Germany. While this third stage saw the largest single deportation and planned action against the Carinthian Slovenes during the war, the local population was continuously terrorized by arrests, torture, executions, and individual deportations up until the final days of the war.

Various forms of resistance to Nazi policies began as early as 1940 in the region. By the early part of that year, Carinthians (and Styrians) had made contact with the Slovene anti-fascist organization TIGR (Trst-Istra-Gorica-Reka) and British intelligence. With the help of Carinthian Slovenes, they had begun to sabotage German military infrastructure and collect much-needed intelligence for the Allies.[46] While there had been limited numbers of Wehrmacht deserters and draft-dodgers taking to the mountains of southern Carinthia, armed, politically organized resistance under the auspices of the Slovene Liberation Front did not start in southern Carinthia until the summer of 1942 after the mass deportations.[47] By 1944, the Liberation Front had approximately 900 partisans in the region. By the end of the war, approximately 3,000 Yugoslav partisans had fought in southern Carinthia, around 1,000 of whom had been Carinthian Slovenes.[48] Those who did not join the partisan groups supported them through various other means, for example, by providing them food and medicine or by acting as couriers of important information. Women and children, since they could move much more openly in public, had critical roles in the resistance network as well.[49] The Liberation Front was the most successful armed movement to have operated within the German Reich during the war.[50] With its effective attacks on German personnel and infrastructure, an estimated 10,000 German soldiers and police were tied down in the region and could not be deployed elsewhere around Europe.[51] The Liberation Front inflicted upwards of 500 casualties on German forces, appropriated material that would have been shipped throughout the Reich (e.g., agricultural products, cattle), provided much-needed intelligence to the Allies, and rescued Allied pilots shot down over the region.[52]

While the Liberation Front's effectiveness as a military organization is beyond debate, its political ideology is one reason why its legacy could be quickly and effectively delegitimized in Carinthia after the war. As part of the wider, communist-led resistance movement throughout Yugoslavia, the Liberation Front had several goals. While its primary aim was to defeat the Nazis and their collaborators throughout the region, it also wanted to unite the regions where Slovene-speakers lived (parts of Austria, Italy, and Hungary)[53] and govern a liberated Slovenia as part of a federated, socialist Yugoslavia.[54] As I show in my analysis of various commemorative structures in chapter 2 and my interviews with memory activists in chapter 3, Carinthian Slovenes have been struggling with this aspect of the resistance's legacy since 1945. It has led German-nationalist organizations and the Carinthian state government to assert that the partisans did not fight to liberate Austria from Nazism or to resist fascism but only to make Carinthia a part of communist Yugoslavia.

There is, of course, some truth to this claim. In the immediate postwar period, Carinthian Slovene Liberation Front activists indeed agitated for Yugoslav annexation of southern Carinthia and tried to mobilize the Slovene population for it.[55] But this agitation has to be seen within the context of what Carinthian Slovenes had just experienced: They had been discriminated against as an ethnic group in the 1920s and 1930s and then persecuted and deported to concentration camps in the 1940s.[56] Then, in the aftermath of the war, denazification efforts in Carinthia were only ever carried out half-heartedly, with former Nazis being able to vote by the time the 1949 election came around.[57] Even the British occupation authorities, who were by no means sympathetic to the Liberation Front, recognized that Slovenes did not have much faith in the new post-war Carinthian government.[58] For the Liberation Front, as one British intelligence report put it, "'the situation seems to be exactly the same as in 1919 and at the beginning of the Nazi regime, when lavish promises were made to the Slovene population, none of which were later fulfilled.'"[59] With this context in mind, this desire on the part of some Carinthian Slovenes to have wanted to make southern Carinthia part of Yugoslavia after the war is not very surprising.

Rather than highlighting the efforts of Carinthian Slovenes, critics of the resistance have traditionally emphasized events that occurred after the British and Yugoslav armies occupied Klagenfurt/Celovec on 8 May 1945. Just as the Allies did in other regions of liberated Europe, both of these armies arrested former Nazi party functionaries and supporters over the ensuing weeks.[60] Among Carinthians, 263 were arrested by the Yugoslav intelligence services and taken to Yugoslavia.

Of these, 106 were released or escaped, 59 eventually were returned to Austria, and 96 were never found and are assumed to have been executed.[61] These arrests and executions occurred in the wider context of mass repatriations that took place in southern Carinthia in May 1945 in the fields around Bleiburg/Pliberk, where the British army repatriated tens of thousands of Nazi-allied collaborationist soldiers, as well as civilian refugees, from Croatia, Slovenia, Serbia, and Montenegro back to Yugoslavia.[62] Thousands of Cossacks, who had fought in Croatia on the side of the Germans and were stationed in this part of Austria, were also repatriated to the Soviet Union.[63] While the exact number of those affected is still hotly debated, an estimated 70,000 of those sent back were subsequently executed in various locations around northern Slovenia by the Yugoslav intelligence services.[64] Alongside this violence, Yugoslavia was also demanding territorial concessions of 2,600 square kilometres (an area in which 180,000 people lived) from the defeated Austrians.[65] In the immediate aftermath of the war, this terrified Carinthians who were reminded of the territorial claims a generation earlier during the Defence Struggle.[66] Thus, the post-1920 plebiscite parole, "Carinthia, free and undivided," soon found use in the post-1945 world as well.

Unfortunately for the Yugoslavs and their Carinthian Slovene supporters, it was not just the Carinthian government that was against these border shifts. The policy did not sit well with the Allies either, who had rejected any calls for border changes two years earlier in the 1943 Moscow Declaration. These territorial demands soon became a key sticking point between Liberation Front activists and British occupation authorities.[67] Although the British and Yugoslavs had been allies during the war, the wartime working relationship quickly dissipated after the war. The British almost immediately banned the Liberation Front's publications, spontaneously enacted search warrants of houses sympathetic to it, closed border crossings into Yugoslavia, and even arrested Karel Prušnik-Gašper, the secretary of the Regional Committee of the Liberation Front, in 1947 for criticizing the British occupation authorities during the unveiling ceremony of the first monument dedicated to the partisan resistance to be built in Carinthia after the war, a monument I examine more closely in chapter 2.[68]

Within this context, perhaps it is unsurprising that victory for the Yugoslavs, and for the Carinthian Slovenes who had actively supported them, was soon delegitimized in Carinthia. Instead of commemorating the twin pillars of persecution and resistance, Carinthia's official post-war memory culture emphasized the resistance's communism and post-war occupation violence, a discursive framework that Carinthian Slovene memory activists have been struggling with ever since. Kurt Bauer's rhetorical move in his history of Austria during the Third Reich is a typical one and captures this framework well. While acknowledging the communist-organized resistance in Austria (but, tellingly, omitting the Liberation Front), he simultaneously undermines its importance by arguing "if the communist resistance had been successful, it would have simply replaced one totalitarian system with another one."[69] While this sentence may sound as if it was written at the height of the Cold War – Bauer published his book in 2017 – it is representative of the difficult environment in which Carinthian Slovene organizations have been trying to commemorate the resistance over the last several decades. As I show in chapter 2, this has led to Carinthian Slovenes building numerous memorials and monuments throughout southern Carinthia, away from the economic and political centres of the state.

Carinthian Official Memory

Almost 80 years after the war, the Carinthian government has still not built a memorial to those who fought with the Liberation Front. Instead, Carinthian official memory has had two components since 1945, both of which are still firmly intact in the twenty-first century. The first consists of commemorating the Defence Struggle (1918–9) and the ensuing Carinthian plebiscite (1920) as one event. The date of the plebiscite, 10 October, has been Carinthia's official state holiday since the inter-war years, and the Carinthian state anthem commemorates the conflict with a controversial fourth verse that honours those who defended Carinthia's borders during the conflict (as the anthem goes: "where the borders were drawn in blood"). Today, most towns in southern Carinthia still have a prominent memorial to those who fought for Austria during the Defence Struggle, and streets and squares named after 10 October – political symbols that infuse the everyday landscape with "political meaning and an ideological message" – are ubiquitous in the region.[70] Even today, more than a century after the conflict, the Defence Struggle still plays a prominent and controversial role in Carinthia's official memory culture, commemorated by the German-speaking majority as well as German nationalist organizations as a fight for freedom and democracy, while seen by Carinthian Slovenes as an annual, hostile reminder that they are outsiders in the region.

Although you can observe this official memory culture in various towns around southern Carinthia, it is best expressed in Klagenfurt/ Celovec, the state capital. Here, the first component finds salience at the

Figure 1.2: Courtyard of Carinthian Parliament in Klagenfurt/Celovec.
The Site of Carinthia Unity is on the right, while the provincial parliament
building is on the left.

Site of Carinthian Unity (Figures 1.2 and 1.3), a memorial site dedicated
to the unity of Carinthia and the events from 1919–1920.

The memorial occupies a prominent position in the Carinthian state
parliament's courtyard, which itself is located just a few steps from the
main pedestrian shopping avenue in the city. With no entrance barri-
ers, the square is a popular cross-through area among those in the city
centre, so the memorial gets more footfall than others in the city. At
first glance, the memorial's framing strategies seem uncontroversial.
The large marble slab that grabs your attention has the Carinthian state
emblem on it, underneath of which the words "freedom," "encounter,"

Figure 1.3: Site of Carinthian Unity in Klagenfurt/Celovec.

"unity," and "peace" are inscribed; all worthy concepts around which to build a memorial that commemorates a complicated time in Carinthia's history when large parts of the population wanted to join another country.

Beneath these abstract concepts, however, there is a large bronze cross with the inscription "Carinthian Freedom Struggle" (Kärntner Freiheitskampf) engraved onto it, an effective sleight of hand that carefully shifts the nature of the armed conflict from one of defence to one of freedom. By doing so, the memorial supports a competitive memory dynamic in which those who died for Carinthia (i.e., for freedom) get memorialized, while those who died for Yugoslavia (i.e., for dictatorship) do not. This section of the memorial site, moreover, grabs the

Figure 1.4: Close-up photograph of the Site of Carinthian Unity in Klagenfurt/ Celovec.

attention of most visitors. It is raised off the ground, its script is clear and can be read from a distance, and its shiny white marble attracts your eyes. To the left and right of the marble, five bronze plaques, which can easily go unnoticed, flank the memorial. If their respective texts are simplifications of history, they also seem relatively benign ones to visitors not well versed in Carinthian history. One, for example, reads: "Site of Carinthian unity. Memorial for perpetual, equitable, and peaceful cooperation of all Carinthians" (Figure 1.4). Another reads: "The right to people's self-determination gave us the undivided Carinthian homeland." Who could be against such statements?

But all the memorial site's inscriptions are only in German, a choice that turns what could have been an actual space of "encounter" between German speakers and Slovene speakers into one of German nationalism. Omitting Slovene from official government spaces does not just happen by accident in Carinthia. The Carinthian government, and those that have supported its mission to remove Slovene from the public sphere, understands the "performative power of language" and the message it sends when both German and Slovene are not used in these spaces.[71] The commemorative plaques described earlier, moreover, were donated by Carinthian Heimat Service (Kärntner Abwehrkämpferbund), the Carinthian League of Resistance Fighters (Kärntnerheimatdienst), and the Ulrichsberg Association (Ulrichsberggemeinschaft), three prominent German nationalist organizations that have long been criticized for their cozy relationships with right-wing extremist politicians and their steadfast refusal to recognize the Slovene minority's language-use rights.[72] One of them, the Carinthian League of Resistance Fighters, still refuses to accept the legitimacy of Article 7 of the Austrian State Treaty, which guarantees Slovene-language protections, while another, the Carinthian Heimat Service, has consistently agitated, at times violently, against Slovene topographical signs for Carinthian towns since the 1970s.[73] Moreover, the Ulrichsberg Association is most well known for organizing an annual gathering of neo-Nazis a few miles from Klagenfurt/Celovec every year to commemorate Austria's fallen soldiers from the First and Second World Wars (including those that were in the SS).[74]

If the Defence Struggle and the plebiscite make up one component of Carinthia's official memory culture, memorials to "the kidnapped" (die Verschleppten) make up the other. These memorials commemorate those Carinthians who were arrested and executed without trial by Yugoslavia in 1945. Although recent research has revealed that those taken to Yugoslavia immediately after the war were overwhelmingly members of the Nazi Party or individuals who had committed crimes during the war against Slovenes in Austria or in Axis-occupied Slovenia,[75] their fate has been instrumentalized to downplay and marginalize the Liberation Front's contributions to the defeat of fascism during the war. Just a short walk from the Site of Carinthian Unity and the parliament, you can find the Memorial for the Victims of the Partisan Revenge Justice on Carinthians (Figure 1.5), which has had its location in front of the city's cathedral since 2002.

Initiated by the German-nationalist organizations in Carinthia like the ones mentioned earlier, the inscription – "In memory of the children, women, and men who were kidnapped and murdered by partisans during and after the Second World War. We do not want to forget so that it never happens again" – emphasizes only Carinthian suffering during the Second World War. To be clear, there is nothing wrong with building a memorial to those who were arrested and executed at the end of the war. Extrajudicial killings of the type that happened throughout former Nazi-occupied Europe as the tide of the war shifted should be criticized and can be memorialized. But how the message of the memorial is framed downplays the brutality of Nazi policy in southern Carinthia and Yugoslavia. Just in Slovenia, around 80,000 Slovenes died during the Axis occupation, and the Nazis "outlawed Slovene culture, mandated German education, and burned Slovene literary collections," and planned to deport about one-third of the country's population.[76]

Figure 1.5: Memorial for the Victims of the Partisan Revenge Justice on Carinthians in Klagenfurt/Celovec. Originally built in 1990 and renovated in 2002. The inscription reads "In memory of the children, women, and men who were kidnapped and murdered by partisans during and after the Second World War. We do not want to forget so that it never happens again."

With the simple omission of this context, the memorial conflates general Carinthian victimhood with those who suffered directly from Nazi policies. By doing so, it produces a type of "Bitburg history" in Austria, Charles Maier's term for a type of German memory politics that, in the 1980s, obscured moral categories and historical agents for Germans to also be considered victims of Nazism and war violence.[77]

This interpretation of the past is also on display at the site during the annual commemorations hosted by the Carinthian Defense Fighter League in May. Every year, the Carinthian Defense Fighter League tells the story of the Second World War by beginning their narrative in May 1945, producing an account of the war in which neither the Nazi's war of extermination nor the invasion of Yugoslavia is mentioned. Instead, commemorations emphasize the innocence of those kidnapped and their love of Carinthia. As Hanspeter Traar, the vice governor of Carinthia, put it in 2014: "They had to die because they loved and fought for their homeland."[78] These commemorations also produce the same type of problematic binary between loyal Carinthians and disloyal partisans that the Site of Carinthian Unity generates. The Carinthian Slovene contribution to the partisan resistance is diminished by linking their motives for joining the Liberation Front not to persecution or deportations but rather due to a desire on their part to make Carinthia part of Yugoslavia. "You have to be aware of the historical truth that the Tito-communist partisans never advocated for an independent Austria," said the Carinthian Defense Fighter League at a typical event in 2019, "but vehemently advocated for separating southern Carinthia and annexing this area to Yugoslavia."[79]

These commemorations, along with several other memorials in the region, effectively tie together events that occurred 25 years apart to create one overarching narrative of Carinthians being under threat from the Slavic south.[80] In Bleiburg/Pliberk, for example, a town 30 miles to Klagenfurt's/Celovec's east, there is a prominent memorial located directly in front of the town's elementary school that merges all of these events onto one piece of stone and, as seen by the wreath in front of it, is actively commemorate by the Austrian Armed Forces. On the front, you see an image of a fallen soldier with the inscription, "They fell for the homeland. Bleiburg, Loibach, Moos." On the back, in addition to the names of soldiers who died during both World Wars, the names of the "kidnapped" are also listed. The inscription on the back reads "In memory of those civilians kidnapped on May 12, 1945" (Figure 1.6).

This strategy of linking the First World War, the Defence Struggle, the 1920 plebiscite, and the Second World War and its aftermath into one historical experience is not only incredibly historically problematic (see Figure 1.7 for another example), but it also has let Carinthia's official memory culture produce a troubling dichotomy between German speakers, who fought and died for Carinthian unity and freedom during all four conflicts, and Slovene speakers, who fought to make Austria part of communist Yugoslavia, in other words German-speaking patriots and Slovene-speaking traitors.[81]

Although there has been a memorial to those executed by the Nazi judicial system outside of the Carinthian state courthouse since 2013 in

Figure 1.6: Memorial in Bleiburg/Pliberk. An example of a memorial that combines the events of the world wars with the *Verschleppung* after the Second World War. On the front, an image of a fallen soldier with the inscription "They fell for the homeland. Bleiburg, Loibach, Moos." On the back, in addition to the names of soldiers who died during the world wars, below is a list of the *Verschleppten*. The inscription reads "In memory of those civilians kidnapped on May 12, 1945." Notice, too, the wreath placed in front by the Austrian Armed Forces for All Saint's Day. The memorial is located directly in front of the Bleiburg/Pliberk Gymnasium.

Klagenfurt/Celovec, those tasked with commemorating the past at the official level in Carinthia have yet to commemorate the Slovene armed, organized resistance to Nazism. Walking around Klagenfurt/Celovec, it is clear that the city offers, to go back to Richard Schein, "a selective story of regional identity which reverberates in ideas about belonging (who does; who does not); a story that ultimately writes *out* of the picture certain people."[82] To discover how the Carinthian Slovenes have written themselves back into this story, we have to leave the Carinthian capital and head south to the Peršmanhof memorial site, which is the topic of chapter 2. But before we do that, let us first turn our attention to some theoretical concerns.

Figure 1.7: Memorial in Köttmannsdorf/Kotmara vas. The memorial blends the First World War, the Abwehrkampf, and the Second World War together. On the back of the memorial, there is also an inscription (difficult to read because of the trees that block it) that reads, "In memory of all those citizens of the German and Slovene ethnic groups who were victims of war and violence." The memorial is on the main square.

Theoretical Overview

This book reveals what happens when a minority group's collective memory of a past event is pushed to the periphery of the official memory of the region in which the group resides. In Austria's official collective memory of the war, the persecution and resistance of the Carinthian Slovenes has largely been ignored. My chance encounter with this *Geschichte* – the German term is apt here, as it has kept the double meaning of "history" and "story" that has now been separated into two words in English – shows the benefits of shifting our lens as German studies scholars from the centre to the periphery, those "sites or spaces on the outskirts or margins of the centres of power" like southern Carinthia.[83] Although plenty of ink has been spilled describing the development of Germany's memory culture as well as the victim myth in post-war Austria, exploring peripheral memories of the Second World War in Austria is still beneficial for a few reasons.

On one level, investigating how peripheral memories "challenge, enrich, divert, stretch, re-evaluate, support and ignore narratives that address and shape memory" can be an effective engine for re-energizing our research agenda on how aspects of the Second World War are being remembered in specific parts of contemporary Europe.[84] Particularly in the case of Austria, emphasizing Carinthian Slovene vernacular memory adds a new, regional perspective to our understanding of post-war Austrian collective memory, something that has usually been explored from a national perspective and rarely from the point of view of one of its protected minority groups. But there is also an ethical drive to my study, too, one that is embedded in recent scholarship's call for a "right to memory."[85] In this avenue of research, reframing a society's memory of the past is one way to challenge injustices in the present.[86] "The power," as Sharon K. Hom and Eric K. Yamamoto argue, "resides in the potential for constructing collective memories of injustice as a basis for redress."[87] While I am certainly not a memory entrepreneur like those individuals I interview in chapter 3, I do hope my study can help push back against the "repressive erasure"[88] of the Carinthian Slovene resistance within Carinthia's official memory culture and, by doing so, reaffirm the group's existence in contemporary Austria.[89]

By moving my lens to the Austrian periphery, on another level, I offer a case study that productively grapples with some of the assumptions and approaches that have become popular in memory studies in the wake of the transcultural turn that hit the field of memory studies in the early 2000s.[90] Since this turn, a whole host of transcultural approaches to memory have been developed that have tried to move memory studies beyond its original research agenda, perhaps best illustrated by Pierra Nora's groundbreaking work in the 1980s, of examining collective memory's role in the national identity building process.[91] While a full engagement with the transcultural turn is outside the scope of this book, these approaches share two underlying principles that are relevant for my study. First and foremost, transcultural perspectives on memory see memory as inherently mobile, fluid, dynamic, and mediated. In contrast to older studies, which tended to focus on (supposedly) stable, bounded national sites of memory, transcultural memory explores how collective memories are circulated, borrowed, cross-referenced, and received beyond and between different cultural, ethnic, or national groups.[92] No less important, however, is the ethical imperative often found in transcultural perspectives on memory that try to move memory politics away from zero-sum, competitive models of memory in which memory politics – that sphere of politics engaged in struggles over what is and what is not to be remembered – is theorized as being highly contested between groups trying to have their particular interpretation of the past remembered at the expense of other ones.[93]

Since the advent of the transcultural turn, this first tenet – that we look for ways that memory processes move beyond group boundaries – has become memory studies orthodoxy. Historical events, after all, are never constrained by constructed national or ethnic borders, so why should the memory of them be? "Memory," as Astrid Erll pointedly puts it, "is fundamentally transcultural. *No* version of the past and *no* product in the archive will ever belong to just one community or place, but usually has its own history of 'travel and translation.'"[94] This is especially the case for the memory of something like the Carinthian Slovene resistance, which was part of a wider multinational anti-fascist army that operated throughout Yugoslavia during the Second World War. As I demonstrate in my analysis of various sites of memory in chapter 2, many of the memorials in southern Carinthia are similar to those built in Yugoslavia in the early post-war years. But "doing" transcultural memory is not just about uncovering, exploring, and describing memory processes that go beyond cultural, ethnic, or national borders. Such an approach to memory also tends to involve ethical claims about how we should be "doing" memory.[95] "Collectively," as one recent edited volume on memory studies' transcultural turn puts it, these approaches "construe a model of memory as a fluid, inclusive, and open-ended process, rather than a fixed and exclusionary narrative, embracing the possibility that the intersection of disparate commemorative discourses might offer an opportunity to forge empathic communities of remembrance across national, cultural, or ethnic boundaries."[96]

The first time I moved to Carinthia to conduct fieldwork, however, I noticed a disconnect between this second tenet of transcultural memory and what I was observing in the field. Inclusive, fluid, empathetic – these were not words that captured what I was seeing in southern Carinthia. In stark contrast to this more idealistic side of transcultural memory, the region's landscape of remembrance, almost 80 years after the end of the Second World War, is still heavily fractured along ethnic lines and contested between Slovene speakers and German speakers. There is still a thriving official memory culture – government-sponsored memorials and official commemorations – that relativizes the persecution of Carinthian Slovenes and maligns the Slovene resistance's role in bringing an end to Nazism in Europe. This has led to Carinthian Slovene organizations commemorating their own past in a manner that is diametrically opposed to what you find at official sites of memory throughout the state, which has resulted in southern Carinthia having a highly competitive memory landscape that commemorates two very different interpretations of the Second World War in two very different ways.

At first, as someone who arrived in southern Carinthia socialized and trained in German studies from a US university, I was initially surprised by how contested this memory landscape was. With such a focus on how Germany has commemorated the Holocaust within German studies, I had connected a German-style memory culture, with its prominent memorials to victims and seemingly endless debates about memory, with memory of the Second World War in general. But Germany's well-known memory culture is much more an exception on the continent than a rule when it comes to memories of the Second World War. As much as the European Union has tried over the last few decades to forge a transnational European identity through a shared memory of the European past centred on the Holocaust and the Second World War, this is far from being reality on the ground.[97]

Since the European Union's eastern expansion in the early 2000s, there has been a contentious debate at the supranational level as to what crime of the twentieth century – the Holocaust or Soviet communism – should take centre stage in the European Union's memory politics.[98] In a twenty-first-century redux of the "Historikerstreit" of the 1980s, when West German academics passionately debated the role of the Holocaust in German history and whether or not the Holocaust could be compared with the crimes of Soviet communism, memory politics in central and eastern Europe has been largely caught in a "competition of evil and victimhood" discourse over the last 30 years in which memories of the Holocaust clash with nationalist narratives about the Second World War in an extremely contested environment.[99] Throughout the region, this discourse revolves around belated confrontations with the Holocaust and the crimes of Soviet communism, both of which had been suppressed during the Soviet era.[100] With this "outburst of competing and discorand memories," as two scholars phrase it, post-1990s memory politics in this region has been dominated by a two-way focus on national resistance to Soviet communism as well as national suffering at the hands of an imported Soviet communism in the war's aftermath at the expense of remembering the Holocaust and these countries' role in it.[101]

At the national level, there have also been sustained memory wars over the last 30 years as to what should be remembered about the Second World War and its aftermath.[102] Just as the myth of the Great Patriotic War helped hold the multi-ethnic, multilingual Soviet Union together in the post-war period, the myth of the People's Liberation War helped forge a pan-Yugoslav identity in post-war Yugoslavia.[103] But Yugoslavia's hegemonic post-war memory culture of Brotherhood and Unity (bratsvo i jedinstvo) collapsed alongside the country with the wars of the 1990s. In its place came extreme nationalist interpretations of the war throughout the former Yugoslavia that have tried to "rank" which ethnic group suffered the most during the war as well as a general rehabilitation of the Nazi-aligned fascist movements from the time.[104] "Memory wars" have been occurring throughout the region ever since.[105] In Croatia, there have been contentious memory debates about the nationalist rehabilitation of the Ustaša, the Nazi-aligned fascist movement that controlled the Independent State of Croatia from 1941 until 1945 and was responsible for carrying out genocide against the region's Jews and Serbs.[106] Across the border in Serbia, the Second World War has been recast into a war of Serbian victimhood, with commemorations of the partisan resistance and the Holocaust pushed aside for a more positive spin on the Četniks, the Serbian nationalist movement that collaborated with the Nazis during the war.[107] A similar process has been happening in Slovenia as well, something I touch on in more detail in chapter 4.

Elsewhere in Europe, too, this competitive dynamic has managed to linger into the twenty-first century. With ethnic Russians in the east still clinging on to the Soviet post-war heroic narrative of the Second World War and ethnic Ukrainians in the west commemorating nationalist narratives that memorialize figures like Stepan Bandera – a Ukrainian nationalist who, allied with the Nazis, fought against the Soviets and, while doing so, collaborated in the Holocaust as well as the mass murder of Poles during the war – Ukraine is a classic example of a country with a "divided memory."[108] In the case of Ukraine, this dynamic has pushed Holocaust memory to the margins.[109] A similar dynamic has been found to exist in the Julian March, the region split between today's Italy, Croatia, and Slovenia, among Italians and Slovenes.[110]

Although Austria has recently been put next to Germany as one of the few countries in Europe that has built a culture of official memory around the crimes of Nazism, southern Carinthia actually has much more in common with these other contested zones of memory around Europe than it does with Germany's.[111] Because of the contested nature of this environment, the commemorative strategies that Carinthian Slovenes use are radically different from what memory studies scholars consider effective commemorative work in the twenty-first century. In an environment where the basics of the past are still heavily contested, the commemorative strategies that are often applauded in memory studies – think counter-memorials, stumbling stones, dialogical museum exhibitions, and multilayered museum exhibitions with multiple perspectives about the past – are simply not found in the southern Carinthian context, the reasons for which I discuss in chapters 2 and 3 in more detail.

Although I rely on a range of methods for this book from various fields – critical geography, literary and cultural studies, and museum studies – my goal throughout is to "extend" our horizons of German and Austrian studies. German studies, as anyone who became interested in Austria through a German department can attest to, has long kept all things Austrian at the margins of its research agenda.[112] From experience, if you study German studies in the United States, you rarely come across Austrian topics, and if you do, distinctions are (at best) flattened out or (at worst) ignored, which leads to studies of Austrian cultural products being simply labelled as belonging to Germany. Suffice to say, German studies "in the USA almost uncritically aggregates Austrian and Austro-Hungarian authors and filmmakers with Germans" and "the damage caused by such scholarly imperialism is ongoing and real."[113]

Likewise, Austrian studies also tends to flatten out the field and only emphasize German-language topics. It speaks volumes about how "Austria" is perceived in the field that the Austrian Fulbright Committee – one of the leading institutional grant providers for Austria studies topics – initially did not want to fund my fieldwork for the research that went into this book because I, as someone from a German department, wanted to write about the Carinthian Slovenes. Because the Carinthian Slovenes do not speak German, the committee argued, how would I be able to communicate with them? This perception is still deeply unsettling to me. Not only does it reveal how secluded the Carinthian Slovene community is from the rest of Austria, but it also shows, 80 years after the end of the National Socialist era in Austria, highly influential Austrians – and academics no less – are still problematically equating Austrian identity with being a monolingual German speaker. By shifting my focus from the streets and neighbourhoods of Vienna to the ravines and mountainsides of southern Carinthia, then, I am also advocating for a broader understanding of what Austrian studies is today. Although small, Austria is such a diverse country, and it is crucial that Austrian studies be opened up in the twenty-first century to include the cultural artefacts of its ethnic and linguistic minorities. Klaus Zeyringer's point about Austrian literature – that it is "not only literature in German but, as the example of contemporary Austria shows, it is all the literature of ethnic minorities such as the Slovenians, Croats, Magyars, and Czechs" – applies to all of Austrian studies.[114]

This book is also a useful case study for memory study's scholars interested in how historically marginalized minority groups remember forgotten pasts in unsupportive environments. While scholars were already criticizing what they called a "surfeit of memory" in the early 1990s, debates about public memory have once again become major topics of political debate in Europe and North America over the last decade.[115] Across both continents, issues of remembrance – specifically, how to publicly commemorate violent and oppressive (often colonial) pasts – have once again shifted into the centre of public attention. As I show in the ensuing chapters, minorities like the Carinthian Slovenes have various arrows that they can pull from their memory strategy quiver. Literature can be written that navigates traumatic histories and provides space to forgotten voices within its pages. Monuments and memorials can be constructed that activate heroic discourses about the past. Museums can be designed that are simultaneously places of pedagogy and spaces of mourning. Activists can hold seminars and events that not only commemorate the past but also use this past to help forge a more just present.

But as anyone who has lived in a city with monuments and memorials knows, commemorating the past is no simple process. The tension that has been observed around the world over the last several years regarding which past gets publicly commemorated shows that there are often stark differences between "official" memory cultures and "vernacular" ones. The term vernacular, perhaps most widely understood in the context of language – that is, "writing, using, or speaking the native or indigenous language of a country of district" – has been used productively across numerous academic disciplines to denote the "everyday," the "ordinary," or a type of "localness" in some shape or form.[116] In memory studies, the term refers to John Bodnar's concept of "vernacular memory," with which he described various American commemorative practices originating from "vernacular culture," or the memory constructed and maintained by community-based, grassroots groups operating in local areas.[117] In his work, Bodnar juxtaposes this vernacular memory to "official memory," which emanates from a society's cultural and political elite. This elite embodies an "official culture" and occupies positions in a society's official institutions (e.g., in education, government, or the military). For Sabine Marschall, who has demonstrated the continued usefulness of Bodnar's approach to memory in her more recent analyses of public memory spaces in post-apartheid South Africa, official memory is the "officially sanctioned markers and spaces of memory, mostly government-endorsed memorials, museums, street names, commemorative monuments, and statues in the public domain" while vernacular memory "includes a diverse range of collective memory practices, often highly localized, informal, spontaneous, ephemeral, community-based, or rooted in tradition, local custom, or popular culture."[118]

There is often a stark difference between vernacular and official memory, stemming largely from why the respective group (the vernacular or the official) wants to commemorate a past event. Vernacular memories, because they derive from the community in question and are created by what Bodnar calls "ordinary people," convey the realities of social life and are thus more authentic versions of the past. Official culture, however, tries to co-opt these vernacular memories for official purposes to create ideal versions of the past based on what the past "should be" rather than what it really was. By relying on concepts like patriotism, official culture seeks to flatten out the diverse experiences and interests of the vernacular, and, by doing so, tries to create a memory of the past that can be used to support, among other goals, national unity and the construction of a national identity. It is through this interaction between the vernacular and the official that what Bodnar calls "public memory" is created.[119]

This distinction between the official and the vernacular is not without its critics, particularly his claim that vernacular memories produce an "authentic" memory while its official counterpart is only interested in abusing memory for its own goals.[120] More recent research asserts that these two forms of memory are actually quite fluid. Sabina Mihelj, for example, argues that "there are several possible ways for vernacular and official memories to interact – sometimes they are openly opposed, in other instances they might mirror each other."[121] Likewise, the domineering and manipulative picture of official memory in Bodnar's framework has also been challenged, with scholars demonstrating that official memory is never as hegemonic as it seems and itself is highly contested.[122] Likewise, Jenny Wüstenberg, in her study on memory in post-war Germany, cautions against characterizing either "the state" or "civil society" as monolithic groups of actors.[123] Still others have warned against characterizing grassroots groups as somehow more ethical or principled than their counterparts working for the state. As Marschall reminds us, "just as officially sanctioned forms of memory have their limitations and are often criticized, vernacular memory practices can equally be problematic and lend themselves to abuse. Because vernacular practices are community-based and often anchored in specific ethnic or religious traditions, they can be exclusive, offensive, and dangerous in culturally heterogeneous societies, especially when being imposed on diverse audiences."[124] These critiques notwithstanding, distinguishing between these two types of memory is useful when applied to Carinthia. As I show throughout the book, there is a meaningful difference, along with a lingering tension, between the official memory culture in Carinthia and its vernacular counterpart in the Carinthian Slovene community.

Because they diverge from Carinthia's official memory culture so radically, the media of memory that make up Carinthian Slovene vernacular memory and I examine in this book (except Maja Haderlap's *Angel of Oblivion*, for reasons I explain in chapter 4) have been marginalized and delegitimized within it. But no memory culture is closed to contestation, and there are always other alternatives as to what can get remembered; these alternatives just have to be uncovered and mobilized. Such a process is at work (and ongoing) in southern Carinthia. The media of memory that I explore throughout this book contain the memories are told from the perspective of those who were "silenced or obscured, or whose interests were repressed during the construction of official memory by the agencies, institutions, and discourses of the state."[125]

In the context of Carinthian Slovene memories of the partisan resistance, these counter-memories have much in common with what Gal Kirn has called the "partisan counter-archive" in the post-Yugoslav space. Kirn, who explores how the partisan struggle during the Second World War became a place of artistic and political encounter in different eras of Yugoslav history, argues that these revolutionary leftovers of the partisan counter-archive – artistic remnants from particular revolutionary moments in Yugoslav history that affirm both antifascist struggle and social revolution – can be uncovered and mobilized to achieve emancipatory political goals in the present. The goal of the partisan counter-archive, writes Kirn, is to "excavate moments and (art)works from the past that form emancipatory fragments and that can potentially transfer them into the present. The Partisan counter-archive is a 'construction site,' where semi-forgotten artworks and political acts enter into a more palpable – and, I hope, lasting relationship in and beyond post-Yugoslav context."[126] By "digging"[127] around the landscape of memory in southern Carinthia as well as through the counter-archive within the Carinthian Slovene community, this book, by offering an "alternative view of the past which challenges the dominant representation of the past," can hopefully contribute to this in the Carinthian context.[128]

The Southern Carinthian Landscape of Remembrance

"The landscape is certainly beautiful around here. But without their stories, that's all it is."

– Zdravko Haderlap

"Remembrance," as Jay Winter writes in his introduction to *Sites of Memory, Sites of Mourning*, "is part of the landscape. Anyone who walks through northern France or Flanders will find traces of the terrible, almost unimaginable, human losses of the war, and of efforts to commemorate the fallen. War memorials dot the countryside, in cities, towns, and villages, in market squares, churchyards, schools, and obscure corners of hillsides and fields."[1] While perhaps not as obvious as in other parts of Europe, fragments of a violent past have left their mark on the landscape of southern Carinthia. Almost 75 years after the Nazis surrendered to the Allies, these marks are, of course, no longer visible through physical evidence of war. The remnants of war are almost completely absent from everyday life. The once destroyed train stations and rail networks have all been rebuilt, as have the town squares, schools, and roads. But if you know where to look, you still come across symbolic traces of the war – monuments, memorials, gravestones, and other "objects of remembrance" – that remind you of this violent past.[2] These traces, tucked away in the small towns and valleys between the Drau/Drava river and the Karawank mountains on the border between Austria and Slovenia, form what I call in this chapter a "landscape of remembrance" that is remarkably different than what you find in the rest of Austria.

This landscape of remembrance, tilled by Carinthian Slovene organizations since the end of the Second World War, commemorates those resistance fighters who gave their lives fighting with the Liberation

Front in Carinthia during the war. Fifty-four objects in total, these memorials, called "partisan memorials" in local parlance, are remarkably similar in their simplicity and messaging.[3] In contrast to the prominent, centrally located monuments that states have traditionally built after having been victorious in wars – think, for example, of the Soviet monuments that still linger throughout many European capitals to commemorate the Soviet victory of the Nazis or the US World War II Memorial in Washington, D.C. – the memorials in southern Carinthia are tucked away in remote village cemeteries or built along hillsides and ridges, often located on the site where the commemorated event occurred, hidden from those not aware of where they are. Aesthetically, these memorials look very much like the ones built in Yugoslavia in the immediate aftermath of the Second World War: modest chunks of stone or cairns, often small, inscribed with the names of those who died in the fight against fascism and (sometimes) adorned with the five-pointed star of the Yugoslav partisans.[4] A local veterans organization of former partisans and their widows, the Alliance of Carinthian Partisans (Verband der Kärntner Partisanen/Zveza koroških partizanov), built these memorials (and has been maintaining them ever since) in southern Carinthia. Unlike the official markers of memory you find in Carinthia, these memorials are all inscribed in both Slovene and German, a choice that reveals Carinthian Slovenes' bilingualism as well as their commitment to keeping Slovene visible in the public sphere in a state that consistently tries to erase it.

In the chapter that follows, I explore these memorials to show how this landscape of remembrance – through its symbolism, design, and framing strategies – supports a vernacular memory that is radically at odds with its official counterpart in Carinthia. Relying on methods for how to analyse landscapes from critical geography, I explore several vernacular memorials and read them against their official counterparts in the region. Although numerous sites of memory in the region recall the Carinthian Slovenes' struggles, I foreground one particular landscape that is crucial to constructing and maintaining memories of those struggles: the Peršmanhof, a memorial site in the far south of the province. In the end, this chapter argues that the process of remembrance that has been built into the landscape in and around the Peršmanhof – through a monument, a museum, and the site itself – activates a countermemory for the Carinthian Slovene community that not only provides the site its mnemonic meaning but also enables it to contest Carinthia's official memory culture of the Second World War and intervene in contemporary political debates.

Landscape as Method

When we think of the word landscape, we often think of beautiful, perhaps overpowering, natural scenes of the world, and not without reason. A loanword from the Dutch *landschap*, the original English word, *landscap*, referred to "a painting of a rural, agricultural, or natural scene, often accented by a ruin, mill, distant church spire, local inhabitants, or elite spectators."[5] By the 1700s, once wealthy landowners began commissioning paintings of magnificent rural scenery, *landscape* took on its contemporary meaning, becoming associated with "a pleasing view or panorama in seemingly wild or untouched nature."[6] Since the mid-1980s, however, critical geographers have been conceptualizing landscape much more rigorously. In contrast to a static perception of an area you can see, the term as it is used in critical geography denotes the interaction of humans with their lived environment.[7] Generally speaking, geographers understand a landscape not only as a particular geographic area that can be observed but also as one that is actually a cultural product that can influence and naturalize certain social relations.[8] "The cultural landscape," as Carl Sauer, one of the first US geographers to theorize landscape in this way, puts it, "is fashioned from the natural landscape by a cultural group. Culture is the agent, the natural area is the medium, the cultural landscape the result."[9] If the cultural landscape is the result of groups' social interactions in a natural area, then the landscape holds knowledge about the social groups that have inhabited it and have influenced it over time. In F. Pierce Lewis's classic phrasing, landscape is our "unwitting autobiography," which reflects "our tastes, our values, our ideas, in tangible, visible form."[10]

Seen in this way, analysing a particular landscape can reveal much about the social relations of the area that have not only been created through the landscape but are also maintained by it. Because they "anchor and bring historical legitimacy to the identities of social groups" and serve "as a conduit for debating what (and whose) view of the past should be remembered," landscapes also support the construction and maintenance of collective memories for social groups.[11] Scholars of memory have begun drawing this connection between landscape and memory as well. From the "memory landscape"[12] and the "memoryscape"[13] to the "topography of memory,"[14] terminology from critical geography has slowly entered memory studies. But the adoption of terminology from critical geography has done little to add to our understanding of a particular landscape's influence on collective memory practices. Memory studies' scholars often use the term with its traditional definition, that is, as a spatial metaphor, to capture "a portion of territory that can be viewed at one time from one place."[15] Rather than using landscape solely as a metaphor to convey an image of a set of tangible commemorative objects that share a similar geographic location, I use landscape in this chapter as a method with which to analyse and evaluate several sites of memory located in southern Carinthian. Taken together, these sites of memory – memorials, graves, monuments, and a museum – form the southern Carinthia landscape of remembrance.

To use landscape as a method, I rely on a four-step approach that Richard Schein developed in his analysis of the courthouse square in Lexington, Kentucky.[16] First and foremost, Schein argues that the history of the landscape must be explained through a "thick description" of the site. This means investigating when, why, and for whom the landscape was created and how it has been altered over time. After the landscape's history has been documented, the landscape's meaning – what it means as a space to those "who live in and through" it – can then be investigated. Then, the landscape can be interrogated for how it has facilitated certain social, political, and economic ideologies as well as particular memories. Finally, the landscape should be viewed as "discourse materialized," which allows us to explore not only how the landscape has normalized particular social practices but also how it can also be used as an avenue to challenge these same practices.

While Schein's framework is helpful for guiding an investigation into what he calls an "ordinary scene," how particular collective memories are constructed and maintained in the landscape is not a central aspect of his approach. In contrast, Rudy Koshar, as one of the few scholars of memory who has adopted the more critical definition of landscape described earlier, places collective memory at the centre of his interpretation of German "memory landscapes" between 1870 and 1990.[17] Due to this, I also rely on his "triad" for exploring the process of remembrance in southern Carinthia, which means I also examine (1) the highly resonant parts of a memory landscape, (2) the individuals and groups that compete to invest this landscape with meaning through particular framing strategies, and (3) the themes and symbols – what he calls the "raw material" – for these framing devices. Because understanding the landscape of and around the Peršmanhof is critical for investigating the site for its function in Carinthian Slovene collective memory, my reading of the southern Carinthian remembrance landscape combines both of these frameworks. They should not be understood as exclusionary but rather as complementary. Schein's approach enables a broader, deeper reading of the entire landscape a particular site is situated in. Koshar's triad, however, proves helpful when examining the individual site of memory for how it creates meaning within this landscape, produced by the various framing strategies and references found at the site. By combining both approaches, I can better explore the entanglements of landscape aesthetics and landscape memory for Carinthian Slovenes today.

History of the Peršmanhof Landscape

From the Austrian Alps and the famous Großglockner mountain in the northwest to the Drau/Drava river valley in the southeast, Carinthia's landscape is remarkably diverse. To the northeast, the Noric Alps separate Carinthia from Styria, while the Carnic and Karawank mountains loom over the southern part of the state.[18] It is here, on a south-facing ridgeline in the Karawanks, a quick ride from the Slovenian border, that the Peršmanhof memorial site is located.

Since the end of the First World War, Carinthia has been Austria's southernmost province, sharing a southern border with Italy and Slovenia. While one can easily miss these international borders today – occasionally, as was the case during my fieldwork in 2019–20, border controls, reminiscent of the time before Slovenia's ascension into the European Union and the Schengen Area, will pop up between Austria and Slovenia – natural geographic features have long played the role of both official and unofficial boundary between states and peoples. With an average height of 6,500 feet and a width of nine miles, the Karawank Mountains are not only the official border between Austria and Slovenia today, but they have often been perceived as a "natural" barrier between Germanic and Slavic Europe (see figure 2.1).[19] While the Karawanks make up this official external border, the Drau/Drava river, which flows 125 miles eastward across the state, has traditionally formed an internal, imaginative border in Carinthia, dividing the historically Slovenian-speaking towns and villages in the south from their German-speaking counterparts in the north, a dynamic that continues today (figure 2.2).[20] The further south one travels into this region, south of the Drau/Drava and into the foothills and gorges of the Karawanks, the more you see and hear Slovene (figure 2.3).[21]

The Peršmanhof is located in this wider geographic and linguistic context, deep in the historic bilingual region of the province. The economy of this area, overwhelmingly rural, is largely based on agriculture, which is why Carinthian Slovenes have traditionally been small farmers.[22] Originally, the Peršmanhof was a family farm (figure 2.4). Before the Second World War, it was one of the largest and most economically important for Slovenes in the area. Owned by the Sadovniks, a local Carinthian Slovene family, the farm itself consisted of 11 separate

Figure 2.1: A view of the Karawank mountains, looking south towards Slovenia from Austria.

buildings (including a mill and a forge, along with the living quarters for both the family and farmhands). Close to forests and cleared pastures, the farm's main economic activities revolved around forestry, cattle, and various forms of agricultural work.

The Peršmanhof's function changed dramatically during the Second World War. Over the course of the war, the farm became one of the central support points for partisans operating in southern Carinthia, providing lodging, food, and relative safety for those involved in fighting Nazis in the area.[23] At certain times, up to 250 partisans could be found camped on the farm's grounds.[24] The farm's new wartime purpose placed the Sadovnik family in grave danger, as anyone suspected of aiding partisans could be executed for doing so.

On 25 April 1945, the landscape of the Peršmanhof was forever altered. Although the war was all but over in Austria – the Soviets had already captured Vienna – violence in the south continued, and the Peršmanhof

Figure 2.2: The Drau/Drava river in Carinthia.

became the site of the largest war crime to occur in Carinthia during the war.[25] In the early evening of 25 April, a local SS and police regiment surrounded the farm, where between 100 and 150 partisans were camping, and attacked it. The partisans escaped into the woods under cover of a brief firefight, and the Germans retreated. Upon returning later that night to recover supplies, however, Josef Reischl, the officer in charge of the German regiment, ordered the Sadovnik family to be executed. By the end of the night, 11 people from the Sadovnik (four adults and five children) and neighbouring Kogoj families (two children) had been murdered. The farm, including the Sadovnik's house, was burned to the ground. Three of the children (Ana, Amalija, and Cyril) managed to survive the attack but were badly injured.[26] After that night, the Peršmanhof never returned to its original function as a large-scale farm. Yet already by 1949, Lukas Sadovnik – the oldest brother in the Sadovnik family who had survived the massacre because he happened to be at a neighbour's house that day – had rebuilt the main house, and both he and his sister, Ana, had begun to live in it again. While Ana would continue to live in the house until 2001, Lukas sold the house in 1965 to Ludvik Bornik, a Carinthian Slovene gunsmith from nearby

Figure 2.3: Bilingual topographical sign in southern Carinthia.

Ferlach/Borovlje, who renovated the house and ensured Ana would have a place to live for the rest of her life.[27]

Compared to the integral commemorative role the Peršmanhof has today in the Carinthian Slovene community, immediately after the war, the site was not the location of any type of ritualized remembrance or commemorative ceremonies. Just as concentration camps did not take on commemorative functions immediately after the war in Germany – in fact, most of them were largely forgotten – the Peršmanhof, too, was not the location of a commemoration until 1965.[28] This first commemoration centred on the personal memories of the Sadovnik and Kogoj families. The Alliance of Carinthian Partisans placed a memorial plaque, written only in Slovene, at the site. It took another decade for the next commemoration to occur, and the site took on a new meaning in the early 1970s when the politics surrounding the erection of bilingual topographical signs in the area led to an outbreak of German nationalist violence and terror (the so-called Ortstafelsturm). By this time, the memory of the Sadovniks had been placed into a larger cultural memory of Slovene suffering and persecution.

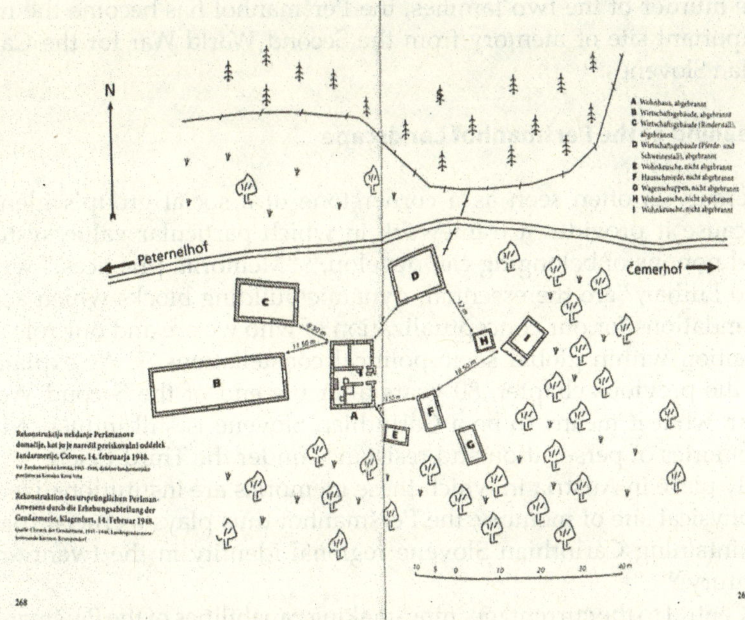

Figure 2.4: Diagram of the Peršmanhof before the Second World War.

Source: Lisa Rettl, Gudrun Blohberger, Zveza koroških partizanov / Verband der Kärntner Partisanen, Društvo / Verein Peršman, Peršman (Göttingen, Germany: Wallstein, 2014), 268–9.

In 1981, Bornik leased half of the house to the Alliance of Carinthian Partisans for 95 schillings and allowed Ana to live in the other half. This was the first step towards the construction of a museum. Getting the original museum off the ground was difficult, particularly when it came to finances. The Austrian federal government provided 5,000 schillings for the project, while the state of Carinthia offered nothing. Mostly due to the leadership of Janez Wutte-Luc, a former partisan and, at the time, head of the Alliance of Carinthian Partisans, the renovation work to get the building into a museum was carried out by volunteers from Carinthia as well as from Yugoslavia and was funded by donations from local Carinthian Slovenes. By the fall of 1981, the renovation was complete, and in April 1982 the museum opened.[29] The original exhibition was designed by Marjan Sturm, a historian and former head of the Alliance of Carinthian Partisans, and Peter Wieser. Since 1987, an annual commemoration has been held at the site in June. Decades after the murder of the two families, the Peršmanhof has become the most important site of memory from the Second World War for the Carinthian Slovenes.[30]

Meaning of the Peršmanhof Landscape

Memory is often seen as a cornerstone of a social group's identity because it provides a framework in which particular value systems and notions of belonging can develop.[31] "Memorial practices," writes Oto Luthar, "are the essential, dynamic building blocks which act as foundations for our conceptualization of who we are and our role and position within global socio-political constellations."[32] As explained in the previous chapter, 80 years after the end of the Second World War, what it means to be a Carinthian Slovene is still influenced by memories of persecution and resistance under the Third Reich. As the only place in Austria in which these memories are institutionalized in a physical site of memory, the Peršmanhof thus plays a crucial role in maintaining Carinthian Slovene regional identity in the twenty-first century.[33]

Central to the current meaning-making capabilities of the Peršmanhof is its location, not only due to its history as a site of terror but also due to its location relative to Carinthia's official memorial culture. The Peršmanhof is secluded from Klagenfurt/Celovec, the economic and political centre of the state. Tucked away on the side of a gorge, 3,400 feet above sea level, the Peršmanhof is seven miles east of Bad Eisenkappel/Železna Kapla, the largest town in the area. Only two small signs reveal the Peršmanhof's existence: one pointing the way from the main road in Bad Eisenkappel/Železna Kapla and a much smaller one, marked "M" for museum, hidden off to the side of a small mountain road, pointing left up a steep, gravel path (figure 2.5). Next to this, a sign urges visitors, due to the poor quality of the gravel path, to park their car on the side of the winding mountain road and walk the rest of the way to the site.

Due to this location, the Peršmanhof attracts little attention from visitors not already aware of its existence (figures 2.6 and 2.7). Even for those interested in visiting the site, reaching it is still difficult. Public transportation does not connect it with Bad Eisenkappel/Železna Kapla or any of the other towns in the area, meaning any possible visitors must arrive by car. This has a negative impact on the overall number of visitors to the site. In 2010, for example, the Peršmanhof only had 700 visitors.[34] I visited the site three times between September 2019 and August 2020 and once again in September 2023. Twice, there were two other visitors, and during one visit, I was there by myself for an

Figure 2.5: Direction of the Peršmanhof from the centre of Bad Eisenkappel/ Železna Kapla.

Figure 2.6: The Peršmanhof memorial site.

Figure 2.7: The wider area of the Peršmanhof memorial site.

afternoon. On my final visit, the museum was simply closed without notice or any sign. According to a volunteer who was operating the site in 2019, an average weekend sees between two and five visitors.

But the location of the Peršmanhof, off the beaten path, high up in the mountains, south of the Drau/Drava river, expresses the physical reality of the Carinthian Slovenes. In 1880, in the Austro-Hungarian Empire's first census, about a third of Carinthians claimed to use Slovene for their "language of everyday use" (around 85,000 people).[35] In 2001, the last time a traditional census was conducted in Austria, only 12,554 people claimed it to be their "language of conversation."[36] The reliability of this census data to determine how many Carinthians can speak Slovene has been heavily criticized.[37] Depending on what source is used (government censuses or local ecclesiastical figures), which country's data are relied on (Austria's or Yugoslavia's), and what question is asked ("language of conversation," "language of thought," or "native language," all of which were asked by census bodies over the decades), competing figures can be found, which has led scholars to take their results with a grain of salt (see figure 2.8).[38] In 1931, even Franz Heiß, the then head of the Austrian Federal Office of Statistics,

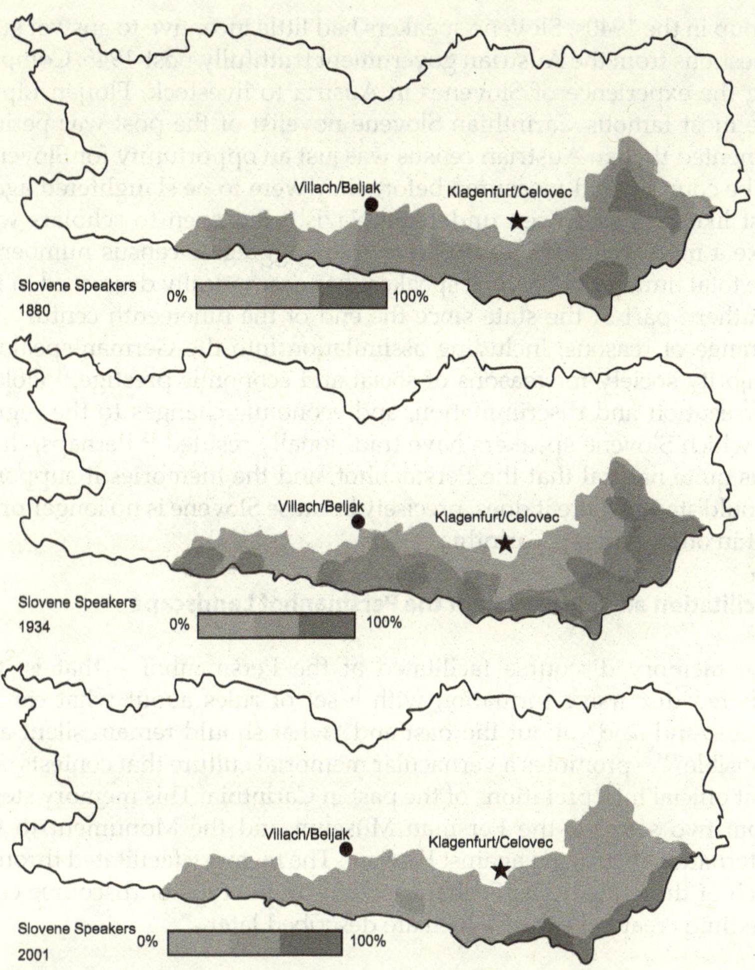

Figure 2.8: Percentage of Slovene speakers in southern Carinthia. From 1880, 1934, and 2011. Map by author. Statistics for maps sourced from relevant census data. See Katharina Prochazka, "Diffusion Modeling of Language Shift in Austria(-Hungary)" (University of Vienna, 2019); Malle, *Die Slovenen in Kärnten*; Statistik Austria, *Volkszählung. Hauptergebnisse I – Kärnten* (Vienna: Verlag Österreich, 2003).

questioned the results of the census from 1910 and chalked up the drastic decline in Slovene language use to how the census was structured and not actual changes within Carinthian demographics.[39] Moreover, in light of National Socialist policies that wreaked havoc on the ethnic group in the 1940s, Slovene speakers had little incentive to answer such questions from the Austrian government truthfully post-1945. Comparing the experience of Slovenes in Austria to livestock, Florjan Lipuš, the most famous Carinthian Slovene novelist of the post-war period, lamented that an Austrian census was just an opportunity for Slovenes to be counted and measured before they were to be slaughtered again just like they had been under the Nazis.[40] But even to scholars who take a more generous approach to these aggregate census numbers,[41] the total number of Slovene speakers has dramatically decreased in the southern part of the state since the end of the nineteenth century for a range of reasons, including assimilation into the German-speaking majority society for reasons of social and economic prestige,[42] violent persecution and discrimination, and economic changes to the region in which Slovene speakers have traditionally resided.[43] Perhaps, then, it is quite natural that the Peršmanhof, and the memories it supports, should stand where it does, precisely because Slovene is no longer present in other parts of Carinthia.

Facilitation and Mediation of the Peršmanhof Landscape

The memory discourse facilitated at the Peršmanhof – that is, the "shared discursive formation with a set of rules about what can be visible and said" about the past and "what should remain silent and invisible"[44] – promotes a vernacular memorial culture that contests current official interpretations of the past in Carinthia. This memory stems from two sources: the Peršman Museum and the Monument to the International Struggle against Fascism. The memory facilitated through each of these mediums is characterized by the type of discourse each medium creates, both of which are described later.

The Peršman Museum: A Pedagogical Discourse

As a museum on the periphery of Carinthia, it is easy to miss the Peršman Museum. The museum is located in the rebuilt Peršman house, but no sign marks an entrance. A normal door, just as you would find on any other house in the area, is all that is there. Upon entering the museum, I was struck by the domesticity of it all: to the left, a kitchen; to the right, a small parlour.

Since 1982, this small museum, run by the Alliance of Carinthian Partisans, has been trying to tell the history of Carinthian Slovene persecution and resistance during the Second World War. The original museum underwent a major update at the end of the 1990s and beginning of the 2000s. New historical details were being uncovered from the events surrounding the 1945 massacre with the opening of archives, and a generational change within the Carinthian Slovene community was occurring: Those who had experienced the war first-hand were slowly dying, which was shifting the Peršmanhof from the realm of communicative memory to cultural memory.[45] A group of Carinthians, largely from outside the Carinthian Slovene community, started the Peršman Association (Društo/Verein Peršman) in 2001 to help the Alliance of Carinthian Partisans manage the museum in light of these changes. From 2003 to 2005, the Peršman Association collaborated with two researchers from the University of Klagenfurt/Celovec, Peter Gstettner (a professor, at the time, in the department of education and a longtime, respected memory activist in the Carinthian context) and Karl Struhlp-farrer (a historian and expert on the Second World War in the region), to modernize the museum with new museological methods and the use of more professional historical sources. In 2012, the museum was renovated and expanded, and the exhibition was redesigned. It now has just over 1,000 square feet of permanent exhibition space, curated by Werner Koroschitz and Lisa Rettl, both of whom are respected independent historians working in the region, and Uli Vonbank-Schedler, a well-known Austrian visual artist. In stark contrast to the memorial sites and historical plaques in Klagenfurt/Celovec, all the information in the museum is presented in both German and Slovene.[46] In the Peršman Museum, English has no presence, perhaps unintentionally revealing that local Carinthians are the main audience and not international tourists.[47]

Mieke Bal's idea of a grammar of exhibition space proves helpful when reading the Peršman Museum. According to her, museum exhibits are "frequently structured and sometimes even presented in terms derived from other media" – including poetry, narrative, theatre, and film – that helps the curator "discriminate between innovation and chaos."[48] The metaphor of narrative leads the visitor through the exhibition from beginning to end as if he or she were following an itinerary. The Peršman Museum adopts the techniques of the narrative to transmit its information and creates a controlled path for the visitor through the exhibition. Large information panels fill the exhibition space. Each one, in chronological order, covers a specific concept and time period (e.g., "1920–1938. The Plebiscite and Germanization"), marking the path you must take through the museum (figure 2.9). By either slowing down or speeding up the visitors' interaction with the objects and texts, these narrative techniques create a rhythm in the exhibition. This rhythm can be intensified by the curator by using structures

Figure 2.9: Exhibition space about the topic of persecution.

in the building that impose "frames like the rules of grammar" onto the visitor.[49] In the Peršman Museum, the hallway takes on this function as it separates the exhibition rooms into two distinct phenomena: "persecution" and "resistance." The first room begins with descriptions of the low-intensity persecution of Carinthian Slovenes in the late nineteenth century, explains the Germanization policies in the wake of the 1920 plebiscite, describes the 1938 Anschluss, the persecution of the area's single Jewish family, and Nazi policies between 1938 and 1941. It concludes with the deportation of Slovenes to concentration camps and their return afterwards. Moving from the first exhibition room into the second, you must pass through the hallway, which provides the structural break to the timeline presented in the museum.

Crossing through this threshold, you move from the years of persecution into the years of resistance. Since the mass deportations of Slovenes in April 1942 was the catalyst many Slovenes needed to take up arms with the partisan units operating in and around the Karawank mountain range, this design break is an effective way to capture this.[50] Resistance, in the second room, is broadly conceived. It includes those engaged in armed resistance as well as the Green Cadre, Carinthian

Slovenes who deserted the Wehrmacht during the war and returned to their homes in southern Carinthia but, after doing so, did not join the Liberation Front. Rather, they remained hidden in the woods and mountains of the region, trying to survive the war.[51] While this group is described under the panel "The First Partisans," the term *Green Cadre* is not explicitly used. Because this loosely organized group of individuals did not actively fight with the partisans, they had a contentious legacy within the Carinthian Slovene community in the post-war era, particularly among former resistance fighters in the Alliance of Carinthian Partisans, which could be the reason they are not explicitly mentioned.

Both exhibition rooms transmit their knowledge without the help of much digital or interactive technology. There is not much of an attempt to create an "experiential museum," or one that uses advanced interactive technology to try and recreate the past for individuals who have no first-hand memory of it.[52] By doing so, these experiential museums try and bring "the visitor into the story that they are telling, making the visitor play an active role and identify with the story's characters."[53] These techniques have become prominent in many museums around the world that try to promote feelings of empathy in their visitors. These types of museums try to affect their visitors in such a way that they do not just come away with a better understanding of the past, but that they also leave the museum space as individuals ready to actively engage in current political debates.[54]

Besides offering the chance to listen to oral histories and watch one video testimony, the Peršman Museum does not rely on any technological innovations. Instead, it uses strategies of a "traditional museum exhibition," that is, it has been designed to transmit knowledge to visitors in a highly authoritative manner. "The curator teaches," writes Graham Black, "the visitors learn."[55] The Peršman Museum follows this didactic approach to transmitting knowledge about the past, creating a "pedagogical space" that proclaims facts to its visitors in an anonymous, authoritative voice.[56] While you can at times feel overwhelmed by the sheer amount of information presented in such a small space, there is a reason for it: It is the only museum in all of Austria that tells this history, which provides the exhibition space a sense of urgency in its textual descriptions.[57] Didactic strategies like these have been roundly criticized by museum studies scholars. As Bal puts it, "their predictability tends to encourage a certain passivity, a consumerist attitude in visitors."[58] Yet for a museum that finds itself in a competitive memory landscape, these techniques are effective. The Peršman Museum – an example of a "minority museum," or a type of museum in which hegemonic narratives of history cannot dominate the exhibition space because the space is controlled by the historically marginalized group that the exhibition is about – uses these traditional, pedagogical techniques to push back against Carinthia's official memory culture.[59] This strategy is effective because the effects of persecution – not just from the Second World War but also from the late nineteenth century and the post-war period – are presented directly to the viewer.

This straightforward approach to displaying the devastating effects of government policy on a minority group in a museum has been extensively analysed by Amy Lonetree, who has explored how colonial violence inflicted on Native Americans by the US government has been presented in various American and tribal museums.[60] According to her, telling the "hard truths" of colonization in a museum dedicated to Native Americans not only allows visitors to gain a clearer understanding of the dynamics of the past, but it also can help members of Native American tribes overcome the legacies of "historical trauma," Maria Yellow Horse Brave Heart's term for the "cumulative emotional and psychological wounding over the lifespan and across generations, emanating from massive group trauma experiences."[61] The US government's historical relationship with Native American tribes is certainly not identical to the Austrian government's with its Slovene minority, and I do not mean to flatten out differences or particularities between the two cases. Yet there are certain parallels – including sustained assimilationist pressure from the end of the nineteenth century onwards, targeted persecution and policies of elimination during the Second World War, and continued discrimination of Slovene speakers into the post-war era and today – that justify applying Lonetree's research to my reading of this facet of the Peršman Museum.

Although in a different context and for a different community, the Peršman Museum presents the history of this "long" persecution of Carinthian Slovenes in a direct manner. It refuses to shy away from the effects that discrimination, Germanization, persecution, deportation, and violence have had on the Slovene-speaking community of Carinthia, policies that have over the last 140 years reduced the percentage of Slovene speakers from about a third of the state's population to less than 3 per cent. In the context of narrating these hard truths, however, the museum never loses sight of the fact that persecution and resistance were always experienced by individuals. It effectively weaves together the general history of Carinthian Slovene persecution and resistance with the stories of families from the Bad Eisenkappel//Železna Kapla area. One family name, in particular, appears again and again. Behind a window in the first exhibition room, the jacket and shoes worn by

Marija Haderlap, Maja Haderlap's grandmother, in the Ravensbrück concentration camp are displayed. A family photo album, created by Zdravko Haderlap, a local artist and founder of an organization that offers various workshops regarding the region's history to school classes, is on display in the second room, showing pre- and post-war photos of the Haderlap family, one of the first families in the area to support the partisan resistance.[62]

This linking of the general with the specific is perhaps most obvious with the central role the 11 members of the Sadovnik and Kogoj families that were murdered on 25 April 1945, play in the museum. Those involved in the renovation of the museum in 2012 thought deeply about how best to commemorate these specific families within the wider context of the exhibition space. "It was always clear to us that the family and its history had to have a central place," Gudrun Blohberger, the director of the Peršman Association during the renovation, says. "We always had the idea that somehow the farm had to be given back to them."[63] Along with having their names engraved on a glass panel outside of the house's front door, after entering the museum space, a section of the exhibition space is dedicated to the Sadovnik and Kogoj families. In addition to an information panel that describes what daily life was like at the farm before the war, a large illustration of the victims of the massacre hangs on the wall. The placement of this illustration directly by the entrance of the exhibition ensures no one can enter the museum space without first being confronted with the fact that the building in which the museum is housed – the building through which they are about to walk – was, before it became the site of a mass murder, a domestic space in which a family lived its life. While neither these 11 individuals nor their surviving family members were ever given any type of justice by the Austrian judicial system – although the post-war Carinthian government investigated the murder after the war, no one was ever charge with a crime – by granting them such a prominent location in a museum with so little space, it ensures, at the very least, that their personal histories have a prominent location in the museum.[64]

Across from the illustration, there is a small reflection area carved out of a small corner in the hallway. There is a small bench, big enough for one or two people, with a marble headstone with members of the Sadovnik family engraved onto it. Here, visitors can sit and contemplate the exhibition they just experienced while reading through one of the many books about the Carinthian Slovenes and their experience during the war. The reflection corner acts as the final stop in the narrative of the exhibition, reinforcing the curators' commitment to providing as much historical information as possible while also connecting this history to individual experience.

Due to its ability to weave together the history of both the persecution and resistance and the memory of these individual families, the Peršman Museum shares certain characteristics with what scholars have come to call "memorial museums," which are structures that combine attributes of memorials (as places of remembrance) and museums (as transmitters of knowledge) into one building.[65] While the Peršman Museum certainly does not play nearly as large a role as national memorial museums – think, for example, of the US Holocaust Memorial Museum in Washington, D.C. – it is indeed a space that offers a straightforward narrative of persecution and resistance as well as one that acts as a site of remembrance for the Carinthian Slovenes around Bad Eisenkappel/Železna Kapla. Zdravko Haderlap, who grew up just below the Peršmanhof and still operates a family farm in the area, described this dual role of the Peršmanhof in an interview I conducted with him:

> Something that is very positive is that the Sadovnik and Kogoj family members have also accepted this museum now as their memorial place. But it is also a memorial place for locals, those that suffered during the National Socialist era. They come to the Peršmanhof again and again.[66]

Providing this space lets the building take on the role of a site of mourning for both the descendants of the Sadovnik and Koboj families and the wider Slovene community, turning it into a place where past historical trauma, perhaps, can be overcome.[67] Yet while the Peršman Museum acts as a site of pedagogy and a site of mourning, an entirely different kind of discourse – what I call a heroic discourse – is facilitated by the monument that sits right outside of the museum's exit, overlooking the valley below.

Monument to the International Struggle against Fascism:
A Heroic Discourse

When it comes to my reading of the Monument against Fascism, I follow other scholars of memory who draw a distinction between "monuments" and "memorials." Within these approaches, monuments tend to be considered sites of celebration and connected with past military victories or historical moments of national triumph, while memorials are often seen as sites of contemplation and reflection.[68] Arthur C.

Danto, in his analysis of the Vietnam Veterans Memorial in Washington, D.C., puts it this way:

> We erect monuments so that we shall always remember, and build memorials so that we shall never forget. … Monuments commemorate the memorable and embody the myths of beginnings. Memorials ritualize remembrance and mark the reality of ends. …Very few nations erect monuments to their defeats, but many set up memorials to the defeated dead. Monuments make heroes and triumphs, victories and conquests, perpetually present and part of life. The memorial is a special precinct, extruded from life, a segregated enclave where we honor the dead. With monuments we honor ourselves.[69]

While Danto's classic distinction between monuments and memorials is a good starting point for anyone interacting with a commemorative structure for the first time, scholars over the last 30 years have vigorously questioned these structures' abilities to commemorate violent and traumatic pasts. Perhaps most famously, James Young, in his 1992 essay on (then) current German commemorative practices, coined the term "counter-monument" to describe the structures used by a younger generation of German artists who, weary of classic monumental aesthetics because they had been tainted by National Socialism, searched for new ways to commemorate the Holocaust and Germany's role in it.[70]

While there is no exact definition of what counter-monuments are, they share a range of characteristics that cut against the grain of what a monument is supposed to do in Danto's sense of the word. These structures, as Young sees them, dismantle the didactic role monuments have traditionally had with viewers through a wide range of methods that try to produce a more equal relationship between the structure and the viewer. Instead of communicating a fixed message for posterity, counter-monuments are open to interpretation and can even shift their meanings over time through ingenious strategies such as disappearing over time, changing their colours, and using light to reveal hidden textual inscriptions. Rather than being sealed off from everyday life through fences or special commemorative sites, they open themselves up to interaction from those living around it. Counter-monuments also avoid the aesthetics of traditional national monuments and, by doing so, question monuments' reliance on heroic and master narratives. This lack of narrative, while perhaps unsettling to the uninitiated passerby, is a crucial characteristic of the counter-monument.

The counter-monument developed in the wider context of a shift that occurred at the end of the twentieth century, becoming a possible solution for the difficult problem of how a state should commemorate past crimes it had committed.[71] While the phenomenon of the counter-monument has perhaps best been analysed in Germany, it has also been advocated for by a wide range of scholars writing about a whole host of different memorial contexts, ranging from South African commemorations of apartheid to US attempts to commemorate the Vietnam War and slavery.[72] Thirty years after having been introduced, Young's concept has become a foundational idea in memory studies and has developed into a generalized prescription for the complicated problem of "how to find a form for monuments dedicated to groups that had suffered at the hands of the society commemorating them."[73]

But while the counter-monumental form has largely been praised in the academic arena, a critical point has often been overlooked: How a nation that perpetrated mass crimes against a certain group would like to commemorate this past can be different than, even at odds with, how the group itself would like to see it commemorated. It is important to note, for example, that for all the positive coverage Berlin's and Vienna's Holocaust memorials have received – both interpreted as counter-monuments – neither of these projects originated from within the cities' respective Jewish communities.[74] Although by no means am I arguing that only members or descendants of victim groups can commemorate those who were once victimized, commemorative goals can vary depending on who commissions the structure and for what purpose, a point often neglected by advocates of the counter-monument. Young's classic argument, for instance, that it would be better to have had an everlasting debate about fascism in Germany than any one final memorial to the Holocaust, is illustrative and worth quoting in full. According to Young:

> Better a thousand years of Holocaust memorial competitions in Germany than any single "final solution" to Germany's memorial problem. ... In the end, the counter-monument reminds us that the best German memorial to the fascist era and its victims may not be a single memorial at all – but simply the never-to-be-resolved debate over which kind of memory to preserve, how to do it, in whose name, and to what end. That is, what are the consequences of such memory? How do Germans respond to current persecutions of foreigners in their midst in light of their memory of the Third Reich and its crimes? Instead of a fixed sculptural or architectural icon for Holocaust memory in Germany, the debate itself – perpetually unresolved amid ever-changing conditions – might now be enshrined.[75]

At first glance, this style of commemoration – that is, a never-ending discussion about the past that keeps the event in the public's consciousness – seems gratifying. After all, keeping issues of the past relevant to current politics is often a core demand of memory activists and others advocating for the construction of structures to commemorate violent pasts. But in such a world, no structure would have ever been built, and it is hard to imagine a German public willing to engage with such a topic on a never-ending, annual basis.

When seen in this light, counter-monuments, while ideally being spaces that provoke viewers into a critical engagement with their nation's past, can also become ones that marginalize the group it is supposed to be commemorating. If it is only ever debated as to whether a memorial should be built or not, this style of monument can end up actually ignoring the original goal of the structure: To commemorate, in public, a historical wrong and, by doing so, jolt a passerby into reflection. A society that is trying to commemorate past crimes is filled with both descendants of perpetrators and descendants of victims, both of whom have commemorative needs that often diverge from one another. Particularly in situations in which vernacular memories have been disparaged and silenced, the counter-monument could actually continue this process of marginalization. As my analysis of the Monument against Fascism at the Peršmanhof demonstrates later, it is exactly what scholars such as Young find so objectionable about traditional monuments – their didacticism, their "authoritarian" claims to truth, their mythologizations of the past – that actually gives the Monument against Fascism its mnemonic power.

As the first commemorative structure dedicated to the partisan resistance to be built after the war, the Monument against Fascism carries immense symbolic meaning for the wider Slovene community.[76] This mnemonic meaning comes largely from two sources: the monument's design, which glorifies the partisan resistance against Nazism, and the monument's own history. The monument's aesthetics are fundamentally different from the other commemorative structures found throughout southern Carinthia. As mentioned at the outset of this chapter, most partisan memorials, often located in small village cemeteries or on the side of narrow mountain roads, are simple, rugged memorials, with the names of victims nearby inscribed on them. The memorials that mark the sites of former atrocities rely on aesthetic choices from traditional funeral practices such as stone monoliths, earth mounds, and cairns.[77] In contrast to Yugoslavia, where such memorials had their heyday in the immediate post-war period but had begun to be replaced by classical, realist monuments by the 1950s, these rugged partisan memorials

Figure 2.10: Memorial space on the Kömmelgupf/Komeljski Vrh.

were mostly built in the 1970s.[78] Although they range in size, their purpose, gleaned from their inscriptions and locations, are truly memorials in Danto's sense of the term. An example of one of these is the memorial in Kömmel/Komelj, which is shown in figure 2.10.

Built in 1972 on the site where, 30 years earlier, 12 partisans, 10 of whom were Carinthians, were arrested, tortured, and then murdered by German police, the memorial was blown up in 1976 by unknown perpetrators and rebuilt in 1978 by the Alliance of Carinthian Partisans. The stone monolith sits off the side of the small road, across from the Cimprc family farm, a short distance from the Slovenian border. A small wooden fence, showing mould and damage of years gone by, keeps the dense forest at bay, separating the memorial from the element that was the partisan's most trusted friend during the war. There are no grand slogans here, no mythologizing of the partisan resistance through heroic, communist symbolism. The location and design of the site, instead, creates a small space to mourn the dead and honour the sacrifice they made. There is a short, direct inscription: "In honor of the twelve partisans who fell at the Apovnik's. October 12, 1944."

Figure 2.11: Memorial on the Kömmelgupf/Komeljski Vrh. The inscription reads "In honour of the twelve partisans who fell at the Apovnik's. 12 October 1944. The monument was built on 28 May 1972. Blown up on 31 October 1976." The wreaths were placed by the Alliance of Carinthian Partisans and the government of Slovenia for All Saints' Day in 2019. Notice the absence of any symbolic objects from the Austrian government.

Although the small site, I imagine, is only seen by those living in the area or those who, every July, participate in an annual commemorative hike organized by the Alliance of Carinthian Partisans, a close reading of memorial reveals an interesting transnational aspect occurring within the Carinthian Slovene's memory culture. I did my memorial site visits in the days following All Saint's Day (1 November), a holiday in Austria during which it is quite popular for people to go to cemeteries and memorial sites and lay flowers to commemorate the dead. For the holiday, as you can see in figure 2.11, two wreaths were placed next to the memorial for the holiday, one by the Alliance of Carinthian Partisans and one by the Slovenian government. At first, seeing the wreath laid by the Slovenian government surprised me. Throughout the Cold War and even into the early twenty-first century, the Carinthian state government, as well as the German nationalist groups I touched on in chapter 1, asserted that Carinthian Slovene organizations like the Alliance of Carinthian Partisans were largely fronts for Yugoslav influence.[79] Within this context, the partisan memorials like the one in Kömmel/Komelj were perceived as proof of Carinthian Slovenes' lingering support for communist Yugoslavia as well as symbolic territorial claims on the part of the Yugoslavs. The SHS state had, after all, quickly invaded and occupied large parts of southern Carinthia in 1919, and Yugoslavia, too, had demanded territorial annexations after 1945.

Although I had rejected such readings of these memorials early on in my fieldwork more as propaganda than anything else, seeing the wreath from the Slovenian government made me wonder how close the relationship was between the Alliance of Carinthian Partisans and the official institutions of Slovenia. When asked about this relationship in a later interview, Andre Mohar, the head of the Alliance of Carinthian Partisans, admitted that the Slovenian government indeed plays a crucial role in the Alliance of Carinthian Partisans' memory work by providing the group with most of its budget, which lets them maintain older memorials and build new ones.[80] The Slovenian government sends an official representative from its consulate in Klagenfurt/Celovec to the Alliance of Carinthian Partisans' annual commemorative ceremonies on All Saint's Day as well as the ones that it holds on Austria's national holiday (26 October). Some of these are even attended by Slovenian parliamentarians.[81] Certainly, one could read Slovenia's (and during the post-war period, Yugoslavia's) financial support for these memorials – as others have read the Soviet Union's Second World War monuments in Eastern Europe – as symbolic territorial claims.[82] In reality, however, it stems largely from the fact that the Liberation Front was indeed a Slovene organization (so it is relatively unsurprising that Slovenia takes an active role in its continual commemoration) and the Austrian government, in clear violation of Article 19 of the State Treaty that commits it to maintaining the graves of Allied soldiers, has never provided the Alliance of Carinthian Partisans funds for this type of memory work. Notice in figure 2.11, for example, the absence of any symbolic remembrance object left by the Austrian or Carinthian governments.

Although the wreaths and candles that were placed by the memorial revealed who the main caretakers of the memorial were, some may find it surprising that these objects were there in the first place. After all, All Saints Day, a prominent Catholic holiday, does not seem like a day that an organization dedicated to commemorating the partisan resistance would take too seriously, considering that the Liberation Front was a communist organization. However, reading Carinthian

Slovene memory work in such a way would be a mistake. It would greatly simplify the reasons for why Carinthian Slovenes fought with the Liberation Front during the war by implying that they were all "just" communists and, in this line of thought, could not be religious, which was far from the case. For "many rank-and-file partisans," writes Peter Pirker, "many of whom came from a traditional Catholic milieu, this [resistance] was simply a struggle for survival – theirs and their families' – that could be waged most effectively by joining" the Liberation Front.[83]

Such a reading would also "exotify" partisan memorial culture in a way that detaches it from its broader European context. In reality, both Carinthian Slovene partisan memorials and Yugoslav ones (of the immediate post-war period) have many more similarities with pre-war European funerary aesthetics than they do differences. Nineteenth-century European war memorials, as well as post-1945 Yugoslav ones, "presented names of the dead" and added "rhymes, short messages, sculptural reliefs, and other three-dimensional ornaments" onto the memorials.[84] Moreover, it is by no means surprising to see prominent religious symbols on the graves of buried partisans throughout the former Yugoslavia.[85] The partisan memorials around Trieste/Trst (Italy) often link "revolution and tradition" on one memorial by adding both "a traditional cross together with a more revolutionary red star."[86] The two partisan memorials in Carinthia shown in figures 2.12 and 2.13 are a good examples of this. Along with the names of the fallen partisan fighters, for example, the memorial in the cemetery of St. Jakob im Rosental/Šenktjakob v Rožu has a traditional cross etched into one of its corners, while the memorial in the cemetery in Velden on the Wörthersee/Vrba na Koroškem has the revolutionary five-pointed star (petokratka) on top.

In contrast to the memorial in Kömmel/Komelj, the monument at the Peršmanhof (figure 2.14), designed by the Croatian Marijan Matijević, promotes a heroic narrative of partisan resistance in the classical monumental style.[87] Although Matijević had moved from Zagreb to Vienna in 1943 and never obtained Yugoslav citizenship after the war, his design clearly reflects the architectural style of monumental realism, which had been popular throughout Europe in the nineteenth century.[88] The monument at the Peršmanhof is similar to many early realist Yugoslav war monuments, which, "aimed at creating an image of an idealized or typified historical protagonist – a Partisan fighter – or an idea itself – e.g., the revolution sacrifice, resistance, revenge – expressed through a broad scope of formal explorations and iconographic patterns."[89] Resting on a pedestal on a ridge line, the bronze sculpture portrays three

Figure 2.12: Memorial in St. Jakob im Rosental/Šenktjakob v Rožu. Built in 1970 and dedicated to nine partisans killed in 1945. Exemplary of the memorials found in village cemeteries in the region. The inscription reads "To the partisans who fell in the struggle against fascism, 1941–1945." The names of the fallen partisans are etched into the three smaller marble blocks that surround the main pillar.

Figure 2.13. Memorial in Velden am Wörthersee/Vrba na Koroškem. Built in 1970, this particular one was renovated in 2019. The inscription reads "Andri Ogris, born 17 September 1924, and five other unknown partisans, fallen on 20 November 1944 in Selpritsch/Žopračah. Here rests those partisans fallen in the struggle against fascism, 1941–1945."

partisans, joined together in combat, outfitted with the tools of war. Unlike the static memorial at Kömmel/Komelj, the sculpture depicts movement, with the three partisans moving dynamically forward in unison. The monument faces northwards, with one figure turning his torso backwards – perhaps encouraging his fellow comrades to follow – giving the impression to the viewer that the figures are storming over the Karawank mountain range and towards Carinthia. As in the case of other war monuments built after the war in Yugoslavia, the full spectrum of partisan resistance is represented in the monument. To the left, the professional revolutionary can be seen. Not only is he placed in front of the other two figures and depicted with a command gesture, but he is also the only one dressed in a military uniform and wearing the "triglavka" cap. Named after Mount Triglav, the highest mountain

Figure 2.14: Monument to the International Struggle against Fascism.

in Slovenia, the triglavka was worn by Slovene partisans during the war. In the post-war period, the triglavka came to symbolize "Slovenia" on commemorative structures in Yugoslavia, while Mount Triglav itself was used for the coat of arms of the Socialist Republic of Slovenia.[90] On the far right, the peasant soldier, symbolized by his carrying of an axe instead of a rifle and dressed in civilian clothes, is shown. When compared with the numerous, Catholic-influenced war memorials that you find in Austria commemorating the First and Second World Wars, perhaps the most radical difference here is the figure of the woman, standing in the centre on the pedestal, actively engaged in resistance and holding a rifle.[91] She has been constructed to be the same height as her male counterparts, symbolizing the active role women took in the resistance, a common feature in Yugoslav war monuments as well.[92] Although these figures represent diverse interests and wartime experiences, in the sculpture, they are fused into one revolutionary movement. Their bodies have merged, and they move forward as one.

The monument's history, which takes us down from the Peršmanhof to the Sankt Ruprecht / Šentrupert cemetery in Völkermarkt/Velikovec, a town about 15 miles to the north, is a complicated one. On 17 November 1946, the Liberation Front organized a large ceremony to rebury 83 people – resistance fighters as well as forced labourers and prisoners of war from around Europe who had managed to escape captivity and join the partisans – who had died during the war and had been buried in wartime graves throughout the region. As with many monuments, this one provoked debate during its design process. The controversy over what was to be written on the pedestal – would it be dedicated to those who fell simply for "freedom" during the war or to those who had died during the "struggle against fascism" – sparked debate in Carinthia already in 1946.[93] Once the monument was unveiled on 26 October 1947, it became the main representation of Carinthian Slovene resistance, what has been called the "corporate identity" of the community.[94]

Once built, however, monuments "can be used in ways that are different from and even contrary to the uses to which their builders or 'owners' intended they be put."[95] In this line of thought, scholars often argue that reinterpreting these public spaces can be seen as a form of popular resistance, as everyday people transform the structure's purpose and destabilize the original narrative.[96] This type of normative argument about everyday people taking back control of public spaces has often been made in studies on post-communist states.[97] Yet this type of reinterpretation can also occur in the other direction, that is, those with dominant positions in society can also deface, derogate, or otherwise damage the commemorative structures built by minority groups. As *the* symbol of partisan resistance in post-war Carinthia, the monument was immediately reinterpreted by German nationalists. Only a week after its construction, the monument was vandalized with pro-fascist slogans. Six years later, on 10 September 1953, the monument was blown up by unknown assailants, which destroyed most of the bronze sculpture but left the pedestal on which it sat largely intact.

If you know where to look, the pedestal can still be seen today in the cemetery. The pedestal and the mass grave, which took me quite a while to find when I visited the site on a rainy autumn afternoon,

Figure 2.15: Sankt Ruprecht / Šentrupert cemetery in Völkermarkt/Velikovec.

are tucked around a corner of the cemetery's small church, cordoned off from the rest of the area (figure 2.15). The cemetery itself is a good example of Carinthia's divided memory culture. To get to the pedestal and the grave for the 83 partisans, you first have to walk by the final resting place, cordoned off in its own pristinely kept section of the cemetery, for 398 Austrian soldiers from the Second World War who had served in both the Wehrmacht and the SS (figure 2.16). At the Sankt Ruprecht cemetery, just as was the case with my other visits to other war memorials throughout southern Carinthia, the Austrian government as well as the Völkermart/Velikovec city government had laid wreaths and flowers next to the graves of these 398 Austrian soldiers but had ignored the pedestal and mass grave of the partisans. Even the Austrian Black Cross (das Österreichische Schwarze Kreuz), a non-partisan organization that, in cooperation with the Austrian Ministry of the Interior, maintains graves of soldiers (from the First and Second World Wars) along with victims of political persecution (nationality notwithstanding), had only maintained the Austrian soldiers' graves.

Of course, the destruction of the monument in 1953 was not perceived to be a random act of vandalism or simply as the "reinterpretation" of

Figure 2.16: Restored pedestal in Völkermarkt/Velikovec. It is located on the side of the church in the Sankt Ruprecht/Šentrupert cemetery and next to a mass grave of 83 fallen partisans, the main inscription reads, "For those who fell in the fight against fascism." The smaller inscription below the cross reads, "In this grave rests 83 anti-fascist resistance fighters from eight countries," followed by a list of these countries. The name of Alfgar Hesketh-Prichard is also included, the British intelligence officer who parachuted into the region as part of the Clowder mission, organized by British intelligence, and was executed by a partisan commander in December 1944.

one community's monument by another, but rather as a political act of terrorism. Even the Carinthian state government, no ally of the Liberation Front or Slovenes in the post-war period, recognized the motives of those behind the bombing and used the word *terrorist attack* (*Attentat*) to describe the event in a telegram to the Ministry of Interior in Vienna. The perpetrators were never found, and while the monument was rebuilt in the St. Ruprecht / Šentrupert cemetery in 1962, the sculpture was never replaced, and for the next 30 years, its remains were stored in a warehouse in Kühnsdorf/Sinča vas by Luka Sienčnik.[98] It was not until 13 August 1983, after Janez Wutte-Luc and Johnan Hanin restored the sculpture with limited funds from the Alliance of Carinthian Partisans and donations from the wider Slovene community, that the reconstructed monument was placed at the Peršmanhof.[99] In the original sculpture, the partisan peasant (on the right) had his arm stretched out behind him, with his hand open, palm facing the sky, gesturing for others to join him in the struggle against fascism. When the sculpture was restored in 1982, a grenade was placed in his palm. The peasant partisan's hand no longer offers a gesture of solidarity to others wishing to join but now symbolizes the continuing struggle of the Carinthian Slovenes.

The response that the monument provoked in German-nationalist circles alludes to the controversial nature of the partisan resistance in the immediate post-war period. Even today, however, the partisan's legacy is still contentious. It remains, in how the legacy of the Vietnam War has been described in US collective memory, a "zone of contested meaning."[100] On one hand, German-nationalist organizations and even some historians maintain that the partisans did not fight for an independent Austria free from Nazism but rather *for* Yugoslavia, and hence for communist totalitarianism. On the other, Carinthian Slovene organizations continue to emphasize Austria's persecution of Slovene speakers, the deportations, and the effectiveness of the Liberation Front.

The monument's framing strategies clearly promote this latter interpretation of the partisans' role in the war. At first glance, due to its "demagogical rigidity and certainty of history," the monument seems to have little in common with the counter-monument aesthetic described earlier.[101] In fact, one could argue that the monument, while not part of Carinthia's official memory culture, actually has several attributes of the "traditional" state-sponsored monument these authors have criticized. It is didactic, telling the viewer what they should think while looking at it. It is spatially separated from everyday life, built in a space designed for commemoration. Perhaps most offensive to critics of these types of monuments, it is self-aggrandizing and heroic, commemorating the mythical nature of the partisan resistance.[102]

Yet focusing solely on these traditional characteristics, that is, criticizing these types of monuments solely on formal grounds, overlooks the radicalism of the Monument against Fascism. In a state that still refuses to officially commemorate the Slovene resistance, this monument does explicitly that. By doing so, it challenges current hegemonic memory practices in Carinthia that highlight historic Slav aggression and partisan reprisals and instead celebrates the partisan resistance. If the message of the sculpture of the three figures heroically fighting fascism is not clear enough for the viewer, the inscription on the pedestal – which, due to its small size, forces the viewer to get close to the structure and lean forward in a posture of acknowledgment – removes any room for doubt:

> In 1947, the Carinthian partisans, in the presence of Allied representatives, unveiled this monument in St. Ruprecht / Šentrupert near Völkermarkt/ Velikovec dedicated to those partisans from eight nations who fell on the Saualpe [a mountain in the region]. The monument is a symbol of the Carinthian and international struggle against fascism. Unknown perpetrators blew it up at night on 11 September 1953. Austrian authorities did not restore the monument to its original form so the Alliance of Carinthian Partisans restored it in 1983 and put it at this location.[103]

Certainly, this direct, didactic form of commemoration has become more and more uncommon since the 1980s and has been substituted for more abstract forms of commemoration.[104] Monuments, moreover, have long been criticized for their rigidity and their mythologization of complex historical events. Already in 1938, for example, Lewis Mumford made the oft-cited observation: "The notion of a modern monument is veritably a contradiction in terms. ... If it is a monument it is not modern, and if it is modern, it cannot be a monument."[105] As James Young has more recently argued, the "imposition of a single cultural icon or symbol onto a host of disparate and competing experiences, as a way to impose common meaning and value on disparate memories" offends our "modern sensibility" that have become accustomed to more pluralistic interpretations of the past.[106] Some scholars contend, perhaps too dramatically, that "the age of monumentality, or meaningful memorials and memorialization in the public sphere, is over."[107] Monuments constructed with the aesthetics of socialist realism have been even more criticized for this rigidity. "Socialist realism," argues Michael Ignatieff, "has such a narrow range, such a limited command of the registers of human experience: the monuments manage to convey the heroic and the grandiose, never the humble and the particular."[108] Paul Stangl, likewise, contends that, due to their construction in totalitarian states, these types of monuments should "be viewed as little more than propaganda etched in stone."[109] While I doubt that the monuments to the defeat of Nazism built under communist regimes are any more propagandistic than monuments built under democratic ones, it is indeed this straightforward glorification of resistance in a country that had so little of it that provides the Monument against Fascism much of its symbolic power.

The power of this direct style of commemoration has been noticed elsewhere, too. Responding to critics who said he should have used more abstract forms of design, Nathan Rapoport, the architect of the "Monument to the Ghetto Heroes" in Warsaw, Poland, told James Young during an interview that a realistic, direct style was required for his work. In his words:

> Could I have made a stone with a hole in it … and said, "Voila! The Greatness of the Jewish People?" No, I needed to show the heroism, to illustrate it literally in figures everyone, not just artists, would respond to. This was to be a public monument after all. And what do human beings respond to? Faces, figures, the human form. I did not want to represent resistance in the abstract: it was not an abstract uprising. It was real.[110]

Just as the Warsaw Uprising was real, so was the partisan resistance. Whether the monumental form should be used for nations or groups commemorating past wrongs is an open question. Yet when a minority group commemorates its own victims and victories, both of which have yet to be incorporated into the official memory culture of the state in which they live, the monument – with its triumphal aesthetics, its glorification of heroes, and didactic messaging – carries significant symbolic power and achieves its goal: To celebrate those who fought with the partisans during the war.

The Peršmanhof as Discourse Materialized

As I have shown, the Peršmanhof is a central location for discussions of the legacy of National Socialism in southern Carinthia, particularly its impact on the Carinthian Slovene community. The Peršmanhof produces a certain type of discourse about Carinthian Slovene persecution and resistance that is at odds with the discourse found in Carinthia's official memory culture described at the outset of this chapter. Outside of the Peršmanhof, one is hard-pressed to see any physical traces of Slovene resistance and/or persecution from the war. The memorial sites that have been created throughout the state have been constructed to naturalize and promote the history and memory of Carinthia as German-speaking Carinthia. To understand the Peršmanhof's meaning, then, is to first acknowledge its absence within the official memory of Carinthia.[111] This absence from the state denotes a silence, an unwillingness to commemorate a particular period in history in which the Austrian government, as part of Nazi Germany, perpetuated mass crimes against its own population. Simultaneously, it also demonstrates a refusal to commemorate the most effective armed, organized resistance to operate within Austria during the war.

When this absence is noticed, however, it speaks volumes about what official memory culture has deemed worthy of commemorating in Carinthia. Because memorials, particularly the ones that occupy prominent public spaces, can be read as "symbols of community values, attitudes and beliefs," they also reflect the political discourses and ideologies of those powerful enough to build them.[112] The Peršmanhof's location is a product of these discourses. It is a product not only of active attempts to "forget" the history it tells and the memories it supports, but it is also the product of an active, at times even violent, strategy to keep these discourses and structures on the periphery of Carinthia's memorial culture.

Being on the periphery of a country's official memory culture tends to not be considered a positive thing. "Memory actors," Jenny Wüstenburg's term for the individuals and organizations involved in the process of constructing memorials, tend to demand that sites of memory be built in significant economic and transportation locations to magnify the structure's importance.[113] In particular, minority communities demanding the memorialization of past crimes or violence often argue that the state in question should acknowledge its past wrong by placing memorials in prominent sites, often in the capital.[114] In this line of argument, occupying a prominent location in a state's official memory culture makes a symbolic statement that the minority community is indeed an integral part of the nation.[115] While it is clear that commemorating past wrongs at the centre can carry symbolic power, there are also several dangers to this centralization of memory. "Place-making activities," as Till writes, "tell us more about the people building a memorial than the peoples and pasts being commemorated."[116] In this line of thought, then, it begs the question: Why would a state commemorate its past wrongs "in the center"? In the case of Germany's memorialization of the Holocaust, Till shows how some German activists worry that this strategy could be used to cordon off this part of the country's past to oblivion and transform the city into a place where national guilt can be commemorated and expiated. Simply by occupying prominent positions in national capitals, these sites of memory can also run the risk of being co-opted by the state, becoming places of "in and for the center" instead of for the people they were built for.[117] Secluded on the side of a mountain and marginalized in Carinthia's official memory culture, the Peršmanhof does not have to worry about its message being absorbed and perhaps neutralized by the state. On the periphery, the Peršmanhof can produce a counter-narrative of the partisan past that is squarely at odds with the official ones it competes with.[118]

As Schein emphasizes in most of his work, however, landscapes do not just reflect the legacies of human activity but are also about "intervention, about promising the possibility for human action in order to change the status quo."[119] While a counter-memory of the Second World War in southern Carinthia is certainly constructed at the Peršmanhof – the narrative of the partisan resistance told at the Peršmanhof is such a radical alternative to the stigmatized, blighted, and generally negative discourse dominant in Carinthian official memory about it – the memory work that occurs in and around the Peršmanhof is not secluded to the specific geographic space nor is it limited to commemorating events from the war. Multiple activist organizations in the area use the landscape of the Peršmanhof – the historical facts of the museum, the heroic aesthetics of the monument, and the geographic site itself – as an avenue to engage visitors in workshops, seminars, and other activities to "reclaim the Partisan legacy."[120] Through their work, these organizations are not only destabilizing Carinthia's official memory culture, but they are also mobilizing these uncovered counter-memories to intervene in contemporary political life. To discuss how these memories are used in and around the Peršmanhof, however, is to grapple with how memory works "on the ground" in southern Carinthia, which is the topic of my next chapter.

The Struggle of Everyday Memory in Southern Carinthia

As I showed in chapter 2, the landscape of the Peršmanhof – the museum, the monument, and the location itself – creates a counter-memory for the Carinthian Slovene community of southern Carinthia, and, by doing so, offers an alternative discourse to the generally negative official one about the Slovene partisans from the Second World War. Foregrounding the discourse sustained by the landscape of the Peršmanhof, however, is only one aspect of understanding the cultural landscape of an area. The other aspect of it, as Richard Schein reminds us, is "about intervention, about promising the possibility for human action in order to change the status quo."[1] In southern Carinthia, several community activist organizations have taken up this challenge, treating these counter-memories as important tools with which to intervene in contemporary Carinthian political life and challenge dominant political discourses in the region. The active intervention of these organizations is the subject of this chapter, which is based on interviews I conducted with five memory entrepreneurs, Elizabeth Jelin's term for creative, passionate individuals who, through a range of innovative strategies, "seek social recognition and political legitimacy of *one* (their own) interpretation or narrative of the past" and are "engaged and concerned with maintaining and promoting active and visible social and political attention on their enterprise."[2] These memory entrepreneurs were from four activist organizations currently trying to influence the official memory of National Socialism in southern Carinthia.

The interviews I conducted reveal that the tangible places and objects of the southern Carinthian landscape of remembrance that I visited during my fieldwork – largely created, maintained, and curated by the activist organizations presented in this chapter – are only a small part of these organizations' memory activism. Through the interviews, I was introduced to their larger educational and political efforts that aim, in various ways, to activate the region's heritage as a political resource for today. Through the development and deployment of these pedagogical efforts, these activist organizations use counter-memories to not only teach visitors about the legacies and consequences of National Socialism in the region. They also use these memories to activate a new political consciousness in them for the present.

But this chapter does more than just reveal a hidden side of these organizations' activism that animates the past for a variety of pedagogies. It also adds multiple voices to my exploration of memory in twenty-first-century southern Carinthia. An often-made critique of memory studies is its overemphasis of individual interpretations of commemorative rituals and mediums at the expense of probing how these are enacted and/or received on the ground from individuals living in the actual area under analysis.[3] As one critic puts it, these studies often boil down to an individual's "reflections on a representation of the past – a memorial, a film, a heritage site – that they feel is flawed or biased in some way."[4] In what follows, I include the perspectives of these memory entrepreneurs, and by doing so, I am able to present a fuller picture of the practices and techniques activist organizations use in order to advocate for an interpretation of the past that has long been marginalized in the state's official memory culture.

Over the course of my fieldwork, in general, and during the interview process, in particular, I developed a deep respect for all the memory entrepreneurs presented in this chapter. Through this process – visits to the various memorials and graves that dot the countryside, interviews, and my process of learning Slovene – a bond developed between those engaged in this memory activism and myself. This bond was not based on language or national identity but rather on a feeling of solidarity with a group of individuals who engage in memory activism not only to create more public salience for a past that has been largely ignored but who also use this past as a tool to "struggle against injuries inflicted on others" in the present.[5]

Advocating for an interpretation of the past that occupies a marginal position in a society's official memory culture is difficult. It requires creativity to develop projects, vast organizational skills, the ability to generate "buy in" from others, perseverance, courage, and determination.[6] Doing this activist work in Carinthia – the state that is often seen as having done the least to memorialize the Nazi era in Austria – is even more so, which is why I found my conversations with these individuals not only rewarding and enlightening but also worthy of inclusion as an entire chapter in this book.[7] In "an attempt to obtain systematic and complete information"[8] on the process of remembrance relating to the Second World War in Carinthia, I conducted qualitative, semi-structured, expert interviews with them.[9] This form of interview

> involves the implementation of a number of predetermined questions and/or special topics. These questions are typically asked of each interviewee in a systematic and consistent order, but the interviewers are allowed freedom to digress; that is, the interviewers are permitted (in fact expected) to probe far beyond the answers to their prepared and standardized question.[10]

During the interviews, I treated each one of the memory activists as an "expert," that is, someone with a highly specialized set of knowledge that was unavailable to me as an outside researcher.[11] Due to this expert position, it was important for me to let the memory entrepreneurs speak for themselves as best as I could and reproduce their statements verbatim.

In consultation with a mentor from the Slovene Institute of Sciences (Slowenisches wissenschaftliches Institut/Slovenski znanstveni inštitut) and the University of Graz, eight memory organizations operating in southern Carinthia were identified and contacted by email. If an organization did not respond, I waited three weeks and contacted them again. Of the eight, four agreed to participate in my project. The following criteria were used: (1) they possessed "expert knowledge" about Carinthian commemorative practices relating to the Second World War; (2) they were in a position to influence official memory policies about the Second World War; and (3) they currently occupy, or have occupied in the past, a leadership position in a Carinthian-based memory organization that engages with Carinthian memory politics of the Second World War. I define "expert knowledge" as an individual possessing the following: (1) practical experience (many years of experience working in a memory organization), (2) organizational knowledge (awareness of the practical information of the respective organization), (3) functional knowledge (an understanding of how the organization functions on an everyday basis), and (4) contextual knowledge (knowledge of the other actors and organizations active in Carinthian memory politics).[12] While my interview sample is too small to explore how all Carinthian memory organizations operate – I did not interview any of the right-wing German nationalist organizations, for example, nor did I interview any organizations from outside of southern Carinthia – the memory entrepreneurs I interviewed represented diverse professions (a farmer/artist, historian, journalist, museum curator, and a retired schoolteacher), and both ethnic groups (Slovene and German). These entrepreneurs represented four organizations, which are described in the following discussion.

Founded in 2001 in Klagenfurt/Celovec by individuals largely from outside the Carinthian Slovene community, the Peršman Association supports the work of the Alliance of Carinthian Partisans at the Peršmanhof memorial site. Since these two organizations signed a cooperation agreement in the early 2000s, the Peršman Association has been in charge of the museological work at the Peršman Museum (creating the exhibition, training volunteers, etc.). From 2003 to 2004, the Peršman Association carried out a large research project, based on newly accessible archival files, to better understand the massacre from 25 April 1945 as well as the history of the farm itself. The findings from this research project formed the basis of the museum renovation, which occurred between 2011 and 2012. Since 2017, in addition to its museological work, the Peršman Association has been offering seminars and workshops to school classes. Membership in the organization is open to anyone and costs €25 for adults and €10 for students. From the Peršman Association, I interviewed the current director, Andrej Mohar. I also interviewed Gudrun Blohberger, who, while no longer involved in the organization's work, was its director during the renovation project.

In contrast to the relatively recent founding of the Peršman Association, the Alliance of Carinthian Partisans is one of the oldest Carinthian Slovene organizations in the state. Founded in 1948 to unite former partisans in the post-war period into one organization, the Alliance, in its early years, took a staunch pro-Yugoslav line on the so-called Carinthian border question after the war – that is, whether southern Carinthia should become a part of the new Yugoslav state – and provided financial assistance to wounded partisan veterans and the widows and orphans of fallen partisans. From its early days, the Alliance of Carinthian Partisans has had an active role in Carinthian public life as one of the main, left-wing representative bodies for Carinthian Slovenes and has taken a leading role in building and maintaining memorials to former partisan fighters in southern Carinthia since its founding. While the organization was originally closed to non-veterans or relatives of veterans, since 1997, membership has been open to anyone wishing to join. Andrej Mohar was also my interview partner representing the Alliance of Carinthian Partisans, as he, at the time of the interview, was the secretary of the organization.

Remember-Villach (Verein Erinnern-Villach) was founded in 1995 in Villach/Beljak by Hans Haider, a local high school math and science teacher. Central to the work of Remember-Villach has been researching the biographies of victims of National Socialism from the Villach/

Beljak area. As of 2020, the organization has managed to publish short biographies of 140 individuals on their website. In addition, Haider has conducted and published interviews with witnesses from Villach about the deportations of the city's Jewish and Roma/Sinti populations. Remember-Villach is best known in the region for successfully building a memorial to victims of National Socialism in 1999. Located in the centre of the town, the Memorial of Names lists the name, date of birth, date of death, and location of death of those from Villach/Beljak killed under National Socialism. Membership is also open to anyone who wishes to join. From Remember-Villach, I interviewed Hans Haider and Alexandra Schmidt in a joint interview.

Since 2002, Zdravko Haderlap has been managing the A-Zone in Leppen/Lepena. Located on the Vinkl-Hof/Vinklnova domačija, the A-Zone offers various workshops to visitors, all of which incorporate the natural environment of the region in various ways. The content of these workshops varies widely, from classes on traditional mountain farming techniques to seminars on autobiographical writing. The A-Zone also produces numerous cultural events during the year (concerts, plays, etc.) and organizes guided hiking tours throughout the region, several of which incorporate the history and culture of Carinthia's Slovene community. From the A-Zone, I interviewed Zdravko Haderlap.

All five of these interviews, which lasted between 53 and 67 minutes, were conducted with a semi-structured interview guide. The guide was prepared beforehand, which ensured that all questions were asked in a consistent manner to the various participants. However, since the questions were open-ended, the participants had a wide range of space for their possible answers. This method enabled me to, when needed, ask follow-up questions and probe the expert for more detail. The guide was developed based on insights gained from five months of fieldwork and in close collaboration with a colleague from the University of Vienna with extensive qualitative interviewing experience. As with any guided interview, this guide provided the starting point for all five interviews, yet the specific phrases and questions varied depending on the context of the individual interview situation.[13]

The interviews were held in a natural setting comfortable for the memory entrepreneur, which took me from a cafe in Klagenfurt/Celovec and a living room in Villach/Beljak to a farm in Leppen/Lepena and an office in Mauthausen. I conducted all these interviews in German and translated them into English, a point that bears emphasis. Although Carinthian Slovenes have historically grown up bilingually and continue to do so, from my personal interactions with the Austrian

Fulbright Committee, the organization that funded my fieldwork, there seems to still be a perception from Austrian academics outside of southern Carinthia that Carinthian Slovenes cannot speak German, which could not be further from the case. As Tom Priestly, the leading linguist on the Slovene dialect spoken in the region, writes:

> Dialect Slovene is the first language of most minority members; there are no monolingual Slovene-speakers still alive. Minority competence in Standard Slovene varies very greatly, depending on, inter alia, education, frequency of church attendance, and strength of ethnic self-identification. All members of the [Carinthian Slovene] minority speak German: they are taught Standard German in school, hear it in the media, and use it for official purposes; nearly all are more or less competent also in some form of Dialect German, and speak this with Germanophones in informal situations.[14]

All interviews were audio-recorded, transcribed, translated into English, coded, and then analysed using qualitative content analysis.[15] To begin this process, I familiarized myself with the data by reading all the transcripts independently from one another. This part of the analysis was "about uncovering, naming, and developing concepts and categories by opening up the text" for the first time.[16] During this stage, I broke the data down into relevant "meaning units," or the "words, sentences or paragraphs containing aspects related to each other through their content and context."[17] Once these meaning units had been isolated, I coded the data, which enabled me to better understand "the meanings of individual sections of data."[18] To ensure consistency, I developed an inductive codebook where the codes, categories, and themes were derived from the interview data themselves.[19] These codes form the backbone of my analysis, and they helped me develop the "concepts around which the data [could] be assembled into blocks and patterns."[20] After the codebook was developed, I labelled each meaning unit with a particular code from this list. To achieve greater rigour, I repeated the coding process three times, adding and deleting codes in the process.

In the end, I developed four main themes based on the data: (1) Why remember the past, (2) Strategies of remembrance, (3) Dynamics of memory, and (4) Transnational memory. The codebook can be found in table 3.1. Before I could develop these themes, the meaning units had to be condensed. From this condensed text, I then developed categories, which helped identify my themes. The coding scheme can be found in table 3.2.

Table 3.1: Codebook

Theme	Category	Code	Definition
R1: Why remember the past?	Goals of organization	Public-oriented commitment	Coding of every text passage that describes a commitment to raising (general) public awareness of National Socialism in Austria, its effects, its legacies, and the perceived return of forms of right-wing extremism (e.g., right-wing extremism, xenophobia, asylum politics).
		Individual-oriented commitment	Coding of every text passage that describes a commitment to increasing individual understanding of issues related to contemporary civics (e.g., what is freedom, democracy, civil society, etc.).
R2: Strategies of remembrance	Strategies used to accomplish goals	Commemorative structure	Coding of every text passage that describes why and/or how structures of remembrance (memorials, monuments, historical plaques, etc.) are built.
		Education	Coding of every text passage that mentions aspects of education. This refers to both techniques of educational learning (e.g., workshops, lectures, seminars, museum visits) to teach about the past and attempts to influence the official educational system.
		Protest	Coding of every text passage that describes the use of organized protests and/or demonstrations.
		Public event	Coding of every text passage that describes the holding of an event open to the public about the organization's work (e.g., commemorative event, public lecture, publishing of book, concerts, theatre, etc.)
		Guided tour	Coding of every text passage that describes organized tours (e.g., city tour, hike).

(Continued)

Table 3.1: Codebook (Continued)

Theme	Category	Code	Definition
		Collaboration	Coding of every text passage that describes efforts to collaborate with other NGOs or initiatives (in the region and internationally) doing similar memory work on the Second World War.
		Parameters of commemoration (broad or narrow)	Coding of every text passage that describes the criteria by which the organization decides who gets memorialized in their work.
R3: Dynamics of memory	Austria's role in Second World War	Awareness (+ or −)	Coding of every text passage that describes the existing or non-existing awareness of the Austrian public about Austria's role in National Socialism.
	Carinthian Slovene experience during Second World War	Awareness	Coding of every text passage that describes the existing or non-existing awareness of the Austrian public about the experience of persecution and resistance in the Carinthian Slovene community during National Socialism.
	Carinthian official memory culture	Description (reasoning, + or −)	Coding of every text passage that describes the dynamics of the contemporary Carinthian official memory regime in relation to the Second World War (e.g., how the Second World War is officially remembered).
R4: Transnational memory	Transnationalism	Visitors	Coding of every text passage that describes international visitors.
		Supporters	Coding of every text passage that describes funding or rhetorical support the organization receives from an international partner.

Table 3.2: Coding Scheme

Meaning unit	Condensed meaning unit	Code	Category	Theme
Auf Basis dieser Ausstellung, natürlich auch zum Besichtigungsprogramm dazugehörend, wenn wir einen Workshop für Schüler anbieten, meistens von den letzten Klassen vom Gymnasium, höheren Schulebenen, 18–19 jährige, die kommen. Ist natürlich auch der Besuch mit dabei. Ansonsten versuchen wir mit ihnen praktisch den Horizont noch zu erweitern, nicht nur den Widerstand zu besprechen, sondern wie es Heutzutage ist, das ganze Spektrum von neuen Formen des Faschismus und Rechtsextremismus, von der Ausländerfeindlichkeit bis … das gesamte Spektrum irgendwie nahe zu bringen oder sie davor zu warnen oder sie bitten darum, dass sie 18 sind, und nicht blind irgendeine Propaganda aufsitzen.	Tries to use the experience of Carinthian Slovene persecution and resistance from the Second World War (as displayed in the exhibition) to influence visitors' political views about contemporary issues; draws a link between National Socialism of the 1930s and 1940s and contemporary right-wing politics.	Public-oriented commitment	Goals of organization	Why remember the past
Es geht um, was basiert Freiheit? Was heißt Zivilcourage? Was heißt Selbstbestimmungsrecht? Sodass alles, was um dich herum passiert, auf den basiert die Demokratie. Von Menschen, von dem Individuum ausgeht und nicht von der Masse. Es geht um die Mündigkeit eines demokratischen pluralistischen Systems, das man hier vermittelt. Und dann kann man das Beispiel nehmen, wo die Menschen das nicht wahrgenommen haben. Man hat hier viele Beispiele was die Auswirkungen sind. Hier geht's praktisch um eine individuelle Bewusstseinsbildung für jeden einzelnen Jugendliche.	Increasing individual understanding of complex civil society issues; uses the past as an avenue to discuss the duties of citizenship in contemporary period; develops individual critical thinking skills for each visitor.	Individual-oriented commitment	Goals of organization	Why remember the past

My social position as a researcher proved to be more complicated in the field than I had initially expected. Interestingly, the feelings of respect I developed for these activists seemed to be mutual, particularly once I had mentioned that I had already conducted five months of fieldwork and had previously lived in the region for a year while teaching English at a secondary school. On multiple occasions, my identity as an American was brought up by my interlocutors in a positive light, something that has rarely occurred in the years I have spent in Austria. The memory entrepreneurs from the Carinthian Slovene community often expressed appreciation that a US researcher was interested in the memory of Carinthian Slovene persecution and resistance, which, in their view, could make this story available to a wider English-speaking audience. While I was certainly grateful for being considered a trustworthy interlocutor for these memory entrepreneurs, in this chapter, I do my best to do the work of a researcher. I negotiate these feelings of mutual respect with detailed, critical analysis of these memory entrepreneurs' activism. To do so, I rely on a close reading of the interview transcripts, and I interpret them with the help of secondary historical material and relevant scholarship from memory studies.

Why Remember the Past?

Before embarking on these interviews, I assumed the memory entrepreneurs would explain the goals of their memory work in relatively similar terms. But the more time I spent with them – and with the transcripts from the interviews – the more I realized their goals differ in small but significant ways, based largely on whether the organization has what I call a "public-oriented" commitment towards its memory work or an "individual-oriented" one.

The memory entrepreneurs who expressed a more public-oriented commitment described the purpose of their memory work in direct connection to contemporary politics. Alexandra Schmidt, from Remember-Villach, and Andrej Mohar, from the Peršman Association and the Alliance of Carinthian Partisans, repeatedly stressed the importance of raising public awareness about the legacies of National Socialism in light of recent Austrian (and, more generally, European) shifts to the right. During our discussions, relatively straight lines were drawn from the fascism of the past to the politics of the present, and memory of this past was perceived as a tool with which to influence these politics. In this approach to memory, the historical experience of fascism is repeatedly invoked not only to give a sense of urgency and importance to the memory entrepreneurs' activism, but to also express a warning that if memory of the Nazi era is not publicly cultivated, fascism could return, a type of memory Michael Rothberg and Neil Levi call "resistant remembrance."[21] Schmidt, for example, connected Remember-Villach's goal of remembering National Socialism to the more publicly oriented goal of confronting these broader right-wing political trends, as can be seen in the following excerpt:

> The goal, of course, is to somehow keep the memory of the Nazi era alive. … Especially now (*emphasis*), when nationalistic tendencies and right-wing extremist tendencies are rising again in Europe. It is just noticeable. You have to work against it.

In the case of the Peršman Association, this publicly oriented commitment was described even more explicitly. According to Mohar, the memory of the Second World War, in particular that of the Carinthian Slovene resistance, is the foundation upon which individuals can become politicized to counter what he calls "new forms of fascism," a term he uses to describe a range of current political issues in Austria ranging from organized right-wing extremism and xenophobia, to the government's asylum policies and integration measures.

In contrast to this public-oriented commitment to memory, Haderlap takes a more individual-oriented approach to his memory work at the A-Zone. While Haderlap is also trying to increase remembrance of National Socialism's impact in the region – particularly on the local Carinthian Slovene community – his description of the purpose of his memory work differs significantly from both Mohar's and Schmidt's. According to Haderlap:

> Of course, this history, especially the history of the war, is important. So is what this region experienced during the war, which is something that's happened again and again throughout history. … How life worked is also important. This region has a long history. But this history is not to be used in a moralizing way, or as a lesson, of what all has happened and what has to be prevented.

In this individual-oriented approach to memory, the past is certainly perceived as important, but it is not seen as something to be used in the present to achieve publicly oriented political goals. It is not to be used as a lesson or as a tool to confront "nationalistic tendencies" (Schmidt) or "new forms of fascism" (Mohar). Rather, it is seen as a starting point to critically reflect on issues facing every individual, to develop, in Haderlap's words, "the ability for each young person to become aware of their surroundings in their own way."

By drawing attention to the differences between a publicly oriented commitment to memory and an individually oriented one, I am not advocating for one approach over the other. By highlighting these differences, my point is to show that these memory entrepreneurs, although all working in a small geographic area and on similar topics, cannot be understood as acting in unison. Just as John Bodnar characterizes vernacular culture as "diverse and changing," the memory activists interviewed in this chapter have a range of motivations and goals for their memory work and represent distinct interest groups. Based on these varying motivations and goals, the memory entrepreneurs adopt an assortment of practices and techniques in their attempts to influence Carinthia's official memory culture. I present these in more detail next.

Techniques and Practices of Remembrance

Memory studies scholars often concentrate on monuments, memorials, museums, and other sites of memory in their analyses – just as I did in the previous chapters. However, these interviews reveal that the objects and places I had visited in the first stage of my fieldwork were merely a small part of a larger educational and political effort aimed at raising critical awareness of contemporary political issues in their visitors. Although physical sites of memory are the most visible element of these organizations' activism, they all perceived other practices presented in this chapter to be just as important in their attempts to influence Carinthia's official memory culture.

Education

The Peršman Association, Remember-Villach, and the A-Zone all perceive the past as something that needs to be *taught* to their visitors. Different educational strategies are used: visits to the Peršmanhof are made, workshops are offered, seminars are organized, and lectures that bring various topics from the past and the present together are held. The Peršman Association offers upwards of 30 workshops per year, mostly aimed at students in the upper level of Austria's secondary school system. In line with the Peršman Association's publicly oriented commitment to memory, Mohar described workshops that incorporate both the history displayed at the museum and current political topics in the following manner:

> We offer a workshop for students, mostly from the last years of high school, 18- to 19-year-old. During these, we try to broaden their horizons. We don't just discuss the resistance, but we also talk about today: The whole spectrum of new forms of fascism and right-wing extremism. We try to bring this whole spectrum closer to home.

The A-Zone, too, offers workshops throughout the year covering a wide variety of topics – from traditional honey cultivation courses to autobiographical writing seminars – all aimed at forcing a type of critical engagement between the visitor and his or her surroundings. In its work with school classes, the A-Zone offers specific workshops intended to stimulate critical thinking about civil society issues by highlighting the history of Carinthian Slovene persecution in the region. Instead of using this past to draw a connection with the present, however, these workshops revolve around difficult civics concepts and what Haderlap sees as existential questions of what it means to live in a free society:

> We're exploring the relationship between humanity and its environment. Several important, existential questions form the basis of our programs. Questions like: What is freedom based on? What does civil courage mean? What does the right to self-determination mean? Our programs talk about what a mature democratic, pluralistic system is. And then we look to when people might not have asked themselves these questions. And we have lots of examples here in southern Carinthia of what the consequences of that were.

Public Events

Holding public events is also an important strategy for achieving the respective goals of these organizations. Remember-Villach, for example, offers two public commemorative events each year, one during May (the end of the war in Austria) and one in November (on the anniversary of the Villach/Beljak pogrom). During these, lectures are held about National Socialism, and various information panels are placed in prominent locations in the city. The Alliance of Carinthian Partisans also organizes various public events throughout the year at the various grave sites and memorials that they maintain. Two of the more prominent ones are the annual memory hike to the partisan memorial located in Kömmel/Komelj – one of the memorials I described in chapter 2 – and the annual commemoration at the Peršmanhof in June. In contrast to the Remember-Villach's public events, which are attended by representatives of the Villach city government, the local Protestant church, and even school classes from around the city, the general public tends not to attend these Alliance of Carinthian Partisan events. These tend to be attended by individuals who are members of the Alliance or other left-wing political organizations in the region.

In addition to offering workshops aimed at a general Austrian audience, the Peršman Association also participates in one of Austria's most well-known cultural events, "The Long Night of the Museums." Sponsored by ORF, Austria's public broadcaster, this event is extremely popular in Austria, with more than 600 museums and cultural institutions keeping their doors open until 1:00 a.m. one night per year. Out of all four organizations, though, the A-Zone has the most diverse offering of public events. Not only does it organize workshops about a wide range of issues (e.g., farming, literature, democracy), but it also stages plays and puts on concerts multiple times a year, many of which engage with the legacies of the Second World War in the region.

Guided Tours

The events of the Second World War occurred at specific places. Although the content of the tours differ significantly – Remember-Villach offers city tours of Villach/Beljak that highlight the history of the city before and during National Socialism, while the A-Zone offers guided hikes through the abandoned farms and houses around Leppen/Lepena – Haider and Haderlap both regard these tours as important tools that can bring to light the "inward turning histories" of the particular places for their visitors.[22] In his tour, Haider takes participants first to the school he used to teach at and then through the centre of Villach/Beljak, narrating histories along the way that are now hidden from view. Haider describes his tour in the following excerpt:

I always start with the school where I taught. I tell those participating what happened after Austria was annexed by Nazi Germany. The school was closed. Six or seven teachers were fired. One teacher committed suicide. A month later, there was already book burnings in the schoolyard. Then I talk about what happened to some of the students who left Villach/ Beljak. I have interviews from them, which I read aloud. Then we go to the city. Then we ask, "What was it like at the pogrom?" We go to the main square, where the people stood during the pogrom. I stand in front of the Glesingers' old store, which of course isn't there anymore because it was Aryanized. We go from stop to stop, from house to house, and I tell the story of what happened.

In contrast to Haider's tour that highlights (predominantly) Jewish places in Villach/Beljak before the Nazi takeover, Haderlap offers various guided hiking programs in the mountains around Leppen/Lepena. Several hikes are available. One takes participants to various abandoned partisan bunkers in the area, while another highlights specific places mentioned in Maja Haderlap's 2011 novel, *Angel of Oblivion*. Haderlap also offers a more general literary hike, during which he leads participants to long-abandoned family farms and homes in the area. Here, he points out the influence these specific places have had on Carinthian Slovene authors from the region, including Florjan Lipuš and Valentin Polanček (both of whom were deeply influenced by personal experiences of the war). During the hike to the specific places, storytelling is also used as a means to unlock these hidden histories. According to Haderlap:

Of course, these literary hikes go through these farms and these small areas out in the countryside. Every corner, every house, every hilltop has a story that touches on literature. I have the books in my backpack, and there are connections from this literature to all kinds of places in the landscape. Then we read aloud and tell stories. The stories become more three-dimensional because you're in the middle of these sentences that have been written down on paper. You experience the language in a third dimension. Then it's really an emotional experience.

School Engagement

While all visitors, independent of age, are welcome to participate in the memory entrepreneurs' events, workshops, and tours, all the memory entrepreneurs perceived their interaction with young people, particularly high school–aged students, as critical for their memory work. Since its founding, Remember-Villach has extensively collaborated with students, and school classes make up about a third of the Peršman Association's annual visitors. Within this context, the role of Carinthia's public school curriculum was repeatedly mentioned by all the memory entrepreneurs. While Remember-Villach, the A-Zone, and the Peršman Association all mentioned the importance of becoming part of the official curriculum in the state of Carinthia – that is, becoming a place that receives an official recommendation from the state board of education as a destination for school-sponsored field trips – the Peršman Association was the only organization actively trying to influence Carinthia's history curriculum. According to Mohar, the association not only creates lesson plans aimed at helping teachers better teach the history of National Socialism in the region, but it has also been trying to turn the Peršmanhof into a memorial site with similar pedagogical value as the Mauthausen Memorial Site in Mauthausen.

The Austrian Ministry of Education recommends that all Austrian students visit Mauthausen, Austria's largest concentration camp, and since 2023, the federal government has been helping cover transportation costs for schools to get to the memorial site. It was not until April 2020, however, that the Carinthian state government began financially supporting these trips.[23] All of the memory entrepreneurs thought it commendable that more and more Carinthian schools now have the financial resources to take their students to Mauthausen. But this centralization of memory was also seen sceptically. Resembling a similar debate that occurred in 1990s' Germany about whether centralized sites of Holocaust memory in Berlin crowded out local initiatives from smaller regions, Gudrun Blohberger felt that the Austrian government's support for visits to Mauthausen could lead to a perception among students that National Socialism in Austria was confined to large, centralized concentration camps like the one in Mauthausen.[24] There is some evidence that is the case. Of the 24 Carinthian teachers interviewed in one study about how schools teach National Socialism, 17 of them said that they took their students on excursions to memorial sites. Of these 17, only 7 had visited the Loibl/Ljubelj memorial site, a memorial on the location of the former concentration camp that is on the border of Carinthia and Slovenia high up in the mountains, and only 2 had visited the Peršmanhof.[25] To counter this, the Peršman Association has been lobbying the Carinthian state government to finance school visits to either Mauthausen or the Peršmanhof for Carinthian-based students, which would show that the effects of National Socialism were actually felt around the country, in large sites and small.

Commemorative Structures

Lobbying the designers of the official school curriculum is certainly one way to influence Carinthian memory politics. But as the "most deliberately designed, official, lasting, and emblematic cultural products codifying memory," one of the most visible ways to take a public position in debates over memory is to build commemorative structures like the ones I analysed in the previous chapter.[26] In Austria, the federal government has a legal responsibility – stemming from its signature on the Austrian State Treaty in 1955, which formed the legal basis for the end of the Allied occupation after the war – to maintain graves, memorials, and other sites that were built by the Allies to commemorate fallen soldiers, prisoners of war, and others who lost their lives to Nazism after having been forcibly brought to Austria.

Although the Liberation Front clearly fulfils these requirements, this obligation has never been fulfilled in relation to partisan memorials in southern Carinthia from chapter 2. This task has fallen solely to the Alliance of Carinthian Partisans. During our conversation, Mohar placed great importance on the Alliance's preservation of partisan memorials in the region – tellingly, he used the word *pflegen* to describe its work, a word meaning "to take care of" that is usually used in the context of caregiving work at nursing homes – which he described as the organization's main activity. These memorials still play a critical role in the Alliance's memory work and are at the centre of their annual commemorative ceremonies. During these ceremonies, the anti-fascist resistance from the Second World War is commemorated and quite explicitly used to politicize the present, to spread what Mohar calls the "values of the resistance" to a new generation of Carinthians.

This politicization of memory was seen critically, but sympathetically, by Haderlap, who, while not a member of the Alliance of Carinthian Partisans, grew up just around the corner from the Peršmanhof and had multiple family members who were active partisans during the war. According to Haderlap:

> Our memorial culture in southern Carinthia is still a bit different than perhaps elsewhere. The Alliance of Carinthian Partisans still sees the Peršmanhof, or this memorial culture, as a symbol of their discrimination. Politically, they also use this as a basis for politicizing. In other words, their politicization is based on this commemorative culture that they themselves cultivate. … On the one hand, I understand it because this is their own history. They have their own stories that happened to their own families. They see this, as well as the monument at the Peršmanhof, as an allegory and as a symbol of their current, existential situation, which they perceive to be a disadvantageous one. "This is what you have to fight for." Sometimes it takes on abstruse, absurd forms. But I think this is also understandable.

That a form of "purposeful remembrance," where the past is used as a tool to forge an identity for a particular group in the present, would be occurring with the help of these memorials is certainly not surprising.[27] Memory has long been recognized as a cornerstone of group identity, and one popular way to support the symbolic link between the two has been through the construction of monuments because of their "high visibility" and "key symbolic value."[28] In the alliance's preservation and commemoration of these memorials, though, a relationship with the past based on what Tzvetan Todorov calls "literal memory" has developed, which makes the historical "event impossible to go beyond" and forces everything in the present to be submitted to the past.[29] Because of the foundational role the memory of resistance plays in the alliance's identity, it runs the risk of creating a type of dead end for its advocates. When the past is viewed in these terms, moreover, it tends to then "be instrumentalized and cited as pretexts for all sorts of political agendas," a dynamic Haderlap alludes to in the previous excerpt.[30]

But when placed in the larger context of the Carinthian post-war period, seeing why the Alliance of Carinthian Partisans places such importance on these commemorative structures is easy. As I detailed in my reading of the Monument against Fascism in the previous chapter, once built, these structures – as symbols not just of an anti-Nazi resistance but also a reminder that Slovene still had a presence in the state – they were often destroyed by German nationalists.[31] They were also targeted during the so-called Ortstafelsturm, the name given to the events surrounding the violent destruction of bilingual city signs by German nationalists in 1972.[32] According to Mohar, most of the alliance's members are on the older end of the "baby boomer" spectrum and were politicized, much like himself, within this post-war context where public symbols of Slovene and wartime resistance were constantly agitated against. This experience, along with the familial connections that most members of the organization still have to the memory of the partisans – "Everywhere," Mohar told me, "there's a deep connection in people's families" – makes it understandable that a form of purposeful remembrance has developed.

Remember-Villach also builds commemorative structures and is best known in the area for having initiated the construction of the Memorial of Names that, since 1999, has been located near Villach's/Beljak's main square. Instead of engaging in purposeful remembrance and forging a social identity through its memorial work, though, Remember-Villach wanted to explicitly challenge the official memorial culture of Villach/Beljak – which, just as in other towns throughout the region, had been based on commemorating fallen German soldiers – by building the memorial.[33] In his description of how he originally became involved in this work, Haider explained how he wanted to directly confront those in Villach/Beljak (and Carinthians more generally) with the consequences of National Socialism in the town. The most appropriate way to do this was to build a memorial:

> I always tried to get involved somehow to change Villach's/Beljak's memory culture. ... We started a group that engages directly with the events of the Nazi era in Villach/Beljak, its surroundings, and in Carinthia. ... And we tried to develop a culture of remembrance here. ... Then this idea just came up that we could make a plaque with names of the victims. ... And then the whole memorial came into being.

Historiography and the Parameters of Commemoration

What does it mean to have a memorial to the victims of Nazism? What exactly is being commemorated through these organizations' memory work? Whom and what gets the privilege of being remembered through these publicly visible structures? As one group of scholars argue, "[m]emorials and monuments are political constructions, recalling and representing histories selectively, drawing popular attention to specific events and people and obliterating or obscuring others."[34] Commemorative structures, it should also be pointed out, are built within particular social contexts and reflect dominant historiographical interpretations of the past.

When it comes to the historiography and commemoration of the Holocaust, a broadening of memory discourses has occurred over the last several decades, which has complicated the traditional Holocaust memory discourse of clear-cut categories of perpetrator, bystander, and victim. Perpetrators are no longer considered just "Nazi Germans," and the label of bystander has "slowly shifted from an exonerating to an incriminating category, especially in Germany."[35] When it comes to victims, moreover, more groups have been added – ranging from Roma/Sinti and homosexuals to Slavic civilians and general political opponents – which "may indicate that 'Holocaust' memory is increasingly a misnomer and that a more general memory of the 'World War II' era or 'Nazi crimes'" may be more appropriate.[36]

You see this broad approach to memorializing the Holocaust in Remember-Villach's approach to memory, particularly in its Memorial of Names. As Haider and Schmidt explained in our conversation, Remember-Villach takes as broad of an approach as possible in its commemorative work, explicitly avoiding victim hierarchies. In response to my question as to whether Remember-Villach struggled with choosing

Figure 3.1: The Memorial of Names in Villach/Beljak.

a particular group to memorialize on its memorial, Haider replied directly:

> No. Who is on this memorial? The victims of the Nazi euthanasia program are on it. Resistance fighters are on it. Jews are on it. So are Jehovah's Witnesses. People who just wouldn't go along with it. Sinti. Why are they on the memorial? Because they lived here in Villach/Beljak.

Built in 1999, Remember-Villach's Memorial of Names reflects this larger evolution in Holocaust memory and collapses all these various victim groups into one, with the only criteria for inclusion on the memorial being a person's connection to Villach/Beljak. The memorial is shown in figure 3.1.

These larger, historiographical debates about the Second World War also influence the memory work of the Peršman Association and the Alliance of Carinthian Partisans. Holocaust historiography, however, is not the main reference point. The memory work of these two organizations reflects a much more limited debate – "limited" both in the sense of historiographical interest and the geographic area – as to how the Carinthian Slovene resistance during the war should be conceptualized and presented today. The historiography of the resistance inside southern Carinthia has concentrated overwhelmingly on the armed struggle led by the Liberation Front.[37] But inside the Peršman Museum, the Peršman Association makes a radical break with this practice and follows the lead of Holocaust scholars, such as Emil Fackenheim and Yehuda Bauer, who have developed more fluid definitions of the term "resistance" to better understand Jewish responses to the Holocaust outside of armed revolt.[38] Alongside information about the Liberation Front, for instance, the exhibition room dedicated to the history of the resistance in southern Carinthia also includes information panels on things like music and education, an approach to resistance that has often been favoured by historians looking to explore "hidden" responses Jews had to the Holocaust.[39] According to Blohberger, who was the director of the Peršman Association during the museum's redesign, the museum did not just want to provide definitions and images of what resistance was, but it also wanted to critically explore the concept itself.

Moving away from the classic image of the armed, heroic partisan – the image that is so well captured in the monument outside the museum – Blohberger wanted visitors to reflect on what resistance meant during the war and why people engaged in it:

> From those that we knew were in the resistance, we wanted to show as many people as possible in the exhibition along with their very different motives for being in it. What does the word resistance even mean? Is it enough to hang up a white sheet to warn somebody of danger? Is that resistance? Or does resistance start when you pick up a gun? It was important to us to explore this whole theme in the exhibition.

The museum's broadening of the concept of resistance was not without controversy, particularly when it came to the inclusion of the "Green Cadre," those soldiers who, while having deserted the German army, did not join the Liberation Front and refused to fight for either side and simply tried to survive the war. According to Blohberger, the decision to include the Green Cadre ignited significant debate between the Peršman Association – made up largely of individuals from outside the Carinthian Slovene community – and the Alliance of Carinthian Partisans – made up largely of former partisans and their descendents:

> We went through all of the content of the exhibition. We did this with the Alliance of Carinthian Partisans as well. And we really discussed the topic of the Green Cadre. Of course, the partisans, the ones that actually

fought with weapons, had always seen the Green Cadre as cowards. ... There were a lot of discussions about this. ... These were definitely intense and difficult, but, in the end, it was clear to everyone that this topic had to be included in order to somehow be able to show the various aspects of resistance. I think that is also the strength of the exhibition. It's not a polarizing exhibition, but one that displays the diversity of the themes so everyone can find themselves in it and still get pushed to maybe think beyond their own limits.

Mohar, as the current director of the Peršman Association, agreed that this broad understanding of resistance is an integral part of the Peršman Museum, and he rejected the notion there is even a question about this in the museum. In our conversation about the commemorative structures built by the Alliance of Carinthian Partisans, he also advocated for a broad approach to memorialization under which all victims of National Socialism are included, not only partisans.

My own fieldwork, too, revealed this to be the case. My interest in Tomaž Olip, a Carinthian Slovene who kept a diary while hiding in the Karawank mountains before being caught and executed by the Nazis in 1943 for desertion, brought me to the district of Zell/Sele, a small collection of several villages near the Slovenian border, where 90 per cent of the population still speaks Slovene.[40] As one of the first areas to offer wide support to the partisans, Zell/Sele (nicknamed the "partisan republic" during the war) played an important role as a partisan support area during the war, and by 1945, 42 men and women from the area had been killed by the Nazis.[41] Olip grew up in one of these villages and, after having read about the ambivalent legacy he left behind in the area due to the Gestapo's discovery of his diary and subsequent arrest of people mentioned in it, I wanted to explore what commemorative structures had been built in the area.[42]

Today, although Zell/Sele has less than 700 people living there, it has a rich assortment of commemorative structures dedicated to those killed during the war, four of which can be found in Zell-Pfarre/Sele-Cerkev. At the entrance to the village cemetery, there has been a memorial – another good example of the similarities between partisan memorials and their classical war memorial counterparts found throughout Europe – of a female medic holding a dying male fighter since 1949 (figure 3.2).

On the entrance to the small church in the cemetery, there are two memorial plaques dedicated to the 13 individuals who either deserted the German army or aided them and were executed in Vienna in April 1943 for doing so (figure 3.3). A memorial, built in 1971 and renovated

Figure 3.2: Early partisan memorial in Zell-Pfarre/Sele-Cerkev.

in 2019, dedicated to fallen partisans in the cemetery maintained by the Alliance of Carinthian Partisans (figure 3.4). Adding to this dense commemorative landscape, the Council of Carinthian Slovenes constructed a memorial to all of the victims of National Socialism from Zell/Sele in 2015 (figure 3.5).

Figure 3.3: Parish church in Zell-Pfarre/Sele-Cerkev. Notice the two memorials dedicated to 13 individuals from Zell/Sele executed on 13 April 1945, in Vienna flanking the entrance. Year of construction unknown.

I visited the Zell-Pfarre/Sele-Cerkev cemetery on 3 November 2019, a day after the commemorative ceremonies of All Saint's Day and a week after those that marked Austria's official national holiday celebrations (26 October). The Alliance of Carinthian Partisans

Figure 3.4: Partisan memorial in Zell-Pfarre/Sele-Cerkev. Memorial dedicated to eight fallen partisans in the cemetery. Constructed by the Alliance of Carinthian Partisans in 1971. Notice the wreaths placed by the alliance and the government of Slovenia for All Saints' Day (2019).

organized commemorative ceremonies on both of these occasions. On 26 October, they held a "counter-ceremony" at the memorial site that commemorated those partisans who helped defeat Nazism and thereby enshrine Article 7 – the one about the Slovene minority's language rights – into the Austrian State Treaty of 1955. For All Saint's Day, it was clear that the focus of the Alliance's commemorative work – they lay candles, flowers, and a wreath at the foot of all 54 partisan memorials with a representative from the Slovene consulate every year – had been on the entire cemetery (i.e., all three of the commemorative structures in it from the war, including that of Olip and the 12 other individuals) and not only partisan graves. Interestingly, however, nothing had been laid by the memorial outside of the cemetery constructed by the Council of Carinthian Slovenes, perhaps revealing that these two organizations approach these commemorative holidays differently.

Figure 3.5: The Memorial to Victims of National Socialism in Zell-Pfarre/ Sele-Cerkev. Built by the Council of Carinthian Slovenes in 2015, designed by Valentin Oman. Notice the absence of wreaths from the alliance or the Slovene government for All Saints' Day. The marble slabs have the names of victims inscribed onto them.

Current Dynamics of Carinthian Memory

In addition to better understanding the strategies of remembrance of each organization, these interviews also helped me explore Carinthia's twenty-first-century "memory politics," that is, the particular sphere of a society's politics in which memories of a past event are negotiated, debated, and contested by various interested actors who tend to have differing interpretations of the past and how it should be publicly commemorated (if at all).[43] When engaging in this particular type of politics, those representing a particular interpretation of the past rely on various strategies to achieve dominance of their respective memory, including both "positive" tactics – persuading others to accept their interpretation of the past – and "negative" ones – marginalizing and delegitimizing other interpretations through polemics and even violence.[44] Understanding this competitive relationship between these various representatives is critical because a "large part of the explanation regarding why a particular memory becomes dominant [in a society] is that representatives of this memory have succeeded in delegitimizing and defeating competing memories."[45]

In southern Carinthia, Second World War memory politics have traditionally occurred in a triad between three constituencies: the Carinthian state government, right-wing German nationalist organizations like the Carinthian Homeland Service, and various Carinthian Slovene political organizations. In the years immediately following the war, the relationship between these three groups was (at best) unproductive and (at worst) combative. Throughout the post-war period, German nationalist groups relied heavily on negative tactics, consistently (and successfully) linking the actions of those Carinthian Slovenes who fought with the Yugoslav partisans to communism. Bolstered by the politics of the Cold War, an effective narrative, supported by the state government, developed that painted them as traitors, while former Nazi Party members – of which there had been an estimated 50,000 by 1943 – were portrayed as loyal Carinthians who had been victimized by the occupying powers.[46]

But much has changed in Austria over the last 30 years. The victim myth, long the leading official interpretation of the Nazi era, has lost its dominance. The geopolitical context of central Europe has also changed dramatically: Yugoslavia is gone, as are the Cold War ideologies that broke Europe into two blocs and placed Austria in the middle. With Slovenia's accession to the European Union in 2004, moreover, the economic and cultural ties between Austria and its southern neighbour have strengthened.[47] In light of these developments, I wanted to explore the memory entrepreneurs' perceptions of twenty-first-century Carinthian memory politics regarding the Second World War. Is the sphere still defined by a combative relationship between the Carinthian state government and the German nationalist organizations, on one hand, and the Slovene organizations, on the other? Or do these groups cooperate to promote a more inclusive official memory of the Second World War in southern Carinthia? How do these memory entrepreneurs characterize Carinthia's official memory culture? Surprisingly, all the memory entrepreneurs suggested that the official memory culture in Austria has changed for the better, even in southern Carinthia.

Blohberger, who, in her current position as the director of pedagogy at the Mauthausen memorial site regularly interacts with school classes from around the country, perceived a fundamental shift to have occurred in the country over the last several decades:

> I think we have now reached the point in Austria where there is an awareness that National Socialism has to be taught and that it is important for society to deal with this topic and this legacy. I think this feeling is here now.

Haider and Schmidt, from Remember-Villach, drew a similar, relatively positive, picture of Carinthia's official memory culture.

> *Haider:* In my view, it's not bad. There's been a paradigm shift in recent years, really a paradigm shift. The quality of the memory culture is high, and its content has developed completely differently over the last 30 years.

> *Schmidt:* Yes, you can also see it here in Villach/Beljak. For the first time, a street has been named after a resistance fighter. That wasn't possible for 75 years, and now all of a sudden it is. A lot of things are breaking open.

Mohar, from the Peršman Association and the Alliance of Carinthian Partisans, also agreed that significant improvements have been made in how the Second World War is remembered in Carinthia. However, in his perspective, these developments have little to do with official initiatives from the state but have rather originated from the efforts of individual Carinthians, particularly certain teachers:

> When 1941 is discussed, which is when the Axis invaded Yugoslavia, it shows that the climate in this state has improved somewhat in recent years.

You also have to acknowledge that in the schools, more and more of the teachers who teach history are quite sensitive to this topic, or at least, are not averse to mentioning this era. Of course, it's far from getting anchored in the curriculum. It's done by individual teachers on a voluntary basis. But the general way of thinking of many teachers has improved. It's much better than it was 20 years ago. But it won't catch on in schools until it is firmly part of the system.

This aligns with recent research about how the era of National Socialism is taught in Carinthian public schools. A recent study shows through interviews and questionnaire data that those teachers who feel confident enough about their knowledge to teach this content well, this content knowledge comes from their own private engagement and not from their formal training when becoming teachers.[48]

Nevertheless, while all the memory activists observed significant improvements in how National Socialism is presented, taught, and commemorated in Carinthia, they also expressed significant disappointment that awareness of the persecution and resistance of Carinthian Slovenes, in particular, remains as limited as it has ever been. According to Mohar, this is largely because the Defence Struggle still occupies a centre stage in Carinthia's official narrative of its past. Haider also sees the commemoration of the Defence Struggle as having a negative impact on the public's awareness of what happened to the Slovenes during the Second World War. In his view, most Carinthians are still unaware of the Carinthian Slovene resistance:

What do people know about it? Nothing. It's really bad. It's terrible. Absolutely no one knows that Upper Carniola, the northern region of today's Slovenia, was part of Carinthia during the war. No one knows that. We only ever talk about the Defence Struggle and having to defend the border with Slovenia in the Karawank mountains.

While Blohberger also perceived Carinthians to have limited awareness of the Carinthian Slovene resistance, in her view, this is largely due to the fact that students rarely encounter this history in school:

I would argue that almost no one knows anything about the Carinthian Slovenes or about their history. It's just not something that is taught. Maybe you bump into it if you're politically active. Maybe if you're at a university, and there's a chance to engage with the topic during your studies. But it's not something that you would just come across at school.

Recent scholarship, too, has come to a similar conclusion. Investigating how National Socialism is taught in Carinthian public schools, scholars discovered that the Nazi era is no longer ignored in history classes. "Resistance" has even become a popular topic in lessons on the Nazi era. But, in an interesting turn, the Carinthian Slovene partisans are rarely mentioned in connection with it.[49]

I was surprised that all five of my interlocutors described Carinthia's official memory culture as being so contradictory: Austria's role in National Socialism is now acknowledged, but the Carinthian Slovene resistance is not. While the Defence Struggle's significance and the absence of Carinthian Slovene history from school curriculum were pointed to as reasons, Haderlap argued this dynamic has developed because the perception of the partisans – symbolized by the Peršmanhof – varies tremendously between Carinthia's two language communities:

> Even today, the Peršmanhof is irrelevant in the region and in the local community. You have to admit that. On the one hand, that's because of the particular memory culture that secludes itself from the rest of the surrounding area. On the other, it has to do with the complete lack of knowledge about what actually happened here in the past. That's typical of southern Carinthia. It's just not talked about. But that way of thinking – "I don't want to have to do anything with it" – keeps progressing from one generation to the next. People push it away and repress it. They think: "I'm not interested in that because I would then have to deal with my own family." Which is why it still isn't well known. Inside the Slovene-speaking community, the history is very much known. There are also a few amongst the German speakers who get it. But these are just individuals. This isn't the case in public or official politics, apart from the *Enotna Lista*, the local Slovene party, or the mayor of Eisenkappel. There is still a riff in the Peršmanhof because [*sarcastically*] some people don't trust historians and like to tell their own stories. On a local level, it's kept at arm's length. When I talk to people in town or to those at the tourism office, they've never been up here. They have no idea about it.

This is a remarkable description in several ways. Most significantly, Haderlap's statement reveals that there is still a "fractured commemorative landscape" in Carinthia regarding the Second World War.[50] The Peršmanhof, as he describes it, is still largely ignored by the German speakers of the area but is widely supported by their Slovene-speaking counterparts. A narrative of the Peršmanhof has been developed within the German-speaking community that not only disputes the specific events of the Peršmanhof massacre but, by doing so, also calls into question the legitimacy of the Carinthian Slovene resistance.

This fracturing of memory along ethnic lines raises doubts about the applicability of the ethical side of transcultural approaches to memory for the study of memory in southern Carinthia that claim diverging memory "discourses might offer an opportunity to forge empathic communities of remembrance across national, cultural, or ethnic boundaries."[51] In her "dialogic model of memory," for instance, Aleida Assmann argues that states can move past the historical violence they have inflicted on each other by "mutually acknowledging their own guilt and empathy with the suffering they have inflicted on others."[52] This type of memory, in her view, could help forge new nations that are "not exclusively grounded in pride" but also accept their "quantum of guilt, thus ending a destructive history of violence by including the victims of this violence into one's own memory."[53] But, as Haderlap's statement above shows, it is extremely difficult for "empathic communities of remembrance" or "dialogic models of memory" to be forged across a cultural boundary when the communities on either side maintain incompatible memories of the same event. To me, it is startling that this dynamic still lingers in Carinthia, 80 years after the Second World War came to an end in the state with the Yugoslav and British armies occupying Klagenfurt/Celovec. As my interlocutors explained, acknowledging Austria's role in the Second World War is one thing. Commemorating victims of National Socialism at the official level, even in Carinthia, no longer seems to be controversial or taboo. But because incorporating Carinthian Slovene memories of resistance into this official memory culture still seems to be a step too far, Omer Bertov and Eric D. Weitz's description of Holocaust memory in eastern Europe, what they call the "shatterzone of empire," seems to fit Carinthia as well: Outright denial of the past is rare, "but a twisting of narratives, obfuscation, insistence on one's own victimization, and attempts to blame one's victims for their own fate" are still common.[54]

Prior to conducting these interviews, I had independently explored the numerous sites of memory that make up the southern Carinthian landscape of remembrance in the previous chapter. Following how most memory studies scholars analyse physical representations of the past, I relied on spatial readings of the various sites, participant observation, and secondary literature produced by local scholars to support my interpretations of these tangible places and objects. But my interviews with memory activists unveiled a hidden side of the landscape of remembrance, revealing that the organizations that have created, curated, and maintained this landscape are also engaged in wide-ranging educational and political efforts intended to affect social change. Unlike the memory work taken on by a museum (like in the previous chapter) or a novel (like in the following one), these organizations' interventions into the landscape do not just try to influence Carinthia's official memory culture of the Second World War. They are also intended to cultivate what can broadly be described as a critical political consciousness in a new generation of visitors that can be used as a political resource for today. In the end, these interviews offer significant insights into contemporary Carinthian memory politics and elucidate the plethora of strategies these memory activists have at their disposal to influence it.

From offering guided tours and public lectures to constructing memorials and maintaining gravesites, I was surprised to discover the range of techniques and practices these organizations employ in their activism. While the respective memory entrepreneurs deemed some techniques more effective than others (e.g., the Alliance of Carinthian Partisans' inclination to memorialize through commemorative structures versus the A-Zone's preference for small seminars), education, particularly of young people, was perceived by all five of my interlocutors to be a critical first step in their work. These educational strategies varied, but there was a consensus that before the larger goals of the respective organization could be achieved, visitors and/or the public had to first be provided historical knowledge of National Socialism, gleaned from the organizations' workshops, seminars, museum visits, and/or guided tours.

All five of these memory activists, moreover, approach the "tangible, visible scene" of the landscape of remembrance – the physical places and objects that compose it – as a resource to be activated in their visitors.[55] For the Alliance of Carinthian Partisans and the Peršman Association, this process of activation, supported by the monuments and memorials to partisans around the region and the museum at the Peršmanhof, is channelled into developing what can broadly be characterized as an anti-fascist political consciousness. Through the seminars and workshops at the Peršman Association, in particular, the memory of the partisan resistance is seen as the foundation on which a new generation of Carinthians can become politicized to confront what Mohar calls the "new forms of fascism" of the twenty-first century. Although Remember-Villach does not deploy the heritage of partisan resistance in its memory activism, it also perceives its commemorative work as being particularly important when seen in the context of the growing popularity of right-wing politics in Europe. In Schmidt's view, by activating a critical memory of National Socialism in its visitors, a new, politically engaged citizenry can be developed that can counter these trends. The A-Zone, too, tries to activate the objects and places of the landscape of remembrance for its visitors. For Haderlap, this activation is achieved not just through workshops and seminars but also through the various hiking tours that incorporate literature written in and about the region. While the A-Zone also challenges its visitors to critically reflect on current political discourse, this political intervention is not guided towards any direct confrontation with Austrian politics but is rather intended to challenge visitors to critically reflect on broader, civil society issues.

However much these activist organizations try, however, it seems clear from my interviews that the traditional narrative of "disloyal" Slovenes who turned their backs on Austria twice – once during the Defence Struggle and once again during the Second World War – remains anchored in Carinthia's official memory. While all of my interlocutors pointed to a lack of awareness on the part of the average German Carinthian about what the Carinthian Slovenes went through in the twentieth century as the main reason for this stagnation in Carinthia's memory culture, perhaps the reason for this is more straightforward. By actively commemorating these individuals, not only would the victim myth have to be called *completely* into question, but celebrating the actions of the Carinthian Slovenes who made this choice would also shine a bright light on the still uncomfortable truth that most Carinthians did not.

Chapter Four

Layers of Memory in Maja Haderlap's
Angel of Oblivion

Angel of Oblivion is an ideal ambassador for the region. People here identify with what's in Maja's novel. It's also their story.

– Zdravko Haderlap

Literature, out of all of all communicative mediums explored in this book so far, is a privileged one for engaging with issues relating to memory, particularly for collective memories not part of a society's official memory culture.[1] Through a variety of strategies – non-linear narration, various narrative points of view, manipulation of chrono-logical time, intertextual references – authors can explore the relationship between individual, communicative memory and collective, cultural memory through literature in a way that is perhaps more difficult in other mediums.[2] The relationship between literature and memory can be explored in three different but complementary ways: We can examine the "literature's memory," that is, the intertextual relations between various literary texts from different time periods and how these texts are transformed across time and rewritten. We can also analyse literature as a "medium of memory" for its ability to transmit memory within a wider cultural context. We can even investigate "memory within literature," or how particular memories are represented and narrated within individual literary texts.[3] Due to the literary context it was written out of, the story it tells, and the narrative techniques it uses, *Angel of Oblivion*, Maja Haderlap's 2011 semi-autobiographical novel about memory, the Second World War, and intergenerational trauma, lends itself nicely to being read through all three of these approaches. Although Haderlap originally published the novel in German (as *Engel des Vergessens*), to ease reading and, hopefully, expand the theme's reach to a wider non-German reading audience, all quotations in this chapter are from Tess Lewis's English translation from 2016.[4]

Situated largely in the bilingual region of southern Carinthia, *Angel of Oblivion's* plot unfolds through the eyes of an unnamed narrator as she grows up – the novel begins when she is six years old and ends when she is an adult woman – and grapples with the scars National Socialism has left behind on her family and the wider Slovene community in the area. This awareness slowly turns the rural area she grows up in from an "idyllic" space deeply connected with its natural surroundings to one burdened by war and violence.[5] In the novel, the narrator encounters remnants of the war largely through her interactions and conversations with her immediate family, in particular her grandmother (Mitzi) and father (Zdravko), both of whom experienced the violence of the war first-hand. Mitzi, the narrator discovers early on, survived the Ravensbrück concentration camp, while Zdravko had been one of the youngest members of the partisans, fleeing to them after having been tortured by German police as a small boy. At the level of language, Haderlap construes the narrator's encounters with the past through two different styles. For the first half of the novel, the plot unfolds through the observations of a child, but, as the narrator ages – we follow her through primary school, Gymnasium, university, and, as the novel closes, her professional life – the past is no longer simply witnessed or heard by the narrator and transmitted to the reader, but it is reflected on and interrogated. This narrative technique lets Haderlap connect the past to contemporary issues of identity, national belonging, gender, and language.[6] Haderlap, of course, is not the first Carinthian Slovene author to write about Nazism, persecution, deportation, and resistance, all of which have long been themes in Carinthian Slovene post-war writing. Although this body of work – what I categorize as memory texts, memory prose, and literary fiction – has a prominent, if often only alluded to, place in Haderlap's novel, scholars of Austrian literature are largely unaware of it because of a tendency in the field to only analyse German-language texts, which makes readings of *Angel of Oblivion* frustratingly incomplete.[7]

Memory texts, the earliest of these three genres, have their roots in post-war community-wide calls for collecting documentary evidence of Nazi war crimes that had occurred during the war. Between 1945 and 1949, when the Austrian State Treaty was still being negotiated and Yugoslavia was pressing its claims for a shift of the southern Carinthian border, various organizations within the Carinthian Slovene community called for their members and readers to collect documents, files, and photographs relating to the war and write down their memories of it.[8] This led to various Slovene-language newspapers and magazines gathering first-hand accounts from former resistance fighters.[9] These documents were meant, first and foremost, to support Allied denazification efforts in Carinthia and to provide evidence of Austria's own contribution to its liberation from Nazi rule (which was a core, but largely ignored, section of the 1943 Moscow Declaration). In the pages of *Slovenski vestnik*, a local Slovene-language newspaper, two columns about Slovene resistance soon made regular appearances: "The Carinthian Struggle" and "Our Woman."[10] In 1951, these essays were edited by the Alliance of Carinthian Partisans and published as *The Carinthian Struggle* (Koroška v borbi), which, as the first collection of first-hand accounts of both the deportations of April 1942 and the partisan resistance to be published, became a foundational memory text in the Carinthian Slovene community.[11]

While these memory texts were produced in the years immediately after the war, it was not until the late 1950s that the first Carinthian Slovene memory prose began to appear. Written by authors who had experienced persecution and resistance firsthand, these texts can broadly be categorized as memoirs of former resistance fighters.[12] Perhaps the most famous example of memory prose is Karel Prušnik-Gašper's *Chamois in an Avalanche*, originally published in 1958 in Yugoslavia.[13] Prušnik-Gašper, one of the leading figures in the Carinthian regional committee of the Liberation Front during the war, was the head of the Alliance of Carinthian Partisans from its founding until his death in 1980. His memoir is not only a personal recollection about his time during the war, but it is also an overarching account of the military operations in the area. When it was translated into German in 1980 (*Gamsen auf der Lawine*), it was the only book written by a Carinthian Slovene author about the partisan resistance to have been published in Austria.[14]

The 1980s proved to be an important decade for books about the Carinthian Slovene resistance as scholars began to search for everyday acts of resistance against Nazism that often left no documented trace behind. To "uncover" these, historians turned to methods of oral history.[15] This led to historians conducting interviews with individuals and then bringing these into narrative form. In 1984, for example, *Jelka. The Life of a Carinthian Partisan* was published.[16] Based on interviews with Helene Kuhar, *Jelka* tells Kuhar's story of growing up a poor farmer in Bad Eisenkappel/Železna Kapla and her joining of the partisan resistance during the war (Jelka was her partisan name). Several edited collections that foregrounded individual experiences of persecution/resistance also appeared in the mid-1980s.[17] Perhaps most prominently, *Looking for Traces. A Narrated History of the Carinthian Slovenes*, a collage of more than 50 interview excerpts from Carinthian Slovenes who had been in the partisan resistance and/or had been persecuted, was published in 1990.[18]

Since the 1980s, memory prose has become an ever more popular medium for Carinthian Slovene authors.[19] In 1996, Andrej Kokot, a renowned Carinthian Slovene lyricist and poet, released a memoir that foregrounded his family's forced deportation in 1942, while, a year later, Lipej Kolenik followed with his own about his desertion from the Wehrmacht and time in resistance.[20] In the late 1990s, the Drava publishing house, which has been based in Klagenfurt/Celovec since 1953 and has focused its work on Carinthian Slovene authors and topics, published several more memoirs from Carinthian Slovenes under the series "Books against Forgetting," which included autobiographies from Anton Haderlap, Tone Jelen, Ana Jug, Franc Kukovica, and Peter Kuhar.[21]

Along with memory texts and prose, Carinthian Slovene authors have also written about the topic of resistance and persecution through literary fiction and drama. In fact, ever since Blaž und Pavla Singer's performed their documentary drama *Our Journey* (Naša pot) in 1947, theatre has long been a popular avenue for Carinthian Slovene authors to negotiate stories of the past in the present.[22] While short literary prose with war motifs began to be published at the end of the 1950s by authors such as Florjan Lipuš and Valentin Polanšek, it was not until the late 1970s and early 1980s that these events became major themes in Carinthian Slovene literary fiction.[23] Lipuš – who would go on to win almost every Slovene literary and artistic award during his career – wrote *Škorenj*, a drama about the Peršmanhof massacre, in 1973.[24] Translated into German three years later, this is considered the first German-language text to mention the Carinthian Slovene resistance during the war. With his novels *The Cross with Crosses* (Križ s križi, 1980), *A Brotherly Autumn I–II* (Bratovska jesen I–II, 1981–2), and *The Urge for Freedom* (Sla po svobodi, 1985), Polanšek is considered the first Carinthian Slovene author to write "war novels" that put the history of the partisan resistance into literary form.[25] Although the novel became less popular as more memory prose was published in the 1990s, the first two decades of the twenty-first century has seen authors return to it as a form through which to write about the past. Lipuš's *Bostjan's Journey* (Boštjanov let), for example, was published in 2003 and was soon followed by Peter Handke's *Storm Still*, a prose drama about Carinthian Slovene persecution and resistance during war.[26]

Handke, of course, is perhaps Austria's most famous contemporary literary figure. Within German-speaking Europe, he is known for his writings from the 1960s and 1970s. Internationally, he is better known for winning the 2019 Nobel Prize in literature despite his outspoken support of Serbia in the 1990s as well of its president and war criminal Slobodan Milošević (he gave a deeply problematic speech at the Serbian president's funeral after the Bosnian War, which many including myself, consider a genocide apology).[27] But he has also had an intimate relationship with Carinthian Slovene literature throughout his career, both as a translator and a public ambassador of sorts. As a translator, Handke has been translating Carinthian Slovene writers into German since the 1980s. In 1981, for instance, he co-translated Lipuš's *The Errors of Young Tjaž*, a story about a young boy's attempts to break away from school and church repression in the Carinthian province, from Slovene into German.[28] A major milestone in Carinthian Slovene literature, *The Errors of Young Tjaž* is considered to be the first Carinthian Slovene novel ever written. Handke's translation not only brought international recognition to Lipuš's work but also ushered in a "golden decade" for Carinthian Slovene literature.[29] Lojze Wieser, the head of the Wieser publishing house in Klagenfurt/Celovec, argues Handke's impact cannot be overstated in this regard: If Handke had not thrown his weight behind Lipuš's translation in the 1980s, it is hard to imagine translated Slovene literature ever getting a foothold on the German marketplace.[30]

Although *The Errors of Young Tjaž* remains Handke's only translated novel, he has also translated Carinthian Slovene writers and lyricists such as Gustav Januš and Fabjan Hafner into German, which has contributed to the increasing critical recognition of Carinthian Slovene literature, particularly in the German-speaking world.[31] He has the ability, as one of the most renowned contemporary writers in the world, to bring wider public attention to Carinthian Slovene literature. Lipuš's *Boštjan's Journey* was published in Slovene in 2003, for example, and translated into German in 2005. The first German edition, however, remained largely ignored in German-language media, even after Lipuš had won Slovenia's Prešeren Award (the country's highest artistic honour). But in a 2011 interview, Handke, when asked what he was currently reading, mentioned it and recommended it to a newspaper's readers. Soon after, the novel was republished, along with a new afterword by Handke. Only after this new edition did the novel receive wide coverage in the German-language press.[32]

Along with his public advocacy of Carinthian Slovene literature and his translations, Handke has also written about his Carinthian Slovene heritage – his mother was a Carinthian Slovene – the Slovene language, and the partisan struggle throughout his career. Already in *A Sorrow beyond Dreams*, his 1972 novel about his mother and her suicide, the attentive reader will pick up references to his mother's Slovene background (e.g., her briefly mentioned language skills help her and her son while living in Soviet-occupied Berlin after the war). These allusions to his Carinthian Slovene heritage and to a broader Carinthian Slovene cultural sphere – nicely hinted at with the final, cryptic sentence of the novel ("Someday I shall write about all this in greater detail") – were taken up more explicitly later in his career in works like *Repetition*, *The Moravian Night*, and, most prominently, in *Storm Still*.[33]

In *Storm Still*, Handke's family history, intertwined with the history of the Carinthian Slovene minority, comes most clearly into view as the narrator meets his deceased Carinthian Slovene ancestors in a magical dream in a field in southern Carinthia.[34] In the text, Handke not only reimagines the biographies of the characters – in the story, two of his uncles join the partisan resistance, while, in reality, they both died in the Wehrmacht during the war – but he also makes explicit references to the memory prose of Prušnik, Kolenik, Jelen, (Anton) Haderlap, and Kuchar, prose he had already brought attention to in the speech he gave upon receiving an honorary doctorate from the University of Klagenfurt in 2002.[35]

All three of these genres – from the early post-war memory texts like *The Carinthian Struggle* to the memory prose referenced by Handke and the literary fiction written by Lipuš and Polanšek – have been referenced and transformed within the Carinthian Slovene literary community over the years. It is out of this wider literary context, moreover, that Maja Haderlap wrote *Angel of Oblivion*. Just as Handke does in *Storm Still*, Haderlap repeatedly references and interweaves various authors and texts mentioned earlier, along with her own family history.[36] But *Angel of Oblivion* marks a significant departure from previous attempts to tell this history through literature in that it was written by an author with no personal experience of the events of the war. Unlike her counterparts, Haderlap is not a "first generation" writer, or someone who experienced the events of the Second World War firsthand. Born in 1961, Haderlap could be classified as either a "second"- or "third"-generation author depending on what criterion is used. If chronological distance to the war years is used as the marker, Haderlap has much more in common with third-generation writers (e.g., Eva Menasse, Doron Rabinovici) than with second-generation ones (e.g., Peter Handke, Robert Schindel). But third-generation authors are usually considered the grandchildren of those who experienced the Second World War first-hand, meaning that these authors tend not to have personal contact with the consequences of the war. While Haderlap is indeed the granddaughter of a concentration camp survivor, she is also the daughter of a resistance fighter, which complicates the clear-cut differences between post-war generations often drawn by literary scholars who have examined similar types of texts. Whichever generation one wants to put Haderlap (and her narrator) in, the interplay of these generations – the interactions between the grandmother, the father, and the daughter – is a core narrative element in the novel, so much so that it should be read as a type of multigenerational novel that reconstructs, in hindsight, a multigenerational story from the perspective of a narrator from the youngest generation.[37] Due to this narrative positioning in the text – the narrator can look back on her family history from the standpoint of the present – how memories are transmitted between generations is a major theme in *Angel of Oblivion*.

Although this genre has its roots in the late nineteenth century, German literature experienced a resurgence in popularity of multigenerational novels around the turn of the millennium.[38] In Germany, these types of novels revolve largely around the intergenerational transmission of memories of National Socialism, the Second World War, and the Holocaust within a family, and how these familial memories interact with larger societal issues.[39] The marked increase in popularity of the multigenerational novel has led to a significant amount of research focused on how the intergenerational transmission of memory works within contemporary German literature.[40]

How this process transpires in contemporary Austrian literature, however, remains either under-examined or subsumed under analyses of German literature. Often, research on how contemporary German authors grapple with the legacies of the Holocaust and National Socialism actually include novels written by Austrian authors.[41] While I am not advocating for a firm split between German and Austrian literature, Austrian authors, particularly ones that write about the Second World War two or three generations removed from it, write about it from a country that has had a much different approach to its Nazi past than their German counterparts. Several German literary critics, perhaps reading *Angel of Oblivion* through the lens of post-war (West) German literary history, seem to have missed this point in their criticism of Haderlap's winning the Ingeborg Bachmann Prize in 2011 for an excerpt of the novel. In contrast to Austria, where her winning of the award was widely met with praise, German critics argued that the novel's story – of Nazi persecution, of the Second World War, of post-war trauma – had already been told numerous times before.[42] Other German critics drew a straight line from early (West) German post-war literature to Haderlap's novel and saw its form and style as just post-war literature packaged in a different story.[43] While it goes without saying that both

German and Austrian writers have written about facets of National Socialism throughout the post-war period, what these German critics miss is that Haderlap's particular story – the persecution and resistance of Carinthian Slovenes and its marginalization in the post-war period – had actually not been told in such a comprehensive way in either German literature or Austrian German-language literature. Analysing Haderlap's *Angel of Oblivion*, then, does not only show how contemporary Carinthian Slovene authors are turning to literature to grapple with the trauma of the Second World War, but it also reveals how Austrian writers are using the multigenerational novel to address the country's specific National Socialist past.[44]

Memory and Generation in *Angel of Oblivion*

We remember the past in two ways: through what Dominick LaCapra calls "primary memory" or "secondary memory." Those of us who have lived through the events we remember operate in the realm of primary memory, while those of us without personal experience with the events remember through secondary memory. This secondary memory results from "critical work" on its primary counterpart, undertaken by "secondary witnesses" such as historians, analysts, or other observers.[45] LaCapra's dichotomy between primary and secondary memory is a helpful starting point for distinguishing how different individuals remember an event. But how exactly those with secondary memory recollect a past they did not experience remains unclear in his framework.

To better understand the difference between primary and secondary memory, the concept of "post-memory" is helpful, as it more fully articulates how individuals born after an event can come to "remember" it. For Marianne Hirsch, the post-memory of a traumatic past is not memory based on lived experience. Rather, it is highly mediated, composed through certain aspects of communicative memory (e.g., family narratives like photo albums and stories).[46] In *Angel of Oblivion*, Haderlap is predominantly concerned with addressing the generational space between those with primary memories of the Second World War and those with post-memories of it. Just as Hirsch describes the relationship between Art Spiegelman and his father's memory of the Holocaust in her famous essay "Family Pictures: Maus, Mourning, and Post-Memory," Haderlap's narrator, born sometime in the post-war period, certainly does not have access to primary memories of the war, but she does grow up in a family environment "dominated by memories of what preceded" her birth.[47] Growing up in southern Carinthia, as the narrator says, "[t]he child understands that it's the past she must reckon with."

As numerous observers have pointed out, the narrator's grand-mother, Mitzi, is one of the main sources of these memories of the war for the narrator.[48] The bookends of the novel – the first sentence and the last paragraph – highlight Mitzi's importance. As the novel opens, the reader enters into the young narrator's world as Mitzi calls her into the kitchen by Mitzi: "Grandmother signals with her hand, she wants me to follow."[49] Almost 300 pages later, the novel closes as the narrator, now an adult, meets Mitzi (who has since passed away) in a dream, providing not only a resolution to the narrated story for the reader but also closure for the narrator's engagement with her own family history. "After many years, Grandmother returns to me in a dream," says the narrator. "I go up to her. She signals with her hand to let me know I shouldn't make any noise. Not so loud, she says, or you can't hear anything."[50]

Between these two plot points, much of the narrative is concerned with the transmission of memory from the war generation (represented by Mitzi) to the post-war one (represented by the narrator) through Mitzi's "accumulation" of the family's history in front of the narrator through storytelling.[51] For Brigitte Prutti, these intergenerational trans-fers of memory largely occur through social interaction between Mitzi and the narrator in their numerous walks through the forest surround-ing the family farm, during which Mitzi not only reminisces about the past but also teaches the narrator about the partisans. As Prutti shows, these walks are critical narrative knots in the novel through which the narrator learns hidden aspects of her family history.[52]

In one of the first trips into the forest with Mitzi, for example, the nar-rator learns that her grandfather, who has already passed away when the novel begins, was a partisan. Moreover, the narrator slowly gains a broader understanding of the war's connection to the landscape that surrounds her:

> The small wood behind our house … is growing rampant. I thought I knew it inside out. I've walked in this wood countless times and could find my way through it with my eyes closed. Now I have to summon all my courage just to set foot in it. … Now the wood is no longer familiar. … I'm afraid it will overflow its banks one day … flooding our thoughts the way I now feel the forest occupies the thoughts of the men who work with my father or visit us to go hunting with him.[53]

As this passage reveals, already as an eight-year-old child, the forests surrounding her childhood home have become more than just geo-graphic features she must pass through to visit her father's cousin's

(Michi) house. Through Mitzi's stories, the narrator connects the small forests around her home to the large ones, the ones that were the refuges for the Slovenes during the war. Although the narrator never experienced the war, the forest, through stories of the past, has become a place laden with affect:

> Going into the forest, in our language, not only means felling trees, hunting, or gathering mushrooms. It also means – as they're always telling us – hiding, escaping, and ambushing. Men and women slept in the forest, they cooked and ate there, too, not just in peacetime, but also during the war. … Many people took refuge in the forest, a hell in which they hunted and were hunted like game. The stories revolve around the forest, just as the forest encircles our farm.[54]

Certainly, then, the forest plays a crucial role in the memory work that takes place in the novel, as does Mitz's "conversational remembering" with the narrator.[55] Moreover, near the end of the novel, once the narrator has finished her doctorate in Vienna and returned home for her father's funeral, another intergenerational connection is made between the grandmother and narrator based on the narrator's assembling of various "testimonial objects" left behind by her grandmother that she discovers tucked away in her old bedroom.[56] For several pages, the narrator embarks on what she calls a "the abyss of history." She reads her grandmother's journal from when she was in the Ravensbrück concentration camp, which not only sparks memories of her childhood spent in her grandmother's room but also lets her reconstruct her grandmother's experience in the camp through her grandmother's own writing. She studies her grandmother's documents, including her report card from primary school, a certificate of residence given to her after her return from Ravensbrück, letters from fellow camp survivors, and her correspondence with various government ministries requesting (unsuccessfully) to receive money from the victims of National Socialism pension fund in the 1950s. This assembling of objects even pushes the narrator to visit Ravensbrück, where she visits the museum's archive and discovers the document noting her grandmother's arrival in the camp on 13 November 1943.

Keeping all of this in mind, I do not want to downplay the importance of the narrator's interactions with Mitzi. But the symbolic transfer of memory from one generation to the next in the text does not actually occur between these two figures. Rather, it occurs largely between the father (Zdravko) and the narrator, a detail that has been overlooked in readings of the novel.

Intergenerational Memory in *Angel of Oblivion*

In his analysis of testimonies from the Holocaust, Lawrence Langer uses the concepts of "heroic" and "unheroic" memory to better understand how concentration camp survivors narrate their memories through video testimony, a distinction that is helpful in analysing intergenerational memory in *Angel of Oblivion*. For heroic memory to develop, a certain amount of "choice, will, power of deliberation, confidence in predictive certainty" must be available to the individual.[57] This type of memory "searches for a moral vision, a principle supporting the idea of the individual as a responsible agent for his actions."[58] Yet, because this ability to be in control of one's existence was unavailable to those in the concentration camps, the testimonies from concentration camp survivors belong to the realm of unheroic memory. As he argues, the "narratives in these testimonies reflect a partially traumatized or maimed self-esteem, lingering like a nonfatal disease without any cure."[59]

Forced to join the partisans as a small boy, the narrator's father is overwhelmed by these unheroic memories of the war as an adult. Unlike the grandmother, who seems to have been able to assert a certain amount of control over her memories from Ravensbrück, the father is unable to do so and tries to manage these through various self-destructive behaviours. Throughout the first section of the novel, the reader is provided various scenes of a young daughter seeing the consequences of this. In stark contrast to the heroic image of the partisan fighters from the monument at the Peršmanhof, these descriptions fluctuate from scenes in which she sees him as a tragic figure struggling to impose control over his memory to those where she is uncomfortable or embarrassed by his erratic and unpredictable behaviour.

Due to the position of the narrator in the first half of the novel, these scenes are transmitted to the reader through the eyes of a young child. Although she observes her father's actions, neither their consequences nor their underlying causes are understood or commented on. One day, for example, she is puzzled when he stops working in the family's apiary, seemingly depressed, and begins singing with what she thinks is a gun in his hand:

> I hear Father singing *Vigred se povrne*, a sad song about spring that returns every year and brings everything back to life, only for him there will be no more spring, for he will die. … I stare at the apiary's open door and believe I can make out Father with a rifle in his hand. In any case, he comes out of the building without a weapon and sits on the threshold with his head in his hands. Mother whispers that we have to take care of him.[60]

The narrator also witnesses her father's extensive bouts with alcoholism. On weekends during her childhood, she is often sent by her mother (Karla) to go fetch him from the local tavern down the road because he forgets to come home. She sees the effects of his alcoholism (he stumbles home incapacitated multiple times) but is too young to understand what is happening or why and thinks he is simply ill. The most disturbing of these scenes occurs when the narrator describes the game she and her little brother play when they are forced to leave the house because of his threatening behaviour:

> We play partisans when once again Father, hunting rifle in hand, threatens at the top of his voice to shoot us all. We run up the slope into the forest, huddle behind a hazel bush, crawl on our stomachs along the edge of the forest. … One time Mother flees with us, which makes us anxious because we're afraid she'll draw Father's attention to our hiding place. … I look at my brother and hope he doesn't understand everything that's going on, but I'm not quite sure. I watch Father, how he wages war with us in a new form. … A dormant cannon, an undetonated missile has wandered out of the past and on our farm by mistake and is seeking shelter under the plum trees in our wood. … We're the unintended targets. … As soon as Father, overcome with exhaustion, nods off and the gun slips from his hand, we exhale. Mother takes his gun and locks it in the hunting closet.[61]

Not only does the narrator transform what is an extremely volatile situation into a harmless game ("We play partisans") in this passage, but this seems to have happened regularly to her and her brother ("once again"). This time, however, the mother joins them, which makes the narrator more worried, not because her mother's actions could reveal the gravity of the situation (*even* the mother, who has spent years with him, hides) but because the mother could reveal their hiding place.

Although similar scenes occur throughout the novel – one day, the family thinks he kills himself in the apiary – as the narrator ages, she begins to recognize why her father acts the way he does. With what Langer calls "a partially traumatized or maimed self-esteem, lingering like a nonfatal disease without any cure," his personal relationships are tied to those who also suffered at the hands of the Nazis.[62] The narrator's sense that her father has a connection to others who were targeted by the Nazis becomes explicit at particular narrative knots in the novel. When she accompanies him through the woods and to the border of Yugoslavia for the first time, he takes her to an abandoned house, hidden behind overgrown grass and apple trees. Here she meets Jaki, an acquaintance of her father's who has been trying to maintain the Blaj's family farm, which has long since become overgrown because all three Blajs brothers were killed during the war and no one is left to run it:

> Too bad no one is farming the place, he says. Who'd have imagined it would turn out this way.
>
> How many brothers was it who died in the camp? Jaki asks.
>
> The three older ones, Jakob, Johi, and Lipi, Father says. Lipi's ashes were sent from Natzweiler, the others died in Dachau.
>
> I hear the resounding name of Dachau, which I'd heard before, but Naztweiler is a new one, and I forget it again immediately.
>
> His uncle died up there, too, Jaki recalls. He had just deserted, Jaki says to me … and he was wounded in the first battle with the Germans. He dragged himself over the field to the Jekls' and lay bleeding below the road behind a bush. The German patrol passed him without seeing him. But then the last soldier looked down and shot him. The Jekls had to bury him next to the road.
>
> That's right, my father says, I know the spot.[63]

While this passage received attention from critics for the narrator's naive description of Dachau and was (unfairly) criticized for downplaying the severity of the camp experience, it is actually a noteworthy passage because it is through conversation between Jaki and her father that the narrator encounters the larger context of suffering, deportation, and resistance that affects most families in her community and sees it visibly manifested for the first time in the abandoned house.[64]

The grandmother, too, plays a role in weaving together a larger context of the community's shared suffering during the war. During the narrator's weekends home in high school – her mother sends her to the Slovene-language Gymnasium in Klagenfurt/Celovec – she overhears her grandmother and father piecing together the family histories of the region:

> She lists all the neighboring properties and the names of those who lived there and who survived the camps or died in them. She sketches the holdings without writing, weaves a fine net from farm to farm, drawing the names together over the hills, a curious network, a secret community of the overpowered. Grandmother lists the holdings in the Lepena Valley. … The names of the camps hang upon the murdered and on the survivors like small labels with inscriptions and they fade on those who have passed away.[65]

As Prutti argues, Haderlap's listing of these family names becomes an "act of poetic restitution" for families that received very little of it in reality.[66] But within the text, it is also creating the larger context for the narrator's encounter with her father's own personal memory. Although she has heard bits and pieces about her father's experience during the war – he had briefly mentioned being forced to flee the Savinja Valley with partisan couriers, for example, and she overhead Peter, her father's cousin, explaining how he had been the youngest of all the partisans – the narrator's most significant encounter with her father's memories occurs explicitly in one scene that Haderlap places in the middle of the novel in which the narrator hears one specific memory of his wartime experience.

After her grandmother dies, the narrator returns home for her funeral. During the wake, family members, friends, and neighbours all visit her parent's house to pay their respects. During the day, prayers are said and stories told, and the narrator learns more about how her grandmother survived Ravensbrück from Mimi, a neighbour. Yet during the night, after the narrator has woken up and gone into the living room, the stories have shifted from Ravensbrück and her grandmother to the partisans and her father. It is here, sitting in his living room and surrounded by close family and friends, that her father finally describes his suffering from the war in vivid fashion in the presence of his daughter. Encouraged to tell his story by Leni, the narrator's great aunt, the narrator discovers that, during the war, local police came to the family's farm to find out the whereabouts of her grandfather who had been suspected of joining the partisans. While her father was milking cows before school, the police surrounded him. The narrator, through indirect speech and frequent shifts between the father's memory and the daughter's reaction, describes what happened:

> After I protested several times that I didn't know anything, the police officers took ropes out of their knapsacks and tied one around my neck. Then they hanged me from a branch. ... They pulled me up with the rope until I started to faint and then let me down again ... three times in a row. The Grandmother ran out of the house and begged them to let me go ... because I had to go to school. Ain't gonna make it to school, the police said ... At two in the morning, they brought him to the police station. ... In the morning they took me to another room and hung me on a hook in the wall. ... Then a police officer beat me with a whip. ... It was a thick whip with lots of cords ... he kept asking if Grandfather was at home. But I didn't say a thing, Father announced. So they let him go ... I was beaten black and blue ... I was terrified.[67]

Until this point in the narrative, the father had only spoken fleetingly of his past.[68] But once he begins to do so in this scene, he cannot stop.

He himself, as the narrator remarks after he finishes the story, looked "a little surprised that he spoke so long."[69] Haderlap captures this dynamic for the reader by placing it in one long, uninterrupted paragraph across three pages, which allows the father's story to be narrated without interruption. Upon hearing her father's story for the first time, the narrator suddenly remarks:

> I am completely upset and want to leap up and ask questions I can't put into words. ... His story has become mine, I observe, although in the moment I'm not perceiving anything, I merely have the feeling that he told me a part of my own story.[70]

The stuff of post-memory, the father's memories from the war have been transmitted to the narrator after this scene "so deeply and affectively as to seem to constitute memories in their own right" for her.[71]

This scene also acts as a break in the narrative style of the text. Previously, memories of the past were narrated to the reader largely through the observations of a child. For example, after her father returns home from visiting Mauthausen, the narrator sees him cry for the first time after he tells of what he has seen at the camp. Revealing the child's perspective, the narrator does not know what to make of this: "It's the first time I've seen him cry and I feel helpless and confused."[72] After the narrator's encounter with her father's traumatic memory, however, the narrative style shifts significantly, which not only ushers in the second part of the novel but also lets the narrator reflect on larger issues of cultural memory within the narrative.

How the narrator describes, reflects on, and critiques these issues related to cultural memory is complex and reveals one of the major advantages that literature has at its disposal when compared to the other media of memory analysed in the previous chapters. Unlike the other media of memory explored thus far, which have often been built with certain political goals in mind, *Angel of Oblivion*, by its nature of being a literary text, has more discursive space to interrogate, question, and pull apart not just various Austrian memory practices but also the link between Carinthian Slovene identity and memory of the partisan resistance.[73] Although Haderlap reveals the various ways these communicative memories can be transmitted intergenerationally – through photographs, letters, family stories, and, most prominently, conversations – she also shows the limits of communicative memory. As the narrator reflects more on the process of memory in the last third of the novel, it becomes clear that these communicative memories are unable to break out of the social context of the narrator's family or the local Slovene region of Carinthia and into the broader cultural memory of either Austria or Yugoslavia.

In Austria – where, as the narrator describes it, no one "ever welcomed the Nazis, no one longed for the Greater German Reich, no one made themselves guilt, no one assisted the Final Solution, they just took part a little bit in the shooting, the assassinations, the gassing, but that doesn't count, nothing counts"[74] – these memories remained locked in "history's cellar," where those who give voice to them are intimidated and threatened: "Those with stories to tell know this and have learned to stay quiet."[75] This is perhaps best illustrated by a scene in which the narrator, home from university during the winter holidays, picks her father up from a local bar. She sits at the table with her father and his friends as they reminisce about their time as partisans. Tine, a friend of her father's, explains to the others what happened at the Peršmanhof. Overhearing this, a man from the neighbouring table rejects Tine's characterization of the events and calls into question the entire raison d'être of the partisans' existence:

> You did nothing more than terrorize the local population. You all fought for Yugoslavia. You are traitors to your country plain and simple, the man at the next table shouts. ... You should all be called up before a military court ... the English should have locked you up instead of the respectable citizens who did their duty.[76]

With this passage, Haderlap shows what happens when the communicative memories of the Carinthian Slovene resistance – which, up to this point in the novel, had been told within the Slovene community in the private spaces of the family home or among friends – are expressed in the public sphere. Just like the monuments and memorials that I analysed in chapter 2, these memories are pushed, by threat of violence, to the margins. As the narrator remarks, "[e]choes of the war surround us for a moment. The inn is transformed into a battle ground on which the opposing sides are taking stands."[77] Even in Bad Eisenkappel/Železna Kapla, a town with a relatively large Slovene-speaking community and only a few miles from the narrator's home down the road, these communicative memories cannot breach the official memory of Carinthia, represented by the man from the neighbouring table who sees the partisan resistance as violence against the loyal Carinthians.

As the narrator continues with her studies, she begins to place her own family history and the memories of her father and grandmother into this larger political context. She begins to think in "larger, public contexts," and realizes that "[b]etween the official version of Austria's history and its actual history stretches a no-man's land in which it's easy to get lost."[78] It is in this no-man's land that Carinthian Slovene communicative memories are located. Not sustained by the stuff of cultural memory – that is, the institutionalized commemoration of the past through things like museums, archives, history books, or official celebrations – it is only within the social context of the family that these memories can be sustained.

But while these memories are limited to the family in southern Carinthia, the narrator discovers that radically different cultural memory had developed about the partisans in post-war Yugoslavia, where, in stark contrast to Austria, the partisans were national heroes. Although she had accompanied her father into Yugoslavia multiple times – once, to buy cigarettes and another time to take him to the dentist – her first encounter with the official memory of Yugoslavia comes from her father after he returns from a trip to Slovenia organized by a local partisan veterans' organization. To her amazement, he joyfully describes how the Carinthian Slovenes were welcomed during a ceremony:

> On his return home, he raves about how well received the Carinthian partisans were in Yugoslavia. He describes how much pomp and circumstance surround the partisans in Slovenia, how supportive they appear of their state and how conscious of their power, how there is still something militant about them.[79]

The narrator herself explores this memory in more detail later in the novel once she finishes her doctorate in Vienna and moves to Ljubljana. Living for a year in the capital of Slovenia in the late 1980s, she observes the debates about democracy and independence that swept the country before the dissolution of Yugoslavia. In this context, new information comes to light about war crimes committed by the partisans near the end of the Second World War, which not only delegitimizes the (then) ruling communist party but also calls into question the entire "myth of the partisans" upon which a pan-Yugoslav post-war identity had been built.[80]

After an event in Ljubljana, the narrator is asked by a historian what the "Slovene Communists in Carinthia" would say about these new discoveries. Although she explains to him that, unlike in Slovenia, the communists never held power in Austria nor does "partisan" equal "communist," the exchange pushes her to critically reflect on the official memory of the partisans in Slovenia and how, what initially seems to be a place sympathetic to her community's memories, turns out to also exclude them:

> I cannot help but think of the partisans in our valleys, who look like scattered forest rebels from the perspective of centralized power in Slovenia. They have nothing in common with the partisan iconography, the oversized imagery of steely warriors storming forward that determined the partisans' image for decades in Yugoslavian and Slovenian public opinion. Our partisans, in contrast, look like erratic boulders left behind by revolutionary history. Since only the Communists' merits could be praised in Yugoslavian and Slovenian post-War historiography, it is obvious that the other partisans – the believers and non-believers, the apolitical and the half-hearted, the disappointed, the skeptics, and the disillusioned – are absent from the general awareness.[81]

This official history highlights the role of what her uncle Tonči calls the "partisans of conviction" but, as she realizes, omits those from her familial surroundings who do not fit into this narrative. In contrast to this heroic, revolutionary picture of the partisans in post-war Slovenia, most partisans in southern Carinthia actually came from conservative, rural, and Catholic environments, traditionally not very responsive to the Liberation Front's revolutionary rhetoric.[82] As Tonči explains to her after her return to Carinthia, during the war, the Slovene farmers "were glad to see the Slovenian army, finally someone who was on their side! They liked the partisans' uniform, but the red star on the cap, not so much."[83] Surprisingly, for the narrator, what at first glance seems to be an environment that would be supportive of Carinthian Slovene communicative memories of the war is, on closer inspection, actually one that marginalizes it as well but for different reasons. This dynamic leads to the communicative memories being excluded from the public sphere in both Austria and Yugoslavia and only told in the private realm of family and friends. Stuck between a rock and a hard place, these memories fall into the background, stereotyped and marginalized from all sides.[84]

Unfortunately, the cultural memory of the Second World War in both countries does not seem likely to become supportive of Carinthian Slovene communicative memories anytime soon. In today's Slovenia, memory of the Second World War has shifted away from the post-war, pan-Yugoslav emphasis on the heroic partisans to what Gal Kirn calls a "national reconciliation" discourse that commemorates all victims of the war – civilian victims, fascist collaborators, and partisan fighters all in one stroke – so Slovenians can "recognize the guilty parties and, at long last, to learn to live in harmony, in a future free of traumas and upsetting memories."[85] Although this had already begun while Slovenia was still part of Yugoslavia, it accelerated after Slovenia became independent as political elites looked for a way to bury the hatchet of the past so the new nation could move forward, a narrative that is perhaps best captured in the name of the monument that was built in Ljubljana in 2016: the Monument to the Victims of all Wars.[86] Reconciliation, however, has also opened the way, heavily supported by the Catholic Church, to rehabilitate the Home Guard (Domobranci), the group that collaborated with the Nazis during the war, and to lure Slovenia "into a relativistic bog in which no one was to blame and no one was morally qualified to judge" the actors involved in the Second World War.[87] Not only have the partisans now been recast as simply a precursor to communist totalitarianism and post-war dictatorship, the partisan's post-war killing of members of the Home Guard, their families, and their supporters has been used to delegitimize the entire post-war period when Slovenia was part of Yugoslavia.[88] In effect, the partisan resistance has been "criminalized" and "equated with the Nazi regime."[89]

In today's Austria, the situation is complex. While commemorative space has yet to be made for Carinthian Slovene memories of persecution and resistance in Carinthia's official memory culture, *Angel of Oblivion* certainly brought public attention to the plight of the Carinthian Slovenes. In the public reception of the novel, commentators often foreground the political and historical aspects of the text and asserted the novel had shined a bright light on an aspect of Austrian history unknown to many.[90] Some commentators even argue that *Angel of Oblivion* helped initiate a larger shift in Carinthian attitudes towards its Slovene minority.[91] Although measuring such a shift in public attitudes would be difficult, official institutions in Austria did indeed honour Haderlap with various awards. In 2012, for example, she was awarded both the Grand Decoration of Honour in Gold of the State of Carinthia and an honorary doctorate from the University of Klagenfurt. Perhaps most significantly, Haderlap was invited to speak at the Vienna opera during the Austrian government's official 100th anniversary celebrations in 2018, which brought renewed public attention to the novel, the Carinthian Slovenes, and their place in twentieth-century Austrian history.[92]

Whether the popularity of the novel or the more public role Haderlap briefly took on in the wake of its success has had any lasting impact on Carinthia's official memory culture, however, is another question. While, as I sketched out in the introduction to this book, much has improved over the last several decades when it comes to Austria's official stance towards its role in the Second World War, commemorative space has yet to be made for Carinthian Slovene memories of persecution and resistance in Carinthia. Of course, *Angel of Oblivion* itself can act as a "vehicle" of cultural memory for Carinthian Slovenes. In one of the most remarkable sections near the end of the novel, for example, the narrator tells the history of the region by condensing the biographies of individuals and families across six pages in one uninterrupted narrative sequence.[93] Long overlooked in both Austrian and Yugoslav official commemorations of the past, Haderlap places their fates on the page, intertwining her narrative with aspects of the Carinthian Slovene memory texts and prose described earlier in this chapter and thus herself makes a contribution to Carinthian Slovene cultural memory.[94] But what happens to these memories, which have been so clearly transmitted within private social structures in southern Carinthia and are even supported by such a novel, when they cannot be pushed into the realm of the official cultural memory? After all, memories "are dependent on their being recalled in various media by later generations who find them meaningful."[95] Once the "living carriers" of these memories have passed, do these memories simply disappear from the wider social environment? In *Angel of Oblivion*, these questions remain unanswered for the reader.

In the novel, the narrator turns to writing to make sense of the predicament. Near the end of the story, the narrator decides to go to Ravensbrück on 13 November, the day her grandmother was admitted to the camp to see her story one last time before she tries to close this chapter of her life. But walking through the structures of the camp – the roll call square, the commandant's house, the barracks – brings no feeling of relief to her. Instead of respite or deliverance from a traumatic familial past, the narrator's trip to the camp brings her to see this past through the lens of Walter Benjamin's version of history, one that is a never-ending cycle of catastrophe:[96]

> The angel of history will have flown over me. His wings will have thrown a shadow over the camp. I couldn't make out his horrified expression in the half-light, I just believed for a moment that I had heard the beat of wings, a burst of wind in his wings, in which are entangled the storms of what is to come. … The angel of oblivion … led me through a sea in which vestiges and fragments were floating. He made my sentences collide against the drifting shards and debris, so they would be wounded, so they would become sharper.[97]

As the violent storm of the past blows Benjamin's angel of history over the narrator, she briefly hears its wings, caught in the wreckage of the past that the novel has been describing, and one that she just saw for herself at Ravensbrück. But despair is not the answer. For Benjamin, just as for the narrator, there are chances for change buried within the struggle over forgotten or suppressed histories. While Benjamin points to the historian as the individual whose job it is to search through the rubble left behind by these winds, the narrator sees this role being taken on by the writer, the creator of literature and the teller of stories:

> With each step, I move further into the present, I bump into myself, I can hear my voice, a voice I recognize, a voice that has not surfaced from the Babel of sentences for a long time, a voice that was kept hidden. ... I will never meet this angel. He will remain formless. He will disappear into books. He will be a story.[98]

As the narrator closes the novel, she realizes that she must look at the catastrophe of her family's and community's past, just like Benjamin's angel of history, with open eyes and to bear witness to its destruction through writing, which results in the novel that the reader has just finished reading.

Conclusion: The Future of Memory in Southern Carinthia

I want to conclude this book with a brief anecdote to demonstrate that, 80 years after the end of the Second World War, the Carinthian Slovene community is still building memorials to resistance fighters and attending funerals for those who were persecuted under Nazism. In the late summer of 2020, I was walking through a small cemetery in Köttmannsdorf/Kotmara vas, and I noticed a funeral was being held. Not wanting to be disrespectful, I put away my camera and notebook, but I continued searching for the particular memorial I knew was hidden somewhere in the vast row of headstones and flower gardens. When I found it, I quickly took a picture of it. Before I could leave, an older man, dressed in a perfectly put-together suit in the hot afternoon air, came up to me and asked what I was doing. I explained to him no offence was meant but that I had come from the United States to visit the graves of those Carinthian Slovenes who had fought in the resistance and the memorials dedicated to them. To my surprise, he told me to take as many pictures as I wanted. What surprised me even more, however, was what he said next. The funeral service that was being held was what he called a "partisan funeral." The man being buried had survived the Dachau concentration camp, and many of those in attendance were former partisans or their family members. He then asked me what I planned to do with the photographs. Before I could reply, he held up the flyer that had been made for the service and told me to take a picture of it, along with all of those in attendance. My pictures of the graves and of these people, he said, should be published. Considering all that had happened, the man who was now buried would like that.

For every year that passes and for every funeral that is held for someone who survived the Nazi era or fought with the partisans, how Carinthian Slovene vernacular memory of the past is being remembered in the region is being altered. Today, the events from the Second

World War are less likely to be remembered by individuals who experienced them directly and are more likely to be experienced through individuals' engagement with particular media of memory, such as memorials and monuments, museums, and literature.[1] Just like other social groups' collective memory of the Second World War, Carinthian Slovene vernacular memories of the war are currently undergoing a shift from the realm of communicative memory to that of cultural memory.[2] In other words, these are shifting away from being memories that are created through individual experience of everyday life in the immediate past to being memories that are shared across eras with the help of symbolic objects and practices that mediate between generations.

In southern Carinthia, these symbolic objects dedicated to resistance and persecution are still controversial. Although, as I explained in the introduction, the victim myth has lost much of its interpretative power, diverging memories of the war – in particular, competing narratives of the partisan resistance – have created a competitive memory dynamic that has managed to linger on in the region. In chapter 2, I explored the southern Carinthian landscape of remembrance to show how two distinct memory cultures, fractured by ethnic group belonging, have been constructed at various sites of memory throughout the region. On one hand, there is the official one that focuses on the Defence Struggle, the 1920 plebiscite, and the partisan crimes at the end of the Second World War. These events are often fused together at memorial sites and commemorations to create a narrative of a monolingual, German-speaking Carinthia that has been under threat from its Slavic south since the end of the First World War. On the other hand, there is a bilingual, Carinthian Slovene vernacular one that focuses on a century of discrimination and highlights the partisan resistance from the Second World War. These partisan memorials, simple expressions of martyrdom and heroism, send a powerful signal to the viewer: "Here rest partisans who fell in the struggle against fascism, 1941–1945." In the southern Carinthian context, such a signal has two layers of meaning. First and foremost, just as Peter Schneider has written about memorials to the wartime resistance in Nazi Germany, these structures show that "[e]ven in the worst years of state terror, there was a choice, a small choice, and some citizens made that choice."[3] But because *that* choice was made largely by Carinthian Slovenes, they also remind Carinthians, particularly those who would rather keep the era of National Socialism in their blind spot, of Slovene speakers' continual existence in the region. It is because of this "double provocation" that these partisan memorials still carry such power and relevance today.[4]

These Carinthian Slovene memorials and monuments that dot the landscape within this memorial culture are aided by the pedagogical discourse curated at the Peršman Museum, the only museum that tells the history of Carinthian Slovene persecution and resistance in all of Austria. By extending the historical narrative from the late nineteenth century into the present, the museum manages to tell the "hard truths" of the persecution and deportation of the Carinthian Slovenes and the targeted state violence directed at them. The museum offers a broad understanding of the term resistance – enabling it to tell a more complex narrative of the past – letting the visitor grapple with the various reasons individuals joined the partisans. In addition to acting as a site of learning for visitors from outside the Carinthian Slovene community, as a small exhibition space located in the former Sadovnik family home, the museum manages to also act as a site of remembrance for visitors from within it.

At this point, although my analysis of Carinthian Slovene memorials and monuments revealed certain transnational influences in the aesthetics and design of these objects, the clashing of these two memory cultures leads me to question a core claim made by advocates of transnational memory practices. In regions with competitive memory cultures, scholars often see a transformative potential lingering beneath the surface of memory competition.[5] In this line of argument, friction, rather than something negative, holds positive power for the future. Competing memories do not have to push opposing memories to the side; they do not need to be understood as "a zero-sum struggle over scarce resources."[6] Rather, such memories can actually forge new, shared narratives of the past or, at a minimum, mutual respect for each other's suffering.[7] As one group of authors put it: There is a "possibility that the intersection of disparate commemorative discourses might offer an opportunity to forge empathic communities of remembrance across national, cultural, or ethnic boundaries."[8] But how are such "empathic communities of remembrance" to be forged across a cultural boundary when the communities on either side of it maintain incompatible memories of the same event? How can mutual respect for different narratives form when these narratives contradict each other? Just as is the case with the other examples of divided memory in Europe that I discussed at the outset of this book, the memory of the partisan resistance in southern Carinthia still seems far from becoming an event that transcends ethnic group belonging and forms the foundation for an inclusive memory culture. The memory entrepreneurs I interviewed gave two main reasons for this, including a general ignorance on the part of Austrians as to the existence of the Carinthian Slovenes as well as a hesitation to fully engage with what happened in the state during the Second World War because that would force a reckoning with family histories.

While seeing such steps being taken anytime soon by the various German nationalist organizations in Carinthia is difficult – in 2020, the Carinthian Heimat Service built a controversial memorial to Hans Steinacher, a leading German nationalist during the 1920 Carinthian plebiscite and later Nazi Party propagandist – some steps have been taken in this direction by representatives of Austria's and Carinthia's official memory cultures.[9] In 2020, for example, at the official state ceremonies in Klagenfurt/Celovec for the 100th anniversary of the Carinthian plebiscite, Alexander van der Bellen, Austria's president at the time, officially apologized to Carinthia's Slovenes on behalf of the Austrian government for not upholding Article 8 of the Austrian Constitution. After quoting Article 8, which requires the government to respect, safeguard, and support the culture and language of its autochthonous ethnic groups, Van der Bellen, speaking in German, said:

> Have we always kept this promise? Unfortunately, I have to admit that no, many things happened late, only after a long period of pressure. For the injustice suffered and for the failures in the implementation of constitutionally guaranteed rights, I would like to apologize here and now as Federal President to you, respected members of the Slovene ethnic group.[10]

Then, switching to (broken) Slovene in an attempt to send a symbolic message, he repeated that last line and offered the first official apology for the government's failure to uphold these constitutionally protected rights in the post-war period.

Within Carinthia's official memory culture, the story is a bit less straightforward. More controversially, Van der Bellen's apology was complicated by Peter Kaiser, the social democratic governor of Carinthia, participating at a commemorative ceremony for Martin Wutte, a leading Nazi propagandist and academic in Carinthia during the National Socialist era who took on an active Germanizing voice against the Carinthian Slovenes. Kaiser's appearance at this ceremony was caught on camera in a telling scene from *Disappearing* (Verschwinden/ Izginjanje), Andrina Mračnikar's documentary about the slow erasure of Slovene from Carinthia over the last century, during which Kaiser justified his participation at the ceremony with an off-hand remark about not getting stuck in the past.[11] However, two years later, on 12 April 2022, 80 years to the day that 227 Carinthian Slovene families like Katja Sturm-Schnabl's from my introduction were deported to concentration camps, Kaiser officially apologized in the name of the Carinthian governor's office.[12] A year later, in February 2023, Kaiser awarded the Order of Merit to Amalija Sadovnik, one of the still living survivors of the Peršmanhof massacre in April 1945, who symbolically stood in for the rest of the victims.[13] Along with the former president of Slovenia, Borut Pahor, Kaiser also participated in a commemorative ceremony at the local cemetery in Zell-Pfarre/Sele-Cerkev, the one I analysed in chapter 3, to commemorate those individuals executed by the Nazis for resistance in that area. Kaiser also made a break with the past and officially acknowledged the role of those individuals who had joined the partisan resistance.[14]

Such symbolic restitution, unprecedented in Carinthia, speaks to the aesthetic, political, and moral power of a novel like *Angel of Oblivion*, which, out of all the mediums analysed in this book, has likely had the largest influence on Carinthian official memory. The novel marks a significant shift in how the Carinthian Slovene resistance is remembered in Carinthia. As I showed in chapters 2 and 3, the story of resistance, as well as its commemoration in stone, has long been fractured between ethnic groups in Carinthia, almost supported solely by Carinthian Slovenes through a form of purposeful remembrance where the past has been used as a tool to forge an identity in the present. When the past is viewed in these terms, however, it has run the risk of being instrumentalized for a whole host of things that have been disconnected from the event being memorialized, a dynamic that was clear in my interviews with certain memory entrepreneurs in chapter 3.[15] This is the flipside of Gal Kirn's counter-archive: Using the past in such a way can also lead to simplified, obtuse activities that no one from outside the group wants to participate in. But, in a novel like *Angel of Oblivion*, the "powerful linkage between memory and identity that is instrumental for public and communicative memory discourses can be loosened, questioned or even decoupled."[16] By employing techniques like plot and narrative, which gives readers the "illusion of access to other people's minds as they experience and recall events," the story the novel tells – of persecution and resistance, of the ensuing memory wars in the postwar period, of the intergenerational trauma both of these left behind within the Carinthian Slovene community – can be accessed by those without any previous personal link to it, something that is much more difficult when it comes to the monuments and memorials I explored in chapter 2.[17] Without Haderlap's novel, which managed to break the story of partisan resistance out of the traditional ethnic divide in Carinthia and led to a significant amount of sympathetic reportage being produced about the Carinthian Slovenes, imagining such symbolic gestures of restitution having the political space to take place is difficult.[18]

Along these lines, I was on a bus from Klagenfurt/Celovec to Graz in 2023 after having attended a conference at the University of Klagenfurt about representations of the partisan resistance. The woman sitting next to me noticed the conference program in my bag, and we ended up discussing the Second World War, Carinthia, and my book project. She had grown up south of Klagenfurt/Celovec in a small village and, as she recollected, had never really thought much of the Carinthian Slovenes except when they would be spoken about as "criminals" or "traitors" in conversations about the past. But, she said, the story that she had read in Haderlap's *Angel of Oblivion* had a dramatic impact on her. She felt a bit ashamed of what had happened and a bit embarrassed for knowing so little about it. After finishing, she had recommended the novel to her friends and family. Once I told her about the Peršmanhof, which she had never heard of before, she even seemed interested in taking her daughter and husband there for a visit to the museum. Such experiences speak to the power of literature, less politically motivated and overt in its messaging than the other mediums of memory I explored in this book, to open up new, perhaps more inclusive, spaces of memory in the twenty-first century for Carinthian Slovene vernacular memories of the past. The story of resistance that Haderlap tells, and of the partisans who are in it, is not like the monument at the Peršmanhof or the political events put on by the Alliance of Carinthian Partisans. Haderlap's partisans, those "believers and non-believers, the apolitical and the half-hearted, the disappointed, the sceptics, and the disillusioned," do not fit into that heroic mould. "They have nothing in common," she writes, "with the partisan iconography, the oversized imagery of steely warriors storming forward."[19] It is this aspect of her story that makes it relatable and approachable to people like the woman I spoke to on the bus.

With these new developments in mind, what does the future of memory look like in southern Carinthia? You could argue that a politician such as Kaiser has little to lose laying a wreath among a small audience in a village cemetery in the hinterlands of Austria 80 years after the end of the Second World War. Almost nothing is at stake in such a ceremony in 2024. Yugoslavia is gone, as is the general geopolitical context that locked the post-war memory of the partisans within the ideologies of the Cold War. Slovenia is a member of the European Union, which has taken – but not removed – wind out of the German nationalist discourse about the "Slavic threat" from the south. But a more sympathetic reading of the situation would argue that an interaction like the one I had on the bus, alongside the symbolic steps taken by someone like Peter Kaiser, offers hope that going forward into the twenty-first century, Carinthia's official memory will open itself up to a more nuanced narrative of the region's twentieth century past by including aspects of Carinthian Slovene vernacular memory in it. Whether that will be the case or not, only the future will tell.

Notes

Introduction

1 Katja Sturm-Schnabl, "Tito, mein Retter," in *Spurensuche. Erzählte Geschichte der Kärntner Slowenen*, ed. Dokumentationsarchiv des österreichischen Widerstandes, Klub Prežihov Voranc, Institut za proučevanje prostora Alpe-Jadran (Vienna: Österreichischer Bundesverlag, 1990), 153–9.

2 Marjan Linasi, *Koroški partizani. Protinacistični odpor na dvojezičnem koroškem v okviru slovenske Osvobodilne fronte* (Klagenfurt/Celovec, Austria: Hermagoras/Mohorjeva, 2010), 679–80.

3 Lipej Kolenik-Stanko, "Die Kraft, die alles erhalten hat," in Dokumentationsarchiv des österreichischen Widerstandes, ed., *Spurensuche*, 357–68.

4 Brigitte Entner, *Wer war Klara aus Šentlipš/St. Philippen? Kärntner Slowenen und Sloweninnen als Opfer der NS-Verfolgung. Ein Gedenkbuch* (Klagenfurt/ Celovec, Austria: Drava, 2014), 27. Entner, however, makes clear that this number is likely an underestimate.

5 For how Carinthian Slovene organizations have engaged with these stories, see Andreas Leben and Erwin Köstler, "Von den primären Quellen zum publizistischen Diskurs. Über den bewaffneten Widerstand der Partisanen in Kärnten," *Zeitgeschichte* 34, no. 4 (2007): 226–42.

6 Josef Rausch, *Der Partisanenkampf in Kärnten im Zweiten Weltkrieg* (Vienna: Österreichischer Bundesverlag, 1979).

7 For more on the historiography of resistance in Austria, see Peter Pirker, "British Subversive Politics towards Austria and Partisan Resistance in the Austrian-Slovene Borderland, 1938–45," *Journal of Contemporary History* 52, no. 2 (1 April 2017): 320–3.

8 See, for example, Wolfgang Neugebauer, *Der österreichische Widerstand 1938–1945* (Vienna: Steinbauer, 2008), 186; Tim Kirk, "Limits of Germandom: Resistance to the Nazi Annexation of Slovenia," *The Slavonic

and East European Review 69, no. 4 (1991): 666; Linasi *Koroški partizani*, 702; Robert Knight, *Slavs in Post-Nazi Austria: Carinthian Slovenes and the Politics of Assimilation, 1945–1960* (London: Bloomsbury Academic, 2017), 24.

9 The literature here is vast. See, for instance, Matthew P. Berg, "Commemoration versus Vergangenheitsbewältigung: Contextualizing Austria's Gedenkjahr 2005," *German History* 26, no. 1 (January 2008): 47–71; Heidemarie Uhl, "Das 'erste Opfer': der österreichische Opfermythos und seine Transformationen in der Zweiten Republik," *Österreichische Zeitschrift für Politikwissenschaft* 30, no. 1 (2001): 19–34; Günter Bischof, "Victims? Perpetrators? 'Punching Bags' of European Historical Memory? The Austrians and Their World War II Legacies," *German Studies Review* 27, no. 1 (2004): 18; Peter Utgaard, *Remembering and Forgetting Nazism: Education, National Identity, and the Victim Myth in Postwar Austria* (New York: Berghahn Books, 2003).

10 Heidemarie Uhl, "The Politics of Memory: Austria's Perception of the Second World War and the National Socialist Period," in *Austrian Historical Memory & National Identity*, ed. Günter Bischof and Anton Pelinka (New Brunswick, NJ: Transaction, 1997), 66.

11 Robert H. Keyserlingk, *Austria in World War II. An Anglo-American Dilemma* (Kingston, ON: McGill-Queen's University Press, 1988).

12 "Mahnmal unerbittlicher Gerechtigkeit: Die Enthüllung des russischen Heldendenkmals auf dem Schwarzenbergplatz," *Das kleine Volksblatt*, 21 August 1945, 1. Translation my own.

13 Jamie Bulloch, *Karl Renner: Austria* (London: Haus, 2009), 145.

14 Günter Bischof, "Victims? Perpetrators? 'Punching Bags' of European Historical Memory? The Austrians and Their World War II Legacies," *German Studies Review* 27, no. 1 (2004): 18.

15 Günter Bischof, "Founding Myths and Compartmentalized Past: New Literature on the Construction, Hibernation, and Deconstruction of World War II Memory in Postwar Austria," in Bischof and Pelinka, eds., *Austrian Historical Memory*, 302–341.

16 Alon Confino, "Remembering the Second World War, 1945–1965: Narratives of Victimhood and Genocide," *Cultural Analysis* 4 (2005): 50.

17 For how this consensus developed, see Peter Pirker, "The Victim Myth Revisited: The Politics of History in Austria Up Until the Waldheim Affair," *Contemporary Austrian Studies* 29 (2020): 151–72.

18 Jenny Wüstenberg and David Art, "Using the Past in the Nazi Successor States from 1945 to the Present," *The Annals of the American Academy of Political and Social Science* 617 (2008): 78.

19 Matti Bunzl, "On the Politics and Semantics of Austrian Memory: Vienna's Monument against War and Fascism," *History and Memory* 7, no. 2 (1995): 12.

20 For the Waldheim Affair, see Cornelius Lehnguth, *Waldheim und die Folgen: Der parteipolitische Umgang mit dem Nationalsozialismus in Österreich* (Frankfurt, Germany: Campus Verlag, 2013). Here, too, scholars point to the affair as a historiographical "turn" in Austrian history. See, for example, Frank Trommler, "Austria Past, Austria Present: Stages of Scholarship in the American University," *Monatshefte* 111, no. 1 (2019): 4; Heidemarie Uhl, "Culture, Politics, Palimpsest. These on Memory and Society," in *A European Memory?: Contested Histories and Politics of Remembrance*, ed. Małgorzata Pakier and Bo Stråth (New York: Berghahn Books, 2012), 85.

21 For these two programs, see Günter Bischof and Michael S. Maier, "Reinventing Tradition and the Politics of History: Schüssel's Restitution and Commemoration Policies," in *The Schüssel Era in Austria*, ed. Günter Bischof and Fritz Plasser (New Orleans: University of New Orleans Press, 2010), 206–34; Judith Beniston, "'Hitler's First Victim'? – Memory and Representation in Post-War Austria: Introduction," *Austrian Studies* 11 (2003): 1–13.

22 For these various initiatives, see Neil Christian Pages, "Architectures of Memory: Rachel Whiteread's 'Memorial to the 65,000 Murdered Austrian Jews,'" *Austrian Studies* 11 (2003): 102–21; Peter Pirker, Johannes Kramer, and Mathias Lichtenwagner, "Transnational Memory Spaces in the Making: World War II and Holocaust Remembrance in Vienna," *International Journal of Politics, Culture, and Society* 32, no. 4 (2019): 450–54; Heidemarie Uhl, "From the Periphery to the Center of Memory: Holocaust Memorials in Vienna," *Dapim: Studies on the Holocaust* 30, no. 3 (2016): 221–42; Thorben Pollerhof, "Mit Akkubohrer und Cif-Reiniger gegen das Vergessen," *Der Standard*, 9 November 2019.

23 For a recent, detailed accounting of the Austrian federal and Carinthian state governments' refusal to fulfil these duties, see Council of Carinthian Slovenes, "Stellungnahme zum 6. Bereicht des Landes Kärnten/Koroška zur Lage der slowenischen Volksgruppe 2023," 1–21, accessed 31 July 2023, https://www.nsks.at/aktualno_aktuell/detail/de/porochilo-o-polozhaju -slovenske-narodne-skupnosti-na-avstrijskem-koroshkem-2023.

24 For these terms, see John Bodnar, *Remaking America: Public Memory, Commemoration, and Patriotism in the Twentieth Century* (Princeton, NJ: Princeton University Press, 1992).

25 For the organization of Austria's autochthonous ethnic groups, see William E. Sanford, "Government-Minority Dialogue in Austria: The Ethnic Advisory Councils," *International Journal on Group Rights* 3, no. 4 (1995): 261–82.

26 Tom Priestley, "Denial of Ethnic Identity: The Political Manipulation of Beliefs about Language in Slovene Minority Areas of Austria and Hungary," *Slavic Review* 55, no. 2 (1996): 364–98; Karl-Michael Brunner,

"Zweisprachigkeit und Identität: Probleme sprachlicher Identität von ethnischen Minderheiten am Beispiel der Kärntner Slowenen," *Psychologie und Gesellschaftskritik* 11, no. 4 (1987): 57–75.

27 Daniel Wutti, "Identität, Gewalt und 'Brückenfunktionen'. Die Analyse qualitativer Gruppeninterviews mit jungen SlowenInnen," in *Kärnten und Slowenien: getrennte Wege – gemeinsame Zukunft. Koroška in Slovenija: Ločene poti – skupna prihodnost. Jugend zwischen Heimat, Nation und Europa. Mladi o domovini, narodu in Evropi*, ed. Jürgen Pirker (Baden-Baden, Germany: Nomos, 2015), 318–19.

28 For the rise of nationalism in nineteenth-century Carinthia, see Thomas Barker, *The Slovene Minority of Carinthia* (New York: Columbia University Press, 1984), 58–89.

29 These organizations are not political parties but advocacy groups at the state level. The Unity List (Einheitsliste/Enotna lista), which has members from both ethnic groups, is the one Slovene political party that contests elections at the municipal level in southern Carinthia and has had a moderate level of success there. For these organizations, see Boris Jesih, "Political Participation of the Slovene Ethnic Minority in Carinthia," *Slovene Studies* 30, no. 2 (2008): 229–33.

30 For more detail on these other organizations, see Daniel Wutti, "Between Self-Governance and Political Participation: The Slovene Minority in Carinthia, Austria," *Razprave in gradivo: revija za narodnostna vprašanja*, no. 78 (2017): 59–71.

31 Brigitta Busch, "Shifting Political and Cultural Borders: Language and Identity in the Border Region of Austria and Slovenia," in *Culture and Cooperation in Europe's Borderlands*, ed. James Anderson, Liam O'Dowd, and Thomas M. Wilson (Amsterdam: Rodopi, 2003), 133. In 1945, the Liberation Front for Slovenian Carinthia (Osvobodilna fronta za Slovensko Koroško), a body that was a spin-off of the partisan Liberation Front from the Second World War, was set up as the Slovene representative body under the Allied occupation authorities. However, the Liberation Front's communism and its continued support for Yugoslavia's territorial demands (i.e., annexation of southern Carinthia) spurred conservative Slovenes to establish a separate, Catholic-oriented organization in 1949. The Liberation Front ceased to exist in 1949, but left-leaning Carinthian Slovenes soon founded the Association of Slovene Organizations.

32 Lisa Rettl, "'… Dass wir für immer aufgehört haben, Sklaven zu sein …' Erinnerungskultur der Kärntner SlowenInnen am Beispiel des Peršmandenkmals," *Zeitgeschichte* 38, no. 1 (2011): 18n2. See also the introduction, authored by Carinthian Slovene organizations from across the political spectrum, to Marjan Borut Sturm and Črtomir Zorec, eds., *Padlim za svobodo: pomniki protifašističnega boja na Koroškem = Den Gefallenen*

für die Freiheit: Gedenkstätten des antifaschistischen Kampfes in Kärnten (Klagenfurt/Celovec, Austria: Drava, 1987).

33 Wutti, "Identität, Gewalt und Brückenfunktionen," 320. For a fuller discussion on Carinthian Slovene identity, Tom Priestly and Ruxandra Comanaru, "'Identity' among the Minority Slovenes of Carinthia, Austria," *Razprave in gradivo: revija za narodnostna vprašanja*, no. 58 (2009): 6–23; Ursula Doleschal, "Multilingualism in Carinthia: The Case of Slovene and the Slovene Minority," *The Polyphony of English Studies. A Festschrift for Allan James*, ed. by Alexander Onysko et al. (Tübingen: Narr Francke Attempto Verlag, 2017), 145–162.

34 Jenny Wüstenberg, *Civil Society and Memory in Postwar Memory* (Cambridge, UK: Cambridge University Press, 2017), 11.

35 See, for instance, Sabine Marschall, *Landscape of Memory: Commemorative Monuments, Memorials and Public Statuary in Post-Apartheid South Africa* (Leiden, The Netherlands: Brill, 2009); Krystyna von Henneberg, "Monuments, Public Space, and the Memory of Empire in Modern Italy," *History and Memory* 16, no. 1 (2004): 37–85; Federico Bellentani and Mario Panico, "The Meanings of Monuments and Memorials: Toward a Semiotic Approach," *Punctum. International Journal of Semiotics* 2, no. 1 (2016): 28–46; Oto Luthar, "Forgetting Does (Not) Hurt. Historical Revisionism in Post-Socialist Slovenia," *Nationalities Papers* 41, no. 6 (November 2013): 882–92; Wüstenberg, *Civil Society*, 11.

36 Marek Tamm, "In Search of Lost Time: Memory Politics in Estonia, 1991–2011," *Nationalities Papers* 41, no. 4 (2013): 6555.

37 Wüstenberg, *Civil Society*, 12.

38 See, most prominently, Lisa Rettl, *PartisanInnendenkmäler* (Innsbruck: Studienverlag, 2006).

39 Maruša Pušnik, "Common History, Divided Memories: Slovenian and Austrian Struggle for the Carinthian Past," *Anthropological Notebooks* 14, no. 1 (2008): 49–61.

40 Elizabeth Jelin, *State Repression and the Labors of Memory* (Minneapolis: University of Minnesota Press, 2003), 33–4.

Chapter 1: Carinthia, the Carinthian Slovenes, and Memory of the Second World War

1 For more on this history, see Mirko Bogataj, *Ein Volk am Rand der Mitte. Die Kärntner Slowenen* (Klagenfurt/Celovec, Austria: Kitab, 2008), 40–6; Mirjam Polzer-Srienz, "The Slovene Community in Austria," in *The Ethnopolitical Encyclopaedia of Europe*, ed. Karl Cordell and Stefan Wolff (New York: Palgrave Macmillan, 2004), 35–40; Rado L. Lenček, "Carantania," *Slovene Studies* 15, no. 1–2 (1993): 193–4.

2 Tom Gullberg, *State, Territory and Identity. The Principle of National Self-Determination, the Question of Territorial Sovereignty in Carinthia and the Post-Habsburg Territories after the First World War* (Åbo, Finland: Åbo Akademi University Press, 2000), 86.

3 Thomas Barker, *The Slovene Minority of Carinthia* (New York: Columbia University Press, 1984), 51.

4 Stefan Karner and Andreas Moritsch, "Zur Einleitung: der nationale Konflikt," in *Kärnten und die nationale Frage. Aussiedlung*, ed. Stefan Karner and Andreas Moritsch (Klagenfurt/Celovec, Austria), 8–14.

5 Gullberg, *State, Territory and Identity*, 88.

6 Matjaž Klemenčič, "German-Slovene Relations in the Slovene Lands from the Mid-19th Century until Today," *Onomàstica. Anuari de la Societat d'Onomàstica* 3 (2017): 130.

7 For the collapse of the monarchy, see Pieter M. Judson, *The Habsburg Empire: A New History* (Cambridge, MA: Harvard University Press, 2016), 385–441.

8 Peter Thaler, *The Ambivalence of Identity. The Austrian Experience of Nation-Building in a Modern Society* (West Lafayette, IN: Purdue University Press, 2001), 68–71.

9 Judson, *The Habsburg Empire*, 436–7.

10 Gullberg, *State, Territory and Identity*, 106–14.

11 Peter Gatrell, "War after the War: Conflicts, 1919–1923," in *A Companion to World War 1*, ed. John Horne (London: Blackwell, 2010), 558–75.

12 John C. Swanson, "The Sopron Plebiscite of 1921: A Success Story," *East European Quarterly* 34, no. 1 (2000): 81–94; Tamás Révész, "The Land of Peace? The 1921 Borderland Conflict of Burgenland in the International Context," *Südost-Forschungen* 79, no. 1 (2020): 124–50.

13 Christian Koller,"… der Wiener Judenstaat, von dem wir uns unter allen Umständen trennen wollen": die Vorarlberger Anschlussbewegung an die Schweiz," in … *der Rest ist Österreich: das Werden der Ersten Republik*, ed. Helmut Konrad and Wolfgang Maderthaner (Vienna: Gerold Verlag, 2008), 83–102.

14 Georg Grote, *The South Tyrol Question, 1866–2010* (Bern, Switzerland: Peter Lang, 2012), 19–33.

15 Robert Knight, *Slavs in Post-Nazi Austria: Carinthian Slovenes and the Politics of Assimilation, 1945–1960* (London: Bloomsbury Academic, 2017), 13.

16 Ute Weinmann, "Die südslawische Frage und Jugoslawien. Grenzziehungen im süden Österreichs unter besonderer Berücksichtigung der Kärntenproblematik," in *Das werden der ersten Republik … Der Rest ist Österreich*, ed. Helmut Konrad and Wolfgang Maderthaner (Vienna: Carl Gerolds Sohn, 2008), 133.

17 Guido Tiemann, "'Kärnten' = Austria, 'Koroška' = Yugoslavia? A Novel Perspective on the 1920 Carinthian Plebiscite," *Historical Social Research* 45, no. 4 (2020): 334.

18 Nadja Danglmaier and Werner Koroschitz, *Nationalsozialismus in Kärnten: Opfer. Täter. Gegner* (Innsbruck: Studienverlag, 2015), 24.

19 Arnold Suppan, "Kärnten und Slowenien: Die Geschichte einer schwierigen Nachbarschaft im 20. Jahrhundert," in *Kärnten und die nationale Frage. Kärnten und Slowenien – "Dickicht und Pfade,"* ed. Stefan Karner and Janez Stergar (Klagenfurt/Celovec, Austria: Johannes Heyn and Hermagoras/Mohorjeva, 2005), 23.

20 Donald F. Reindl, *Language Contact: German and Slovene* (Bochum, Germany: Universitätsverlag Dr. N. Brockmeyer, 2008), 3.

21 Tim Kirk, "Limits of Germandom: Resistance to the Nazi Annexation of Slovenia," *The Slavonic and East European Review* 69, no. 4 (1991): 650.

22 Weinmann, "Die südslawische Frage," 135.

23 Suppan, "Kärnten und Slowenien," 10–12.

24 Barker, *The Slovene Minority*, 172.

25 Weinmann, "Die südslawische Frage," 134; Barker, *The Slovene Minority*, 172.

26 Barker, *The Slovene Minority*, 172–173.

27 Danglmaier and Koroschitz, *Nationalsozialismus in Kärnten*, 26.

28 Knight, *Slavs in Post-Nazi Austria*, 14.

29 Originally in "Kärntner Landsmannschaft," 15 December 1920, cited in Weinmann, "Die südslawische Frage," 135. Translation my own.

30 Barker, *The Slovene Minority*, 178–9.

31 Matjaž Klemenčič, "German-Slovene Relations in the Slovene Lands from the Mid-19th Century until Today," *Onomàstica. Anuari de la Societat d'Onomàstica* 3 (2017): 138–40.

32 Pieter M. Judson, *Guardians of the Nation: Activists on the Language Frontiers of Imperial Austria* (Cambridge, MA: Harvard University Press, 2006), 240–1. For more detail, see Arnold Suppan, "Zur Lage der Deutschen in Slowenien zwischen 1918 und 1938. Demographie – Recht – Gesellschaft – Politik," in *Geschichte der Deutschen im Bereich des heutigen Slowenien 1848–1941. Zgodovina nemcev na območju današnje Slovenije 1848–1941*, ed. Helmut Rumpler and Arnold Suppan (Vienna: Verlag für Geschichte und Politik, 1988): 171–80, 204–5.

33 Judson, *Guardians of the Nation*, 244–5.

34 Eithne McLaughlin, "Cultural Memory and Regional Identities in Northern Ireland and Southern Carinthia," in *Towards a Dialogic Anglistics*, ed. Werner Delanoy et al. (Münster, Germany: LIT, 2007), 36.

35 Robert Knight, "Ethnicity and Identity in the Cold War: The Carinthian Border Dispute, 1945–1949," *The International History Review* 22, no. 2 (June 2000): 288.

36 Weinmann, "Die südslawische Frage," 135.

37 For Carinthian Slovenes and the Anschluss, see Knight, *Slavs in Post-Nazi Austria*, 17–20.

38 Valentin Sima, "Gewalt und Widerstand 1941–1945," in *Die Kärntner Slowenen 1900–2000. Bilanz des 20. Jahrhunderts*, ed. Andreas Moritsch (Klagenfurt/Celovec, Austria: Hermagoras/ Mohorjeva, 2000), 266–7.

39 Walter Manoschek, "Kärntner Slowenen als Opfer der NS-Militärjustiz.," in *Opfer der NS-Militärjustiz. Urteilspraxis – Strafvollzug – Entschädigungspolitik in Österreich*, ed. Walter Manoschek (Vienna: Mandelbaum, 2003), 359.

40 Marjan Linasi, *Die Kärntner Partisanen. Protinacistični odpor na dvojezičnem koroškem v okviru slovenske Osvobodilne fronte* (Klagenfurt/Celovec, Austria: Hermagoras/Mohorjeva, 2010), 25.

41 Leopoldina Plut-Pregelj and Carole Rogel, *The A to Z of Slovenia* (Plymouth, UK: Scarecrow Press, 2010), 434.

42 Johann Böhm, *Die deutsche Volksgruppe in Jugoslawien 1918–1941. Innen- und Außenpolitik als Symptome des Verhältnisses zwischen deutscher Minderheit und jugoslawischer Regierung* (Frankfurt am Main: Peter Lang, 2009), 37; Philip W. Lyon, "After Empire: Ethnic Germans and Minority Nationalism in Interwar Yugoslavia," (PhD diss., University of Maryland, 2008), 558.

43 For the invasion, see Ben Shepherd, *Terror in the Balkans: German Armies and Partisan Warfare* (Cambridge, MA: Harvard University Press, 2012), 72–82.

44 Manoschek, "Kärntner Slowenen," 359; Maurice Williams, "Another Final Solution: Friedrich Rainer, Carinthian Slovenes, and the Carinthian Question," *Slovene Studies* 19, no. 1–2 (1997): 47.

45 Valentin Sima, "Die Vertreibung slowenischer Familien als Höhepunkt deutschnationaler Politik in Kärnten," in *Pregon koroskih slovencev 1942–2002 = Die Vertreibung der Kärntner Slowenen 1942–2002*, ed. Avguštin Malle (Klagenfurt/Celovec, Austria: Drava, 2002), 149.

46 Tina Bahovec, "Der Zweite Weltkrieg im Alpen-Adria-Raum," in *Alpen-Adria. Zur Geschichte einer Region*, ed. Andreas Moritsch (Klagenfurt/ Celovec, Austria: Hermagoras/Mohorjeva, 2011), 453–69.

47 Barker, *The Slovene Minority*, 198–9. For draft-dodging, see Gregor Kranjc, "Fight or Flight: Desertion, Defection, and Draft- Dodging in Occupied Slovenia, 1941–1945," *Journal of Military History* 81, no. 1 (2017): 133–62.

48 Linasi, *Koroški partizani*, 679–680.

49 Brigitte Entner, "Kärntner Slowenen und Sloweninnen – unbekannte / ungeliebte Minderheit im Süden Österreichs," *Psychologie & Gesellschaftskritik* 39, no. 4 (2016): 16–7.

50 Kirk, "Limits of Germandom," 666; Linasi, *Koroški partizani*, 702;
Neugebauer, *Der österreichische Widerstand*, 182.

51 Barker, "Partisan Warfare," 207.

52 Linasi, *Koroški partizani*, 705–6.

53 In the inter-war period, in addition to the Slovenians living in Austria,
an estimated 1,100,000 Slovenians lived in the Drava Banovina (the SHS
state's northernmost region), around 350,000 in Italy (in Trieste, the Julian
March, and parts of the province of Udine), and 7,000 in Hungary. See
Nevenka Troha, "Slovenia. Occupation, Repression, Partisan Movement,
Collaboration, and Civil War in Historical Research," *Südosteuropa* 65, no. 2
(2017): 334n1; 337.

54 *Temeljne točke Osvobodilne fronte* (Fundamental Principles of the Liberation
Front), first published in *Slovenski poročevalec* (the Liberation Front's
newspaper) in January 1942 in *Dokumenti ljudske revolucije v sloveniji*, ed.
Tone Ferenc, et al., vol. 1, *marec 1941 – marec 1942* (Ljubljana, Slovenia:
Inštitut za zgodovino delavskega gibanja, 1962), 255–6.

55 Knight, "Ethnicity and Identity in the Cold War," 291–2.

56 Brigitte Entner, "Kärntner Slowenen und Sloweninnen," 21.

57 Robert Knight, "Denazification and Integration in the Austrian Province
of Carinthia," *The Journal of Modern History* 79, no. 3 (September 2007):
572–612.

58 Robert Knight, "A No-Win Situation? Gerald Sharp and British Policy
towards the Carinthian Slovenes 1945–1960," in *Widerstand gegen
Faschismus und Nationalsozialismus im Alpen-Adria-Raum. Odpor proti
fašizmu in nacizmu v alpsko-jadranskem prostoru*, ed. Brigitte Entner and
Slowenisches Wissenschaftliches Institut (Klagenfurt/Celovec, Austria:
Drava, 2011), 84–96.

59 Consolidated Intelligence Report 11,3 Oct 1945, FO 1007/296. Originally
cited in Knight, "Ethnicity and Identity," 291.

60 Brigitte Entner, "Vergessene Opfer? Die 'Verschleppten' vom Mai 1945
im Spiegel regionaler Geschichtspolitik," in *Kärnten liegt am Meer.
Konfliktgeschichte/n über Trauma, Macht und Identität*, ed. Wolfgang Petritsch,
Wilfried Graf, and Gudrun Kramer (Klagenfurt/Celovec, Austria: Drava,
2012), 423; Stefan Karner and Susanne Hartl, "Die Verschleppungen von
Kärntnern 1945 durch Jugoslawische Partisanen," in *Kärnten und die
nationale Frage. Aussiedlung – Verschleppung – nationaler Kampf*, vol. 1, ed.
Stefan Karner and Andreas Moritsch (Klagenfurt, Austria: Johannes Heyn
and Hermagoras/Mohorjeva, 2005), 53–78.

61 Linasi, *Koroški partizani*, 672.

62 Gregor Kranjc, "Talking Past Each Other: Language and Post–World War II
Killings in Slovenia," *Journal of Genocide Research* 20, no. 4 (2018): 565–86.

63 Robert Knight, "Kosaken und Kroaten in Kärnten: vernachlässigte
    Perspektiven," in *Zweiter Weltkrieg und ethnische Homogenisierungsversuche
    im Alpen-Adria-Raum/Druga svetovna vojna in poizkusi etnične homogenizacije
    v alpsko-jadranskem prostoru*, ed. Brigitte Entner and Valentin Sima
    (Klagenfurt/Celovc, Austria: Drava, 2012), 127–46.
64 Jozo Tomasevich, *War and Revolution in Yugoslavia, 1941–1945: Occupation
    and Collaboration* (Palo Alto, CA: Stanford University Press, 2001), 765. See
    751–785 for a detailed discussion of the end of the war in the Balkans and
    how it concluded in Carinthia.
65 Knight, "Ethnicity and Identity," 277.
66 Rausch, *Der Partisanenkampf*, 83.
67 Knight, "Ethnicity and Identity," 278; Brigitte Entner, "Zwischen
    Integration und Ausgrenzung. Kärntner SlowenInnen und britische
    Besatzungspolitik bis zu den Novemberwahlen 1945," in *Von Neuem. Die
    Kärntner Slowenen unter der britischen Besatzungsmacht nach dem Jahr 1945.
    Zeitzeugen, Beiträge und Berichte* (Klagenfurt/Celovec: Drava, 2008), 37–38.
68 Avguštin Malle, "Konfrontation mit den ehemaligen Verbündeten.
    Betrachtungen zur Haltung der britischen Besatzungsmächte gegenüber
    den Kärntner Slowenen in den ersten Jahren nach dem Zweiten
    Weltkrieg," in *Von Neuem*, 44–88.
69 Kurt Bauer, *Die dunklen Jahre. Politik und Alltag im nationalsozialistischen
    Österreich. 1938 bis 1945* (Frankfurt am Main, Germany: Fischer, 2017), 410.
    Translation my own.
70 Derek H. Alderman, "Creating a New Geography of Memory in the South:
    (Re)Naming of Streets in Honor of Martin Luther King, Jr.," *Southeastern
    Geographer* 36, no. 1 (1996): 54.
71 Jennifer M. Gully, "Bilingual Signs in Carinthia: International Treaties, the
    Ortstafelstreit, and the Spaces of German," *TRANSIT* 7, no. 1 (2011): n.p.
72 AK gegen den Kärntner Konsens, "Der Ulrichsberg Fakten und Zahlen,"
    in *Friede, Freude, deutscher Eintopf. Rechte Mythen, NS Verharmlosung
    und antifaschistischer Protest*, ed. AK gegen den Kärntner Konsens
    (Vienna: Mandelbaum), 77–120; Brigitte Bailer-Galanda and Wolfgang
    Neugebauer, "Right-Wing Extremism: History, Organisations, Ideology,"
    in *Incorrigibly Right. Right-Wing Extremists, "Revisionists" and Anti-Semites
    in Austrian Politics Today*, ed. Brigitte Bailer-Galanda and Wolfgang
    Neugebauer (Vienna: Stiftung Dokumentationsarchiv des österreichischen
    Widerstandes and the Anti-Defamation League, 1996), 5–21.
73 Kärntner Abwehrkämpferbund, "Organisation," *Kärntner
    Abwehrkämpferbund*; Peter Gstettner, "… 'wo alle Macht vom Volk
    ausgeht': eine nachhaltige Verhinderung; zur Mikropolitik rund um den
    'Ortstafelsturm' in Kärnten." *Österreichische Zeitschrift für Politikwissenschaft*
    33, no. 1 (2004): 81–94.

74 Walter Fanta and Valentin Sima, *Stehst mitten drin im Land. Das europäische Kameradentreffen auf dem Kärntner Ulrichsberg von den Anfängen bis heute* (Klagenfurt/Celovec, Austria: Drava, 2003).

75 Linasi, *Die Kärntner Partisanen*, 338, 421–2.

76 Gregor Joseph Kranjc, "On the Periphery: Jews, Slovenes, and the Memory of the Holocaust," in *Bringing the Dark Past to Light. The Reception of the Holocaust in Postcommunist Europe*, ed. by John-Paul Himka and Joanna Beata Michlic (Lincoln: University of Nebraska Press, 2013), 597.

77 Charles S. Maier, *The Unmasterable Past: History, Holocaust, and German National Identity* (Cambridge, MA: Harvard University Press, 1997), 13.

78 Kärntner Abwehrkämpferbund, "Gedenkfeier für die verschleppten und ermordeten Kärntner durch Tito-Partisanen," *Kärntner Abwehrkämpferbund*, 10 May 2014. Translation my own.

79 Kärntner Abwehrkämpferbund, "Partisanenverherrlichung in Klagenfurt," 20 January 2019, *Kärntner Abwehrkämpferbund*. Translation my own.

80 Valentin Sima, "Das Peršman-Massaker," 119.

81 Knight, "Ethnicity and Identity," 288.

82 Richard H. Schein, "Belonging through Land/Scape," *Environment and Planning A: Economy and Space* 41, no. 4 (April 2009): 821.

83 Fionnuala Dillane and Gunnþórunn Guðmundsdóttir, "Iceland – Ireland Memory, Literature, Culture on the Atlantic Periphery," in *Iceland – Ireland Memory, Literature, Culture on the Atlantic Periphery*, ed. Fionnuala Dillane and Gunnþórunn Guðmundsdóttir (Leiden, The Netherlands: Brill, 2022), 5.

84 Kobi Kabalek, "Memory and Periphery: An Introduction," *HAGAR Studies in Culture, Polity and Identities*, vol. 12 (2014): 8.

85 Anna Reading, "Identity, Memory and Cosmopolitanism: The Otherness of the Past and a Right to Memory," *European Journal of Cultural Studies* 14, no. 4 (2011): 379–94.

86 Sharon K. Hom and Eric K. Yamamoto, "Collective Memory, History, and Social Justice," *UCLA Law Review* 47 (1999): 1759.

87 Hom and Yamamoto, "Collective Memory," 1764.

88 Paul Connerton, "Seven Types of Forgetting," *Memory Studies* 1, no. 1 (2017): 60–1.

89 Philip Lee and Prapid Ninan Thomas, "Introduction: Public Media and the Right to Memory: Towards an Encounter with Justice," in *Public Memory, Public Media and the Politics of Justice*, ed. Philip Lee and Prapid Ninan Thomas (Basingstoke, UK: Palgrave Macmillan, 2012): 15.

90 See, for example, Lucy Bond and Jessica Rapson, eds., *The Transcultural Turn: Interrogating Memory between and beyond Borders* (Berlin: De Gruyter, 2014).

91 Pierre Nora, *Realms of Memory: Rethinking the French Past*, trans. Lawrence D. Kritzman (New York: Columbia University Press, 1996).

92 Astrid Erll, "Traveling Memory," *Parallax* 17, no. 4 (2011): 4–18.

93 See, most prominently, Michael Rothberg, *Multidirectional Memory. Remembering the Holocaust in the Age of Decolonization* (Stanford, CA: Stanford University Press, 2009). For the concept of memory politics, see Marek Tamm, "In Search of Lost Time: Memory Politics in Estonia, 1991–2011," *Nationalities Papers* 41, no. 4 (2013): 651–74.

94 Astrid Erll, "Transcultural memory," *Témoigner. Entre histoire et mémoire* 119 (2014), 178.

95 Aleida Assmann, "Transnational Memory and the Construction of History through Mass Media," in *Memory Unbound. Tracing the Dynamics of Memory Studies*, ed. Lucy Bond, Stef Craps, and Pieter Vermeulen (New York: Berghahn Books, 2017), 65–80.

96 Lucy Bond, Stef Craps, and Pieter Vermeulen, "Introduction: Memory on the Move," in Bond et al., eds., *Memory Unbound*, 6.

97 See, for example, the contributions in Małgorzata Pakier and Bo Stråth, eds., *A European Memory? Contested Histories and Politics of Remembrance* (New York: Berghahn Books, 2010); Stefan Berger and Caner Tekin, eds., *History and Belonging: Representations of the Past in Contemporary European Politics* (New York: Berghahn Books, 2018).

98 Stefan Berger and Caner Tekin, "Conclusion," in Berger and Tekin, eds., *History and Belonging*, 196–7.

99 Omer Bertov, "Conclusion," in *Bringing the Dark to Light. The Reception of the Holocaust in Postcommunist Europe*, ed. John-Paul Himka and Joanna Beata Michlic (Lincoln: University of Nebraska Press, 2013), 663–94.

100 Marek Kucia, "The Europeanization of Holocaust Memory and Eastern Europe," *East European Politics and Societies* 30 (2016): 107–19; Sierp Aline, "Drawing Lessons from the Past: Mapping Change in Central and South-Eastern Europe," *East European Politics and Societies and Cultures* 30, no. 1 (2015): 3–9.

101 John-Paul Himka and Joanna Beata Michlic, "Introduction," in Himka and Michlic, eds., *Bringing the Dark Past to Light*), 6.

102 Tea Sindbæk Andersen and Barbara Törnquist-Plewa, eds., *Disputed Memory Emotions and Memory Politics in Central, Eastern and South-Eastern Europe* (Berlin: de Gruyter, 2016).

103 Heike Karge, "Local Practices and 'Memory from Above': On the Building of War Monuments in Yugoslavia," in *Shaping Revolutionary Memory – The Production of Monuments in Socialist Yugoslavia*, ed. Sanja Horvatinčić and Beti Žerovc (Ljubljana, Slovenia, and Berlin: Igor Zabel Association for Culture and Theory and Archive Books, 2023), 93.

104 Gal Kirn, *The Partisan Counter-Archive: Retracing the Ruptures of Art and Memory in the Yugoslav People's Liberation Struggle* (Berlin: De Gruyter, 2020), 212.

105 For an overview of these, see Anna Milosević and Tamara Trošt, eds., *Europeanisation and Memory Politics in the Western Balkans* (Cham, Switzerland: Palgrave Macmillan, 2020).

106 Mark Biondich, "Representations of the Holocaust and Historical Debates in Croatia since 1989," in Himka and Michlic, eds., *Bringing the Dark to Light*, 131–65; Andriana Benčić Kužnar and Vjeran Pavlaković, "Exhibiting Jasenovac: Controversies, Manipulations and Politics of Memory," *Heritage, Memory and Conflict* 3 (2023): 65–69; Jovan Byford, *Picturing Genocide in the Independent State of Croatia: Atrocity Images and the Contested Memory of the Second World War in the Balkans* (London: Bloomsbury Academic, 2020).

107 Jelena Đureinović, *The Politics of Memory of the Second World War in Contemporary Serbia: Collaboration, Resistance and Retribution* (London: Routledge, 2019); Jelena Đureinović, "Marching the Victorious March: Populism and Memory Appropriation of the Yugoslav Partisans in Today's Serbia," *Nationalities Papers* 51, no. 6 (2023): 1250–62.

108 Julie Fedor, Simon Lewis, and Tatiana Zhurzhenko, "Introduction: War and Memory in Russia, Ukraine, and Belarus," in *War and Memory in Russia, Ukraine and Belarus*, ed. Julie Fedor et al. (Cham, Switzerland: Palgrave Macmillan, 2017), 17–20; John-Paul Himka, "The History behind the Regional Conflict in Ukraine," *Kritika: Explorations in Russian and Eurasian History* 16, no. 1 (2015): 129–36; Eleonora Narvselius, "The 'Bandera Debate': The Contentious legacy of World War II and Liberalization of Collective Memory in Western Ukraine," *Canadian Slavonic Papers* 54, no. 3–4 (2012): 469–90; Timothy Snyder, "European Mass Killing and European Commemoration," in *Remembrance, History, and Justice. Coming to Terms with Traumatic Pasts in Democratic Societies*, ed. Vladimir Tismaneanu and Bogdan C. Iacob (Vienna: Central European University Press, 2015), 34–35.

109 Omer Bartov, *Erased: Vanishing Traces of Jewish Galicia in Present-Day Ukraine* (Princeton, NJ: Princeton University Press, 2007).

110 Pamela Ballinger, *History in Exile: Memory and Identity at the Borders of the Balkans* (Princeton, NJ: Princeton University Press, 2003).

111 See, for example, Jenny Wüstenberg and David Art, "Using the Past in the Nazi Successor States from 1945 to the Present," *The Annals of the American Academy of Political and Social Science* 617 (2008): 72–87; Berger and Tekin, "Conclusion," 196.

112 For a recent contribution about this problem, see Elizabeth Loentz et al., "Forum: Austrian Studies," *The German Quarterly* 89, no. 2 (2016): 221–39.

113 Loentz et al., "Forum: Austrian Studies," 223.

114 Klaus Zeyringer, "Austrian Literature: A Concept," in *Shadows of The Past. Austrian Literature of the Twentieth Century*, ed. Hans Schulte and Gerald Chapple (New York: Peter Lang, 2009), 25–8.

115 Charles Maier, "A Surfeit of Memory? Reflections on History, Melancholy and Denial," *History and Memory* (1993): 136–2.

116 For language, see Leonard Norman Primiano, "Vernacular Religion and the Search for Method in Religious Folklife," *Western Folklore* 54, no. 1, Reflexivity and the Study of Belief (1995): 42. For the traditional definition from anthropology, see Margaret Lantis, "Vernacular Culture," *American Anthropologist* 62, no. 2 (1960): 202–16. For architecture, see Carl Mitcham, "Thinking Re-Vernacular Building," *Design Issues* 21, no. 1 (2005): 32–40.

117 John Bodnar, *Remaking America: Public Memory, Commemoration, and Patriotism in the Twentieth Century* (Princeton, NJ: Princeton University Press, 1992).

118 Sabine Marschall, "Collective Memory and Cultural Difference: Official vs. Vernacular Forms of Commemorating the Past," *Safundi* 14, no. 1 (2013): 79.

119 Bodnar, *Remaking America*, 13–20.

120 See, for instance, Jeffrey K. Olick, "Memory: The Two Cultures," *Sociological Theory* 17, no. 3 (1999): 339; Barry Schwartz, *Abraham Lincoln and the Forge of National Memory* (Chicago: University of Chicago Press, 2000), 13–5.

121 Sabina Mihelj, "Between Official and Vernacular Memory," in *Research Methods for Memory Studies*, ed. Emily Keightley and Michael Pickering (Edinburgh: Edinburgh University Press, 2013), 72–3.

122 Jeffrey K. Olick, "What Does It Mean to Normalize the Past?: Official Memory in German Politics since 1989," *Social Science History* 22, no. 4 (1998): 555.

123 Jenny Wüstenberg, *Civil Society and Memory in Postwar Germany* (Cambridge, UK: Cambridge University Press, 2017), 20.

124 Marschall, "Collective Memory," 89–90.

125 Dora Apel, *War Culture and the Contest of Images* (New Brunswick, NJ: Rutgers University Press, 2012), 63.

126 Kirn, *The Partisan Counter-Archive*, 18.

127 For this metaphor, see Hom and Yamamoto, "Collective Memory," 1764.

128 Barbara A. Misztal, *Theories of Social Remembering* (Maidenhead, UK: McGraw-Hill International, 2003), 158.

Chapter 2: The Southern Carinthian Landscape of Remembrance

1 Jay Winter, *Sites of Memory, Sites of Mourning: The Great War in European Cultural History* (Cambridge, UK: Cambridge University Press, 2014), 1.

2 Norbert Fischer, "Maritime Death, Memory and Landscape. Examples from the North Sea Coast and the Islands," in *Waddenland Outstanding. History, Landscape, and Cultural Heritage of the Wadden Sea Region*, ed. Linde

Egberts and Meindert Schroor (Amsterdam: Amsterdam University Press, 2018), 169.

3 For a tour guide–like approach to these memorials, see Andrej Mohar, *Otoki Spomina/ Gedenkinseln. Partizanska spominska obeležja na južnem Koroškem/Gedenkstätten für die Partisanen in Südkärnten* (Klagenfurt/Celovec, Austria: Drava, 2018).

4 For these memorials that were built during or right after the war in Yugoslavia from what scholars have referred to as "ordinary people," see Heike Karge, "Local Practices and 'Memory from Above': On the Building of War Monuments in Yugoslavia," in *Shaping Revolutionary Memory: The Production of Monuments in Socialist Yugoslavia*, ed. Sanja Horvaticnčić and Beti Žerovc (Ljubljana, Slovenia, and Berlin: Igor Zabel Association for Culture and Theory and Archive Books, 2023), 119–20.

5 Paul Groth and Chris Wilson, "The Polyphony of Cultural Landscape Study: An Introduction," in *Everyday America. Cultural Landscape Studies after J. B. Jackson*, ed. Paul Groth and Chris Wilson (Berkeley: University of California Press, 2003), 2.

6 Groth and Wilson, "The Polyphony of Cultural Landscape Study," 3.

7 F. Pierce Lewis, "Axioms of the Landscape: Some Guides to the American Scene," *JAE* 30, no. 1 (1976): 6.

8 Richard H. Schein, "Normative Dimensions of Landscape," in Groth and Wilson, eds., *Everyday America*, 203.

9 Carl Sauer, "The Morphology of Landscape," *University of California Publications in Geography* 2, no. 2 (1925): 46.

10 Lewis, "Axioms of the Landscape," 6.

11 Derek H. Alderman and Joshua F. J. Inwood, "Landscapes of Memory and Socially Just Futures," in *The Wiley-Blackwell Companion to Cultural Geography*, ed. Nuala C. Johnson, Richard H. Schein, and Jamie Winders (Hoboken, NJ: John Wiley & Sons, 2013), chap. 18. ProQuest Ebook Central.

12 Gunda Barth-Scalmani, "Memory-Landscapes of the First World War: The Southwestern Front in Present-Day Italy, Austria and Slovenia," in *From Empire to Republic*, ed. Günter Bischof, Fritz Plasser, and Peter Berger (New Orleans: University of New Orleans Press, 2010), 222–53; Gordana Božić, "Diversity in Ethnicization: War Memory Landscape in Bosnia and Herzegovina," *Memory Studies* 12, no. 4 (2019): 412–32.

13 Kendall R. Phillips and G. Mitchell Reyes, "Introduction. Surveying Global Memoryscapes: The Shifting Terrain of Public Memory Studies," in *Global Memoryscapes: Contesting Remembrance in a Transnational Age*, ed. Kendall R. Phillips and G. Mitchell Reyes (Tuscaloosa: University of Alabama Press, 2011), 1–26.

14 Eva Kuttenberg, "Austria's Topography of Memory: Heldenplatz, Albertinaplatz, Judenplatz, and Beyond," *The German Quarterly* 80, no. 4 (2007): 468–91.

15 *Merriam Webster Dictionary*, "landscape (n.)."

16 Richard H. Schein, "A Methodological Framework for Interpreting Ordinary Landscapes: Lexington, Kentucky's Courthouse Square," *Geographical Review* 99, no. 3 (2009): 377–402.

17 Rudy Koshar, *From Monuments to Traces: Artifacts of German Memory, 1870–1990* (Berkeley: University of California Press, 2000), 10.

18 Alice F. A. Mutton, "Carinthia: A Province of Austria's Southern Frontier," *Geography* 38, no. 2 (1953): 83–93; Richard R. Randall, "Political Geography of the Klagenfurt Basin," *Geographical Review* 47, no. 3 (1957): 406–11.

19 Mutton, "Carinthia," 87; Brigitta Busch, "Shifting Political and Cultural Borders: Language and Identity in the Border Region of Austria and Slovenia," in *Culture and Cooperation in Europe's Borderlands*, ed. James Anderson, Liam O'Dowd, and Thomas M. Wilson (Amsterdam: Rodopi, 2003), 125–44.

20 Thomas Barker, *The Slovene Minority of Carinthia* (New York: Columia University Press, 1984), 20–4; Martina Berchtold-Ogris, Brigitte Entner, and Helena Verdel, *Die Drau ist eine eigene Frau: ein Fluss und seine Kulturgeschichte. Drava je svoja frava: h kulturi in zgodovini Drave*, ed. Slowenischer Kulturverband/Slovenska prosvetna zveza, trans. Vida Obid (Klagenfurt/Celovec, Austria: Drava, 2001), 7.

21 See, for example, Tom Priestly, Meghan McKinnie, and Kate Hunter, "The Contribution of Language Use, Language Attitudes, and Language Competence to Minority Language Maintenance: A Report from Austrian Carinthia," *Journal of Slavic Linguistics* 17, no. 1–2 (2009): 278–82.

22 Bogataj, *Die Kärntner Slowenen, Ein Volk am Rand der Mitte. Die Kärntner Slowenen* (Klagenfurt/Celovec, Austria: Kitab, 2008), 320; Avguštin Malle, ed., *Die Slovenen in Kärnten. Slovenci na Koroškem. Gegenwärtige Probleme der Kärntner Slovenen. Sodobni probleme koroških Slovencev* (Ferlach/Borovlje: Drava, 1975), 25–27.

23 Valentin Sima, "Das Peršman-Massaker in der Erinnerungspolitik und seine justizielle Untersuchung," in Entner, Sima, and Malle, *Widerstand gegen Faschismus*, 117.

24 Wilhelm Baum, *Peršmanhof 1945. Protokolle eines NS-Kriegsverbrechens* (Klagenfurt/Celovec, Austria: Kitab, 2013), 8.

25 Baum, *Peršmanhof*, 7.

26 Lisa Rettl, "Die Ermordung der Familie Sadovnik am 25. April 1945. Ein Humanitätsverbrechen im zeitgeschichtlichen Kontext. Einleitende Vorbemerkungen," in Rettl et al., *Peršman*, 29–37.

27 Lisa Rettl, "Museum Peršmanhof. Tatort – Erinnerungsort – Lernort," *Neues Museum. Die österreichische Museumszeitschrift* 3, no. 4 (2013): 79.

28 Insa Eschenbach, "Soil, Ashes, Commemoration: Processes of Sacralization at the Former Ravensbrück Concentration Camp," *History and Memory* 23, no. 1 (2011): 134.

29 Rettl, *PartisanInnendenkmäler*(Innsbruck: Studienverlag, 2006), 220–5.

30 Rettl, "Museum Peršmanhof," 78.

31 Tamm, "In Search of Lost Time: Memory Politics in Estonia, 1991–2011," *Nationalities Papers* 41, no. 4 (2013): 651–74.

32 Luthar, "Forgetting Does (Not) Hurt. Historical Revisionism in Post-Socialist Slovenia," *Nationalities Papers* 41, no. 6 (November 2013): 883.

33 Gudrun Blohberger, "Ausstellungsimpressionen. Ein Museumsrundgang in Wort und Bild. Mit Fotos von Zdravko Haderlap," in Rettl et al., *Peršman*, 230.

34 Janine Wulz and Jonas Kolb, "Der Gedenkort Peršmanhof. Ein Stachel in der Kärntner Erinnerungslandschaft," in *Friede, Freude, deutscher Eintopf. Rechte Mythen, NS-Verharmlosung und antifaschistischer Protest*, ed. Arbeitskreis gegen den kärntner Konsens (Vienna: Mandelbaum kritik & utopie, 2011), 322.

35 Barker, *The Slovene Minority*, 88. At the end of the nineteenth century in the Habsburg monarchy, this debate was, of course, not limited to Carinthia but was a main concern of nationalist activists around the empire. See Judson, *Guardians of the Nation: Activists on the Language Frontiers of Imperial Austria* (Cambridge, MA: Harvard University Press, 2006), 23–4.

36 Statistik Austria, *Volkszählung. Hauptergebnisse. Kärnten* (Vienna: Verlag Österreich, 2003), 17.

37 Barker, *The Slovene Minority*, 86–89.

38 See, for example, Andreas Moritsch, "German Nationalism and the Slovenes in Austria between the Two World Wars," *Slovene Studies* 8, no. 1 (1986): 15–20; Katharina Prochazka, "Minderheitensprachen zählen! Über Sprachzählungen und Minderheiten(-sprachen)," *Wiener Linguistische Gazette* 83 (2018): 1–26; Tom Priestly, "Maintenance of Slovene in Carinthia (Austria): Grounds for Guarded Optimism?," *Canadian Slavonic Papers / Revue Canadienne des Slavistes* 45, no. 1/2 (2003): 95–117; Albert F. Reiterer, "The Slovene Language in Carinthia - Symbolic Bilingualism," *Razprave in Gradivo* 43 (2003): 186–201.

39 Franz Heiß, *Methodik der Volkszählungen* (Jena, Germany: G. Fischer, 1931), 143–4.

40 Karl-Markus Gauß, *Die Vernichtung Mitteleuropas. Essays* (Klagenfurt/ Celovec, Austria: Wiesler, 1991), 138.

41 See, for example, Marija Jurić Pahor, "Hidden Identities within National Minority Groups: The Case of Slovenes in Carinthia and in the Province of

Trieste," in *(Hidden) Minorities. Language and Ethnic Identity between Central Europe and the Balkans*, ed. Christian Promitzer, Klaus-Jürgen Hermanik, and Eduard Staudinger (Münster, Germany: LIT, 2009), 35–58.

42 Knight, "Ethnicity and Identity in the Cold War: The Carinthian Border Dispute, 1945–1949," *The International History Review* 22, no. 2 (June 2000): 287.

43 For an excellent explanation on the influence of economic modernization on Slovene usage in one particular village, see Tom Priestely, *From Phonological Analysis at My Desk to Linguistic Activism with Slovene in the Austrian Alps* (Oxford: The University of Mississippi Printing Services for the Southeast European Studies Association, 2014), 21–5.

44 Gal Kirn, *The Partisan Counter-Archive: Retracing the Ruptures of Art and Memory in the Yugoslav People's Liberation Struggle* (Berlin: De Gruyter, 2020), 16.

45 Jan Assmann, "Communicative and Cultural Memory," in *Cultural Memory Studies: An International and Interdisciplinary Handbook*, ed. Astrid Erll and Ansgar Nünning (Berlin: Walter de Gruyter, 2008), 109–19.

46 Lisa Rettl, "Vom Tatort zum musealen Erinnerungsort. Zur Geschichte der Gedenkstätte," in *Peršman*, 202–208.

47 Scholars have often considered using English a critical component of the "transnationalization" of specific museum spaces. See, for example, Annika Björkdahl and Stefanie Kappler, "The Creation of Transnational Memory Spaces: Professionalization and Commercialization," *International Journal of Politics, Culture, and Society* 32, no. 4 (2019): 396.

48 Mieke Bal, "Guest Column: Exhibition Practices," *PMLA* 125, no. 1 (2010): 10.

49 Bal, "Guest Column," 12.

50 Valentin Sima, "Gewalt und Widerstand 1941–1945," in *Die Kärntner Slowenen. 1900–2000. Bilanz des 20 Jahrhunderts*, ed. Andreas Moritsch (Klagenfurt/Celovec, Austria: Hermagoras/Mohorjeva, 2000), 272.

51 Gregor Kranjc, "Fight or Flight: Desertion, Defection and Draft-Dodging in Occupied Slovenia, 1941–1945," *Journal of Military History* 81, no. 1 (2017): 133–62; Brigitte Entner, *"Kaj človek vse doživi! Was der Mensch alles erlebt!" Odpor in preganjanje v občini Sele 1938–1945. Widerstand und Verfolgung in der Gemeinde Zell: 1938–1945* (Klagenfurt/Celovec, Austria: Mohorjeva/Hermagoras, 2018), 14.

52 Alison Landsberg, *Prosthetic Memory: The Ethics and Politics of Memory in an Age of Mass Culture* (New York: Columbia University Press, 2004), 33–34.

53 Amy Sodaro, *Exhibiting Atrocity: Memorial Museums and the Politics of Past Violence* (New Brunswick, NJ: Rutgers University Press, 2018), 24.

54 Silke Arnold-de Simine, *Mediating Memory in the Museum. Trauma, Empathy, Nostalgia* (New York: Palgrave Macmillan, 2013), 13.

55 Graham Black, *The Engaging Museum: Developing Museums for Visitor Involvement* (London: Routledge, 2005), 130.

56 Margaret Lindauer, "The Critical Museum Visitor," in *New Museum Theory and Practice: An Introduction*, ed. Janet Marstine (Hoboken, NJ: Wiley-Blackwell, 2005), 213.

57 To be sure, the Carinthian Slovenes are mentioned as one of the officially recognized victim groups of Nazism in the Haus der Geschichte Österreichs, Austria's first contemporary history museum, which has been located in Vienna's Neue Burg since 2018. But the only mention of the Slovene resistance is found in a small caption underneath an even smaller photo relegated to the side of the exhibition, which can be easily missed due to the spatial constraints of the exhibition. Other scholars have noticed these spatial issues regarding how the Second World War is presented, too. According to one critic, "Austria's problematic role during the Nazi rule is only documented in a small part of the already spatially limited current exhibition, somewhat hidden in the chronological flow of the exhibition and can easily be bypassed." See Stephan Neuhäuser, "Coming to Terms with the Past: The Case of the 'House of Austrian History' (Haus der Geschichte Österreich) in the Wake of the rise of Populist Nationalism in Austria," *Modern Languages Open*, no. 1 (2020): 11. For an extended critique of the museum, see Claudia Teeb, *The Politics of Repressed Guilt. The Tragedy of Austrian Silence* (Edinburgh: Edinburgh University Press, 2018), 167–202.

58 Bal, "Guest Column," 20.

59 Belinda Kazeem, Nicola Lauré al-Samarai, and Peggy Piesche, "Museum. Space. History: New Sites of Political Tectonics. A Virtual Exchange between Belinda Kazeem, Nicola Lauré al-Samarai, and Peggy Piesche," trans. Tim Scharpe, eipcp. European Institute for Progressive Cultural Policies, June 2008.

60 Amy Lonetree, *Decolonizing Museums. Representing Native America in National and Tribal Museums* (Chapel Hill: The University of North Carolina Press, 2012).

61 Maria Yellow Horse Brave Heart, "Historical Trauma Response among Natives and Its Relationship with Substance Abuse," *Journal of Psychoactive Drugs* 35, no. 1 (2003): 7.

62 Blohberger, "Ausstellungsimpressionen," 244.

63 Interview with Gudrun Blohberger, January 15, 2020.

64 Claudia Kuretsisdis-Haider, "Strafsache wegen Verbrechen an der Familie Sadovnik. Das Verfahren des Volksgerichts Klagenfurt und der Umgang der österreichischen Justiz mit den Ereignissen auf dem Peršmanhof," in Rettl et al., *Peršman*, 49–89.

65 Sodaro, *Exhibiting Atrocity*, 23.

66 Interview with Zdravko Haderlap, 21 January 2020.

67 For the transmission of historical trauma specifically within the Carinthian Slovene community, see Daniel Wutti, *Drei Familien, drei Generationen das Trauma des Nationalsozialismus im Leben dreier Generationen von Kärntner SlowenInnen* (Klagenfurt/Celovec, Austria: Drava, 2013).

68 Marita Sturken, "The Wall, the Screen, and the Image: The Vietnam Veterans Memorial," *Representations*, no. 35 (1991): 118.

69 Arthur C. Danto, "The Vietnam Veterans Memorial," *The Nation*, 31 August 1985, 152–5.

70 James E. Young, "The Counter-Monument: Memory against Itself in Germany Today," *Critical Inquiry* 18, no. 2 (1992): 277.

71 Mechtild Widrich, "The Willed and the Unwilled Monument: Judenplatz Vienna and Riegl's Denkmalpflege," *Journal of the Society of Architectural Historians* 72, no. 3 (2013): 382.

72 For Germany, see Cecily Harris, "German Memory of the Holocaust: The Emergence of Counter-Memorials," *Penn History Review* 17, no. 2 (2010): 56. For the other countries, see Andrew Crampton, "The Voortrekker Monument, the Birth of Apartheid, and Beyond," *Political Geography* 20, no. 2 (2001): 243–4; Quentin Stevens, Karen A. Franck, and Ruth Fazakerley, "Counter-Monuments: The Anti-Monumental and the Dialogic," *The Journal of Architecture* 17, no. 6 (2012): 956–8; Cynthia J. Becker, "Confederate Soldiers, Voodoo Queens, and Black Indians: Monuments and Counter-Monuments in New Orleans," *de arte* (2019): 1–24.

73 Mechtild Widrich, "After the Counter-Monument. Commemoration in the Expanded Field," in *The Routledge Companion to Critical Approaches to Contemporary Architecture*, ed. Swati Chattopadhyay and Jeremy White (New York: Routledge, 2019), 59.

74 Abigail Gillman, "Cultural Awakening and Historical Forgetting: The Architecture of Memory in the Jewish Museum of Vienna and in Rachel Whitehead's 'Nameless Library,'" *New German Critique* 93, Special Issue: Austrian Writers Confront the Past (2004): 151; Karen E. Till, *The New Berlin: Memory, Politics, Place* (Minneapolis: University of Minnesota Press, 2005), 172–3.

75 James E. Young, "Memory and Counter-Memory," *Harvard Design Magazine* 9 (1999). Tellingly, when Young was on the selection committee for Germany's National Memorial for the Murdered Jews of Europe, he changed his position on whether a memorial should be built or not. See James E. Young, "Berlin's Holocaust Memorial: A Report to the Bundestag Committee on Media and Culture 3 March 1999," *German Politics & Society* 17, no. 3 (52) (1999): 54–70.

76 Rettl, *PartisanInnendenkmäler*, 54.

77 Sanja Horvatinčić, "From Storytelling to Re-Enactment: Strategies of Monument-Making in Socialist Yugoslavia," in *Shaping Revolutionary*

Memory – The Production of Monuments in Socialist Yugoslavia, ed. Sanja Horvatinčić and Beti Žerovc (Ljubljana, Slovenia, and Berlin: Igor Zabel Association for Culture and Theory and Archive Books, 2023), 129.

78 Kirn, *The Partisan Counter-Archive*, 191–8. By the 1970s, Yugoslav memorial culture was undergoing a dramatic shift in its direction and began to emphasize more abstract, free-formed aesthetics, which led to the proliferation of socialist monumental modernism in the form of the Monuments to the Revolution, a style of monument completely absent in Carinthia. See also Vladana Putnik, "Second World War Monuments in Yugoslavia as Witness of the Past and the Future," Journal of Tourism and Cultural Change 14, no. 3 (2016): 206–21.

79 Lisa Rettl, "Kampf um die Erinnerung – Partisanendenkmäler und antifaschistisches Gedächtnis in Kärnten" (lecture at the Alfred Klahr Gesellschaft, 29 October 2005).

80 Interview with Andrej Mohar, 20 January 2020.

81 Mohar, Interview.

82 See, for example, Sergiusz Michalski, *Public Monuments: Art in Political Bondage 1870–1997* (London: Reaktion Books, 1998), 125–31.

83 Peter Pirker, "British Subversive Politics towards Austria and Partisan Resistance in the Austrian-Slovene Borderland, 1938–45," *Journal of Contemporary History*, 52, no. 2 (1 April 2018): 321. For religion within the wider Yugoslav partisan movement, see Kirn, *The Partisan Counter-Archive*, 108–11.

84 Karge, "Local Practices," 97.

85 Karge, "Local Practices," 97–8.

86 Borut Klabjan, "'Our Victims Define Our Borders': Commemorating Yugoslav Partisans in the Italo-Yugoslav Borderland," *East European Politics and Societies* 31, no. 2 (1 May 2017): 301.

87 Ivan Mirnik, "Marijan Matijević. A Century Tribute," *The Medal*, no. 51 (2007): 23–31.

88 Horvatinčić, "From Storytelling to Re-Enactment," 129.

89 Horvatinčić, "From Storytelling to Re-Enactment," 130.

90 Katja Hrobat Virloget and Neža Čebron Lipovec, "Heroes we Love? Monuments to the National Liberation Movement in Istria between Memories, Care, and Collective Silence," *Studia ethnologica Croatica* 29, no. 1 (2017): 51; Božo Otorepec, "Triglav: ein Symbolberg," *Histoire des Alpes = Storia delle Alpi = Geschichte der Alpen* 2 (1997): 140.

91 Rettl, "'… Dass wir für immer aufgehört haben," 5–6.

92 Jasmina Čubrilo, "Two Monuments by Stretan Stojanović. Continuity and Discontinuity," *Znanstvena revija za umetnostno zgodovino* 18, no. 2 (2013): 70.

93 Rettl, *PartisanInnen*, 124.

94   Rettl, *PartisanInnen*, 54.

95   Linda Hershkovitz, "Tiananmen Square and the Politics of Place," *Political Geography* 12, no. 5 (1993): 397.

96   Schein, "Normative Dimensions," 217–8.

97   See, for example, Jose Segal, *Art and Politics: Between Purity and Propaganda* (Amsterdam: Amsterdam University Press, 2016), 111–7.

98   Rettl, *PartisanInnen*, 152–75.

99   Rettl, *PartisanInnen*, 230.

100   Marilyn B. Young, *The Vietnam Wars, 1943–1990* (New York: Harper Perennial, 1991), 314.

101   James E. Young, "Berlin's Holocaust Memorial: A Report to the Bundestag Committee on Media and Culture 3 March 1999," *German Politics & Society* 17, no. 3 (1999): 57.

102   For more on these traditional characteristics, see Mary Rachel Gould and Rachel E. Silverman, "Stumbling Upon History: Collective Memory and the Urban Landscape," *GeoJournal* 78, no. 5 (2013): 792–3; Young, "Memory and Counter-Memory."

103   Translation my own.

104   Noam Lupu, "Memory Vanished, Absent, and Confined: The Countermemorial Project in 1980s and 1990s Germany," *History and Memory* 15, no. 2 (2003): 130–1; Jay Winter, "Remembrance and Redemption" *Harvard Design Magazine*, https://www .harvarddesignmagazine.org/articles/remembrance-and-redemption/.

105   Lewis Mumford, *The Culture of Cities* (New York: Harcourt, Brace and Co., 1938), 438.

106   James E. Young, "The Memorial's Arc: Between Berlin's *Denkmal* and New York City's 9/11 Memorial," *Memory Studies* 9, no. 3 (2016): 329–30.

107   Michael P. Levine, "Mediated Memories," *Angelaki* 11, no. 2 (1 August 2006): 117.

108   Michael Ignatieff, "Soviet War Memorials," *History Workshop*, no. 17 (1984): 162.

109   Paul Stangl, "The Soviet War Memorial in Treptow, Berlin," *Geographical Review* 93, no. 2 (2003): 213.

110   Quoted in James E. Young, "The Biography of a Memorial Icon: Nathan Rapoport's Warsaw Ghetto Monument," *Representations*, no. 26 (1989): 82.

111   Françoise Vergès, "A Museum without Objects," in *The Postcolonial Museum. The Arts of Memory and the Pressure of History*, ed. Ian Chambers et al. (London: Routledge, 2017), 25.

112   R. W. Stump, "Toponymic Commemoration of National Figures: The Cases of Kennedy and King," *Names* 36 (1988): 215.

113   Wüstenberg, *Civil Society*, 11.

114   Landsberg, *Prosthetic Memory*, 109.

115 Andrea A. Burns, *From Storefront to Monument: Tracing the Public History of the Black Museum Movement* (Amherst: University of Massachusetts Press, 2013), 159.

116 Till, *The New Berlin*, 18.

117 Robin Boast, "Neocolonial Collaboration: Museum as Contact Zone Revisited," *Museum Anthropology* 34, no. 1 (2011): 67.

118 Michael Foucalt, *Language, Counter-Memory, Practice. Selected Essays and Interviews*, ed. Donald F. Bouchard, trans. Donald F. Bouchard and Sherry Simon (Ithaca, NY: Cornell University Press, 1977), 139–64.

119 Schein, "A Methodological Framework," 398.

120 Kirn, *The Partisan Counter-Archive*, 57.

Chapter 3: The Struggle of Everyday Memory in Southern Carinthia

1 Richard H. Schein, "A Methodological Framework for Interpreting Ordinary Landscapes: Lexington, Kentucky's Courthouse Square," *Geographical Review* 99, no. 3 (2009): 398.

2 Elizabeth Jelin, *State Repression and the Labors of Memory* (Minneapolis: University of Minnesota Press, 2003), 33–4.

3 Wulf Kansteiner, "Finding Meaning in Memory: A Methodological Critique of Collective Memory Studies," *History and Theory* 41, no. 2 (2002): 179–97; Sabina Mihelj, "Between Official and Vernacular Memory," in *Research Methods for Memory Studies*, ed. Emily Keightley and Michael Pickering (Edinburgh: Edinburgh University Press, 2013), 60–75.

4 Gabriel Moshenska, "Memory: Towards the Reclamation of a Vital Concept," in *Heritage Keywords*, ed. Kathryn Lafrenz Samuels and Trinidad Rico (Boulder: University Press of Colorado, 2015), 203.

5 Ariella Azoulay, *The Civil Contract of Photography*, trans. Rela Mazali and Ruvik Danieli (New York: Zone Books, 2008), 14.

6 Jelin, *State Repression*, 139n9.

7 Peter Gstettner, "Die Legende von der Selbstbefreiung Kärntens. Alte Töne und neue Varianten am Rande des 'Gedenkjahres 2005,'" in *Jahrbuch 2006. Schwerpunkt Erinnerungskultur*, ed. Dokumentationsarchiv des Österreichischen Widerstandes (Vienna: Lit Verlag, 2006), 80–105.

8 Alexander Bogner and Wolfgang Menz, "The Theory-Generating Expert Interview: Epistemological Interest, Forms of Knowledge, Interaction," in *Interviewing Experts*, ed. Alexander Bogner, Beate Littig, and Wolfgang Menz (Basingstoke, UK: Palgrave Macmillan, 2009), 47.

9 Päivi Eriksson and Anne Kovalainen, *Qualitative Methods in Business Research* (Los Angeles: Sage, 2013), 82.

10 Bruce Berg, *Qualitative Research: Methods for the Social Sciences* (Boston: Allyn and Bacon, 2001), 71.

11 Alexander Bogner and Wolfgang Menz, "The Theory-Generating Expert Interview: Epistemological Interest, Forms of Knowledge, Interaction," in *Interviewing Experts*, ed. Alexander Bogner, Beate Littig, and Wolfgang Menz (Basingstoke, UK: Palgrave Macmillan, 2009), 47.

12 Stefanie Dreiack and Marlen Niederberger, "Qualitative Experteninterviews in Internationalen Organisationen," *Politische Vierteljahresschrift* 59, no. 2 (2018): 298–9.

13 Anja Broda et al., "Perspectives of Policy and Political Decision Makers on Access to Formal Dementia Care: Expert Interviews in Eight European Countries," *BMC Health Services Research* 17, no. 1 (2017): 4.

14 Thomas Priestly, "Maintenance of Slovene in Carinthia(Austria): Grounds for Guarded Optimism?," *Canadian Slavonic Papers / Revue Canadienne des Slavistes* 45, no. 1/2 (2003): 96.

15 Mariette Bengtsson, "How to Plan and Perform a Qualitative Study Using Content Analysis," *NursingPlus*, no. 2 (2016): 11.

16 Eriksson and Kovalainen, *Qualitative Methods*, 164.

17 U. H. Graneheim and B. Lundman, "Qualitative Content Analysis in Nursing Research: Concepts, Procedures, and Measures to Achieve Trustworthiness," *Nurse Education Today* 24, no. 2 (2004): 106.

18 Johnny Saldaña, *Fundamentals of Qualitative Research* (Oxford: Oxford University Press, 2011), 95.

19 Berg, *Qualitative Research*, 245–6.

20 Bengtsson, "Qualitative Study," 12.

21 Michael Rothberg and Neil, "Memory Studies in a Moment of Danger: Fascism, Postfascism, and the Contemporary Political Imaginary," *Memory Studies* 11, no. 3 (2018): 355–67.

22 Michel de Certeau, *The Practice of Everyday Life* (Berkeley: University of California Press, 1984), 108.

23 ORF, "Land fördert Schulbesuche in Mauthausen," *ORF Kärnten*, 21 February 2020.

24 Karen E. Till, *The New Berlin: Memory, Politics, Place* (Minneapolis: University of Minnesota Press, 2005), 22.

25 Nadja Danglmaier and Samo Wakounig, "Zur Methodik und Didaktik in Unterricht und bei Projekten," in *Erinnerungsgemeinschaften in Kärnten/ Koroška. Eine Empirische Studie über gegenwärtige Auseinandersetzungen mit dem Nationalsozialismus in Schule und Gesellschaft*, ed. Nadja Danglmaier et al. (Klagenfurt/Celovec, Austria: Hermagoras/Mohorjeva, 2017), 102–4.

26 Marschall, *Landscape of Memory*, 2.

27 Marschall, *Landscape of Memory*, 2.

28 For the links between group identity and collective memory, see Tamm, "In Search of Lost Time," 651–74.

29 Tzvetan Todorov, "The Uses and Abuses of Memory," *Common Knowledge* 5, no.1 (1996): 14.

30 Nathan Bracher, "History, Memory, and Humanism in the Recent Writings of Tzvetan Todorov," *South Central Review* 15, no. 3/4 (1998): 43.

31 Amann, "Kampfplatz Erinnerung," 82.

32 Gstettner, "'… Wo alle Macht vom Volk ausgeht,'" 85.

33 For this memorial culture based on commemorating the Wehrmacht, see Heidemarie Uhl, "Of Heroes and Victims: World War II in Austrian Memory," *Austrian History Yearbook* 42 (April 2011): 189.

34 Iain Hay, Andrew Hughes, and Mark Tutton, "Monuments, Memory and Marginalisation in Adelaide's Prince Henry Gardens," *Geografiska Annaler. Series B, Human Geography* 86, no. 3 (2004): 204.

35 Eric Langenbacher, "A Plea for an 'Intergovernmental' European Memory," in *Dynamics of Memory and Identity in Contemporary Europe*, ed. Erich Langenbacher, Bill Niven, and Ruth Wittlinger (New York: Berghahn Books, 2012), 211.

36 Langenbacher, "A Plea, 211.

37 Entner, "Komm, miß dich mit uns," 31.

38 Emil Fackenheim, *To Mend the World: Foundations of Post-Holocaust Jewish Thought* (New York: Shocken Books, 1982); Yehuda Bauer, *Rethinking the Holocaust* (New Haven, CT: Yale University Press, 2001).

39 For more on approaches to "resistance," see Douglas Carlton McKnight, "Writing through Crisis: Two Diaries from the Second World War in Carinthia," *Journal of Austrian Studies* 53, no. 1 (Spring 2020): 1–19.

40 Entner, *Kaj človek vse doživi!*, 34. For my reading of his diary, see McKnight, "Writing through Crisis."

41 Entner, *Kaj človek vse doživi!*, 10.

42 E.S., "Vorwort," in *Das Tagebuch des Thomas Olip. Wie ein im Käfig eingesperrter Vogel*, ed. Wilhelm Baum (Vienna: Kitab, 2010), 15.

43 For memory politics, see Tamm, "In Search of Lost Time," 651–2. For contestation of memory, Eric Langenbacher, "Changing Memory Regimes in Contemporary Germany?," *German Politics & Society* 21, no. 2 (67) (2003): 50.

44 Langenbacher, "Memory Regimes," 38.

45 Langenbacher, "Memory Regimes," 50.

46 Knight, "Denazification," 579.

47 Brigitta Busch, "Shifting Political and Cultural Borders: Language and Identity in the Border Region of Austria and Slovenia," in *Culture and Cooperation in Europe's Borderlands*, ed. James Anderson, Liam O'Dowd, and Thomas M. Wilson (Amsterdam: Rodopi, 2003), 125–44.

48 Nadja Danglmaier and Samo Wakounig, "Rahmenbedingungen für LehrerInnen in Hinblick auf Unterricht und Projekte zum Thema

Nationalsozialismus," in *Erinnerungsgemeinschaften in Kärnten/Koroška. Eine Empirische Studie über gegenwärtige Auseinandersetzungen mit dem Nationalsozialismus in Schule und Gesellschaft*, ed. Nadja Danglmaier et al. (Klagenfurt/Celovec, Austria: Hermagoras/Mohorjeva, 2017), 78.

49 Nadja Danglmaier et al., "Fazit und Ausblick," in *Erinnerungsgemeinschaften in Kärnten/Koroška. Eine Empirische Studie über gegenwärtige Auseinandersetzungen mit dem Nationalsozialismus in Schule und Gesellschaft*, ed. Nadja Danglmaier et al. (Klagenfurt/Celovec, Austria: Hermagoras/Mohorjeva, 2017), 241–4.

50 Catherine Switzer and Sara McDowell, "Redrawing Cognitive Maps of Conflict: Lost Spaces and Forgetting in the Centre of Belfast," *Memory Studies* 2, no. 3 (2009): 349.

51 Bond, Craps, and Vermeulen, "Introduction," 6.

52 Aleida Assmann, "From Collective Violence to a Common Future: Four Models for Dealing with a Traumatic Past," in *Justice and Memory: Confronting Traumatic Pasts: An International Comparison*, ed. Ruth Wodak (Vienna: Passagen Verlag, 2009), 40.

53 Assmann, "From Collective Violence," 43.

54 Omer Bertov and Eric D. Weitz, "Introduction: Coexistence and Violence in the German, Habsburg, Russian, and Ottoman Borderlands," in *Shatterzone of Empire: Coexistence and Violence in the German, Habsburg, Russian, and Ottoman Borderlands*, ed. Omer Bertov and Eric D. Weitz (Bloomington: University of Indiana Press, 2013), 13.

55 Lewis, "Axioms of the Landscape," 6–9.

Chapter 4: Layers of Memory in Maja Haderlap's *Angel of Oblivion*

1 Ann Rigney, "Portable Monuments: Literature, Cultural Memory, and the Case of Jeanie Deans," *Poetics Today* 25, no. 2 (2004): 368–9.

2 Eigler, "Writing in the New Germany," 25–6.

3 Astrid Erll and Ansgar Nünning, "Literaturkonzepte von Gedächtnis: Ein einführender Überblick," in *Gedächtniskonzepte der Literaturwissenschaft: Theoretische Grundlegung und Anwendungsperspektiven*, ed. Astrid Erll and Ansgar Nünning (Berlin: Walter de Gruyter, 2010), 1–9.

4 Maja Haderlap, *Angel of Oblivion*, trans. Tess Lewis (New York: Archipelago Books, 2016).

5 Jožica Čeh Steger, "Die zerstörte Dorfidylle an der österreichischslowenischen Grenze: Maja Haderlaps Engel des Vergessens," in *Imaginäre Dörfer: zur Wiederkehr des Dörflichen in Literatur, Film und Lebenswelt*, ed. Nell Werner and March Weiland (Bielefeld, Germany: Transcript, 2014), 339–56.

6 Marjan Horvat, "Maja Haderlap im Gespräch mit Marjan Horvat," in *Literatur/a. Jahrbuch. 2010/2011*, ed. Fabjan Hafner, Klaus Amann, and Doris Moser (Klagenfurt/Celovec, Austria: Robert Musil-Institut der Universität Klagenfurt and Kärntner Literaturarchiv, 2012), 134.

7 While not a close reading of the novel, for an exception, see Brigitte Entner, "Eine Familie, zwei Sprachen, drei Erzähltypen," in *Storylines and Blackboxes. Autobiographie und Zeugenschaft in der Nachgeschichte von Nationalsozialismus und Zweitem Weltkrieg.*, ed. Johanna Gehmacher and Klara Löffler (Vienna: New Academic Press, 2017), 149–74.

8 Avguštin Malle, "Erinnerung an Vertreibung und Widerstand," in *Pregon koroških slovencev 1942–2002 = Die Vertreibung der Kärntner Slowenen 1942–2002*, ed. Malle (Klagenfurt/Celovec, Austria: Drava, 2002), 213–14.

9 Avguštin Malle, "Der Widerstand der Kärntner Slowenen," in *Widerstand gegen Faschismus und Nationalsozialismus im Alpen-Adria-Raum. Odpor proti fašizmu in nacizmu v alpsko-jadranskem prostoru*, ed. Entner et al. (Klagenfurt/Celovec, Austria: Drava, 2011), 75–82.

10 Andreas Leben and Erwin Köstler, "Von den primären Quellen zum publizistischen Diskurs. Über den bewaffneten Widerstand der Partisanen in Kärnten." *Zeitgeschichte* 34, no. 4 (2007): 232.

11 Franc Peter, ed., *Koroška v borbi. Spomini na osvobodilno borbo v Slovenski Koroški* (Klagenfurt/Celovec, Austria: Zveza bivših partizanov Slovenske Koroške, 1951).

12 Amann, "Kampfplatz Erinnerung," 94–5; Franc Zadravec, "Die slowenische Gegenwartsliteratur," in *Die slowenische Literatur in Kärnten. Ein Lexikon*, ed. Verband slowenischer Schriftsteller/innen, Übersetzer/innen und Publizist/inn/en in Österreich (Klagenfurt/Celovec, Austria: Drava, 1991), 140.

13 Karel Prušnik-Gašper, *Gamsi na plazu. Zapiski in spomini* (Ljubljana: Glavni odbor zveze borcev NOV Slovenije, založba Borec, 1958). Translation of title into English my own.

14 Robert Buchacher, "Tod dem Faschismus," in *Materialien zu Karel Prušnik-Gašper. Gämsen auf der Lawine*, ed. Lojze Wieser (Klagenfurt/Celovec: Wieser, 2015), 20.

15 Brigitte Entner, "Verortung des slowenischen Widerstandes in Kärnten," in *Widerstand gegen Faschismus und Nationalsozialismus im Alpen-Adria-Raum. Odpor proti fašizmu in nacizmu v alpsko-jadranskem prostoru*, ed. Brigitte Entner, Valentin Sima, and Avguštin Malle (Klagenfurt/Celovec, Austria: Drava, 2011), 54–56.

16 Helene Kuchar, *Jelka: Aus dem Leben einer Kärntner Partisanin*, ed. Thomas Busch and Brigitte Windhab (Basel, Switzerland: Verlag API, 1984). Translation of book title into English my own.

17 Notable examples include Karin Berger et al., eds., *Der Himmel ist blau. Kann sein. Frauen im Widerstand. Österreich 1983–1945* (Vienna: Promedia, 1985); Karin Berger, et al., eds., *Ich geb Dir einen Mantel, daß Du ihn noch in Freiheit tragen kannst. Widerstehen im KZ. Österreichische Frauen erzählen* (Vienna: Promedia, 1987).

18 Dokumentationsarchiv des österreichischen Widerstandes, Klub Prežihov Voranc, Institut za proučevanje prostora Alpe-Jadran eds., *Spurensuche. Erzählte Geschichte der Kärntner Slowenen* (Vienna: Österreichischer Bundesverlag, 1990). Translation of book title my own.

19 Leben and Köstler, "Von den primären Quellen," 230.

20 Andrej Kokot, *Ko zori spomin. Otroška doživetja v pregnanstvu* (Klagenfurt/Celovec: Drava, 1996); in German as *Das Kind, das ich war. Erinnerungen an die Vertreibung der Slowenen aus Kärnten*, trans. Andre Kokot (Klagenfurt/Celovec, Austria: Drava, 1999); Lipej Kolenik, *Mali ljudje na veliki poti. Spomini na predvojni, vojni in povojni čas na Koroškem.* (Klagenfurt/Celovec, Austria: Drava, 1997); in German as *Für das Leben, gegen den Tod. Mein Weg in den Widerstand*, trans. Erwin Köstler (Klagenfurt/Celovec, Austria: Drava, 2001).

21 For these, see Judith Goetz, *Bücher gegen das Vergessen – Kärntnerslowenische Literatur über Widerstand und Verfolgung* (Klagenfurt/Celovec, Vienna: Kitab Verlag, 2012).

22 Erwin Köstler, "Institutionen, Akteure, Modelle: das Kärntner zweisprachige literarische Feld als Anziehungspunkt für deutschsprachige Autor_innen," in *Literarische Mehrsprachigkeit im österreichischen und slowenischen Kontext*, ed. Andreas Leben and Alenka Koron (Tübingen, Germany: Narr Francke Attempo, 2019), 84.

23 Andrej Leben, "Koroške (slovenske) vojne pripovedi med reprezentacijo in diskurzom," *Primerjalna književnost* 38, no. 3 (2015): 123.

24 Klaus Amann and Johann Strutz, "Florjan Lipuš. Kleines Porträt mit Hintergrund," in *Lipuš Lesen. Texte und Materialien zu Florjan Lipuš*, ed. Klaus Amann and Johann Strutz (Klagenfurt/Celovec, Austria: Wieser, 2000), 9.

25 Leben, "Koroške (slovenske) vojne," 129.

26 Leben, "Koroške (slovenske) vojne," 125.

27 Alexsander Hemon, "The Bob Dylan of Genocide Apologists," *The New York Times*, 15 October 2019.

28 Florjan Lipuš, *Der Zögling Tjaž*, trans. Peter Handke and Helga Mračnikar (Salzburg, Austria: Residenz, 1981).

29 Fabjan Hafner, "Der „exemplarische Epiker" der Kärntner SlowenInnen: Florjan Lipuš," in *Und (k)ein Wort Deutsch … Literaturen der Minderheiten und MigrantInnen in Österreich*, ed. Nicola Mitterer and Werner Wintersteiner (Innsbruck: Studienverlag, 2009), 140.

30 Barbara Maier, Franz V. Spechtler, and Peter Handke, eds., *Lojze Wieser. Die Zunge reicht weiter als die Hand. Anmerkungen eines Grenzverlegers* (Vienna: Czernin, 2004), 86–87.

31 Klaus Amann, "Peter Handkes Poetik der Begriffsstutzigkeit," in Amann, Hafner, and Wager, *Peter Handke*, 247.

32 Felix Oliver Kohl, "Nemški prevodi Lipuševih del ob in po Tjažu v luči konsekracije," *Primerjalna književnost* 41, no. 3 (2018): 26–27.

33 Fabjan Hafner, "Slowenien, die Slowenen, das Slowenische im Werk Peter Handkes," *Manuskripte* 46, no. 172 (June 2006): 111–117; Fabjan Hafner, "Es ist die Muttersprache, aber die Mutter ist lange tot … Slowenisches im Werk von Peter Handke," in *Peter Handke – Poesie der Ränder*, ed. Klaus Amann, Fabjan Hafner, and Karl Wagner (Vienna: Böhlau, 2006), 47–63.

34 Peter Handke, *Immer noch Sturm* (Berlin: Suhrkamp, 2010).

35 Peter Handke, "Wut und Geheimnis. Rede zur Verleihung des Ehrendoktorats der Universität Klagenfurt am 8. November 2002," in Amann, Hafner, and Wagner, eds., *Peter Handke*, 253–8.

36 See Leben, "Koroške (slovenske) vojne," 132.

37 Eigler, "Writing in the New Germany," 27.

38 Friederike Eigler, *Gedächtnis und Geschichte in Generationenromanen seit der Wende* (Berlin: Erich Schmidt, 2005), 9–12, 29–38.

39 Ulrike Vedder, "Erblasten und Totengespräche. Zum Nachleben der Toten in Texten von Marlene Streeruwitz, Arno Geiger und Sibylle Lewitscharoff," in *Literatur im Krebsgang: Totenbeschwörung und memoria in der deutschsprachigen Literatur nach 1989*, ed. Arne de Winde and Anke Gilleir (Amsterdam: Rodopi, 2008), 229; Aleida Assmann, "Limits of Understanding: Generational Identities in Recent German Memory Literature," in *Victims and Perpetrators: 1933–1945. (Re)Presenting the Past in Post-Unification Culture*, ed. Laurel Cohen-Pfister and Dagmar Wienroeder-Skinner (Berlin: De Gruyter, 2006), 32.

40 The literature here is vast. See, for example, Matteo Galli and Simone Costagli, eds., *Deutsche Familienromane: Literarische Genealogien und internationaler Kontext* (Munich: Wilhelm Fink, 2010); Bernhard Jahn, "Familienkonstruktionen 2005. Zum Problem des Zusammenhangs der Generationen im aktuellen Familienroman," *Zeitschrift für Germanistik* 16, no. 3 (2006): 581–96; Goran Lovrić and Marijana Jeleč, eds., *Familie und Identität in der Gegenwartsliteratur* (Frankfurt am Main, Germany: Peter Lang, 2016).

41 For an example of this, see Anne Fuchs, Mary Cosgrove, and Georg Grote, eds., *German Memory Contests: The Quest for Identity in Literature, Film, and Discourse since 1990* (Rochester, NY: Camden House, 2006).

42 Richard Kämmerlings, "Bachmann-Preis für Haderlap – eine Fehlentscheidung," *Die Welt*, 10 July 2011.

43 Dirk Knipphals, "Bedächtige Nachkriegsliteratur," *taz*, July 10, 2011.

44 For recent studies, see Yannick Müllender, "Generationenkonzepte in zeitgenössischen österreichisch-jüdischen Romanen," *Journal of Austrian Studies* 46, no. 2 (2013): 23–47; Christina Guenther, "The Poetics of Ritual in Diaspora: Anna Mitgutsch's 'Familienfest' and Vladimir Vertlib's 'Letzter Wunsch,'" *Journal of Austrian Studies* 45, no. 1 (2012): 93–118; Dagmar C. G. Lorenz, "Intersection Vienna: Crime and Transnationalism in Post-Shoah Austrian Fiction and Films," *Journal of Austrian Studies* 47, no. 4 (2014): 65–87.

45 Dominick LaCapra, *History and Memory after Auschwitz* (Ithaca, NY: Cornell University Press, 1998), 20–1.

46 Marianne Hirsch, *The Generation of Postmemory: Writing and Visual Culture after the Holocaust* (New York: Columbia University Press, 2012), 33–6.

47 Marianne Hirsch, "Family Pictures: Maus, Mourning, and Post-Memory," *Discourse* 15, no. 2 (1992): 8.

48 Jelena Spreicer, "Geschichte aus dem slowenischen Blickwinkel – Maja Haderlaps 'Engel des Vergessens,'" in *Narrative im (post)imperialen Kontext. Literarische Identitätsbildung als Potential im regionalen Spannungsfeld zwischen Hubsburg und hoher Pforte in Zentral- und Südosteuropa*, ed. Matthias Schmidt et al. (Tübingen, Germany: Narr Francke Attempto, 2015), 253; Bernard Banoun, "Schmalspur-Bahn der Erinnerung: Aspekte des kommunikativen Gedächtnisses in Werner Koflers 'Tanzcafe Treblinka' und Maja Haderlaps 'Engel des Vergessens,'" in *Literatur-Politik-Kritik. Beiträge zur Österreichischen Literatur des 20. Jahrhunderts*, ed. Harald Jele and Elmar Lenhart (Göttingen, Germany: Wallstein, 2014), 17–24.

49 Haderlap, *Angel*, 7.

50 Haderlap, *Angel*, 289.

51 Marijana Jeleč, "Formen der Vergangenheitsbewältigung in ausgewählten zeitgenössischen österreichischen Generationenromanen," in Lovrić and Jeleč, eds., *Familie*, 158.

52 Brigitte Prutti, "Ist es nicht ein finsterer Wald, in den wir gerieten?" Waldgänge und Waldgänger in Maja Haderlaps Roman 'Engel des Vergessens,'" *Studia Theodisca* 21, no. 85 (2014): 85–137.

53 Haderlap, *Angel*, 75.

54 Haderlap, *Angel*, 76.

55 Lucas M. Bietti, *Discursive Remembering: Individual and Collective Remembering as a Discursive, Cognitive and Historical Process* (Berlin: De Gruyter, 2014), 35–7.

56 Hirsch, *The Generation of Postmemory*, 206.

57 Lawrence Langer, *Holocaust Testimonies: The Ruins of Memory* (New Haven, CT: Yale University Press, 1991), 177.

58 Langer, *Holocaust Testimonies*, 186.

59 Langer, *Holocaust Testimonies*, 176.

60 Haderlap, *Angel*, 53–4.

61 Haderlap, *Angel*, 95–96.

62 Langer, *Holocaust Testimonies*, 176.

63 Haderlap, *Angel*, 83–84.

64 According to Mieke Feßmann, one of the Ingeborg Bachmann Prize jurors from 2011, "… diese Kinderperspektive führt dazu, dass man zum Beispiel so eine Formulierung verwenden muss wie 'der klingende Name Dachau'. Ich finde, das geht nicht. Auch wenn der Name Dachau für dieses Kind einen guten Klang hat, weil es sich nicht vorstellen kann, was dort passiert ist, kann man als Erzähler diese Zusammenfügung nicht nennen." See Hubert Winkels, ed., *Klagenfurter Texte. Die besten 2011. Die 25. Tage der deutschsprachigen Literatur in Klagenfurt* (Munich: Piper, 2011), 35.

65 Haderlap, *Angel*, 139–40.

66 Prutti, "Ist es nicht ein finsterer Wald," 94.

67 Haderlap, *Angel*, 152–4.

68 Haderlap's father, Valentin (Zdravko) Haderlap, participated in the DÖW's oral history project, *Spurensuche*, in which he described this experience. See Valentin Haderlap-Zdravko, "Die Buben werden nicht durchkommen," in Dokumentationsarchiv des österreichischen Widerstandes, Klub Prežihov Voranc, Institut za proučevanje prostora Alpe-Jadran, *Spurensuche*, 291–95. See also Entner, "Eine Familie, zwei Sprachen, drei Erzähltypen," 167–169.

69 Haderlap, *Angel*, 154.

70 Haderlap, *Angel*, 154.

71 Hirsch, *The Generation of Postmemory*, 205.

72 Haderlap, *Angel*, 45.

73 Eigler, "Writing in the New Germany," 25–6.

74 Haderlap, *Angel*, 245.

75 Haderlap, *Angel*, 236.

76 Haderlap, *Angel*, 177.

77 Haderlap, *Angel*, 178.

78 Haderlap, *Angel*, 183.

79 Haderlap, *Angel*, 168.

80 Maruša Pušnik, "Media Memorial Discourses and Memory Struggles in Slovenia: Transforming Memories of the Second World War and Yugoslavia," *Memory Studies* 12, no. 4 (2019): 435.

81 Haderlap, *Angel*, 221.

82 Pirker, "British Subversive Politics," 321.

83 Haderlap, *Angel*, 222.

84 Amann, "Kampfplatz Erinnern," 94.

85 Gal Kirn, "Transformation of Memorial Sites in the Post-Yugoslav Context," in *Retracing Images. Visual Culture after Yugoslavia*, ed. Daniel

Šuber and Slobodan Karamanic (Leiden, The Netherlands: Brill, 2012), 267–8.

86 Gal Kirn, *The Partisan Counter-Archive: Retracing the Ruptures of Art and Memory in the Yugoslav People's Liberation Struggle* (Berlin: De Gruyter, 2020), 227–35.

87 Borut Klabjan, "Memory, Revision, Resistance: Reviving the Monuments along the Slovenian-Italian Border," in *Borderlands of Memory*, ed. Borut Klabjan (Oxford: Peter Lang, 2019), 236.

88 Oto Luthar, "Forgetting Does (Not) Hurt. Historical Revisionism in Post-Socialist Slovenia," *Nationalities Papers* 41, no. 6 (2013): 882–92.

89 Pušnik, "Media Memorial Discourses," 442–3.

90 Paul Jandl, "Katharsis in Kärnten," *Die Welt*, 23 December 2011; Ulrich Greiner, "Gerechtigkeit für die Slowenen," *Die Zeit*, 21 July 2011. Haderlap herself touched on this in an interview as well. See Horvat, "Maja Haderlap im Gespräch," 136.

91 Die Presse, "Maja Haderlap erhielt Rauriser Literaturpreis," *Die Presse*, 22 March 2012.

92 Maja Haderlap, *Im langen Atem der Geschichte. Rede beim Staatsakt anlässlich der 100. Wiederkehr des Jahrestages der Gründung der Republik Österreich* (Göttingen, Germany: Wallstein, 2018).

93 Haderlap, *Angel*, 240–5.

94 Leben, "Koroške (slovenske) vojne," 131–2.

95 Rigney, "Portable Monuments," 368.

96 Walter Benjamin, "On the Concept of History," trans. Dennis Redmond, *Gesammelten Schriften* I:2 (Frankfurt am Main: Suhrkamp Verlag, 1974), https://www.marxists.org/reference/archive/benjamin/1940/history.htm.

97 Haderlap, *Angel*, 287.

98 Haderlap, *Angel*, 288.

Conclusion: The Future of Memory in Southern Carinthia

1 Dora Osborne, *What Remains: The Post-Holocaust Archive in German Memory Culture* (Rochester, NY: Camden House, 2020), 9.

2 Jan Assmann, "Communicative and Cultural Memory," in *Cultural Memory Studies: An International and Interdisciplinary Handbook*, ed. Astrid Erll and Ansgar Nünning (Berlin: Walter de Gruyter, 2008), 109–19.

3 Peter Schneider, "Saving Konrad Latte," *New York Times Magazine*, 13 February 2000, 54.

4 Amann, "Kampfplatz Erinnerung: der Widerstand der Kärtner Slowenen im Zweiten Weltkrieg als politischer und als literarischer Topos," in *Erfundene Erinnerung. Literatur als Gedächtnisildung und Gedächtnisreflexion*, ed. Thomas Eder (Linz, Austria: StifterHaus and BeiträgerInnen, 2013), 82.

5 See, for example, Aleida Assmann, "From Collective Violence to a Common Future: Four Models for Dealing with a Traumatic Past," in *Justice and Memory: Confronting Traumatic Pasts: An International Comparison*, ed. Ruth Wodak (Vienna: Passagen Verlag, 2009), 40.

6 Michael Rothberg, *Multidirectional Memory. Remembering the Holocaust in the Age of Decolonization* (Palo Alto, CA: Stanford University Press, 2009), 3.

7 See, most prominently, Claus Leggewie, *Der Kampf um die europäische Erinnerung: Ein Schlachtfeld wird besichtigt* (Munich: CH Beck, 2011).

8 Lucy Bond, Stef Craps, and Pieter Vermeulen, "Introduction: Memory on the Move," in *Memory Unbound*, ed. Lucy Bond, Stef Craps, and Pieter Vermeulen (New York: Berghahn Books, 2017), 6.

9 ORF Kärnten, "Heimatdienst gedenkt Hans Steinacher," 30 September 2020.

10 ORF, "Van der Bellen entschuldigt sich," *ORF*, 10 October 2020. Translation my own.

11 *Verschwinden/Izginjanje*, directed by Andrina Mračnikar (Vienna: Soleil Film GmbH 2022).

12 ORF Volksgruppen, "Erinnern gegen das Vergessen," 19 April 2022.

13 ORF Kärnten, "Ehrenzeichen für Opfer des Peršmanhofs," 27 February 2023.

14 Land Kärnten, "Grenzenlose Erinnerungskultur gegen das Vergessen," 15 May 2023.

15 Nathan Bracher, "History, Memory, and Humanism in the Recent Writings of Tzvetan Todorov," *South Central Review* 15, no. 3/4 (1998): 43, https://doi.org/10.2307/3189832.

16 Friederike Eigler, "Writing in the New Germany: Cultural Memory and Family Narratives," *German Politics & Society* 23, no. 3 (2005): 25.

17 Ann Rigney, "Fiction as a Mediator in National Remembrance," in *Narrating the Nation: The Representation of National Narratives in Different Genres*, eds. Stefan Berger, Linas Eriksonas, and Andrew Mycock (Oxford: Berghahn Books, 2009): 79–96

18 See, for example, Benjamin Breitegger, "Österreichisch-slowenische Grenzregion. Von geografischen Grenzen und denen im Kopf," 8 December 2019, accessed 26 February 2024, https://www.deutschlandfunkkultur.de/kaernten-und-seine-slowenische-minderheit-das-misstrauen-100.html.

19 Haderlap, *Angel*, 221.

Bibliography

AK gegen den Kärntner Konsens. "Der Ulrichsberg Fakten und Zahlen." In *Friede, Freude, deutscher Eintopf. Rechte Mythen, NS Verharmlosung und antifaschistischer Protest*, edited by AK gegen den Kärntner Konsens, 77–120. Vienna: Mandelbaum.

Alderman, Derek H. "Creating a New Geography of Memory in the South: (Re)Naming of Streets in Honor of Martin Luther King, Jr." *Southeastern Geographer* 36, no. 1 (1996): 51–69. https://doi.org/10.1353/sgo.1996.0014.

Alderman, Derek H., and Joshua F.J. Inwood. "Chapter 18: Landscapes of Memory and Socially Just Futures." In *The Wiley-Blackwell Companion to Cultural Geography*, edited by Nuala C. Johnson, Richard H. Schein, and Jamie Winders. ProQuest EbookCentral. Hoboken, NJ: John Wiley & Sons, 2013.

Aline, Sierp. "Drawing Lessons from the Past: Mapping Change in Central and South-Eastern Europe." *East European Politics and Societies and Cultures* 30, no. 1 (2015): 3–9. https://doi.org/10.1177/0888325415605890.

Amann, Klaus. "Peter Handkes Poetik der Begriffsstutzigkeit." In *Peter Handke*, edited by Amann, Hafner, and Wagner, 239–51. Vienna: Böhlau, 2006.

Amann, Klaus. "Kampfplatz Erinnerung: der Widerstand der Kärntner Slowenen im Zweiten Weltkrieg als politischer und als literarischer Topos." In *Erfundene Erinnerung. Literatur als Gedächtnisbildung und Gedächtnisreflexion*, edited by Thomas Eder, 81–107. Linz: StifterHaus and BeiträgerInnen, 2013.

Amann, Klaus, Fabjan Hafner, and Karl Wagner, eds. *Peter Handke – Poesie der Ränder*. Vienna: Böhlau, 2006.

Amann, Klaus, and Johann Strutz. "Florjan Lipuš. Kleines Porträt mit Hintergrund." In *Lipuš Lesen. Texte und Materialien zu Florjan Lipuš*, edited by Klaus Amann and Johann Strutz, 9–28. Klagenfurt/Celovec: Wieser Verlag, 2000.

Andersen, Tea Sindbæk, and Barbara Törnquist-Plewa, eds. *Divided Memory. Emotions and Memory Politics in Central, Eastern and South-Eastern Europe.* Berlin: De Gruyter, 2016.

Apel, Dora. *War Culture and the Contest of Images.* New Brunswick: Rutgers University Press, 2012.

Arbeitskreis gegen den Kärntner Konsens. "Der Ulrichsberg Fakten und Zahlen." In *Friede, Freude, deutscher Eintopf. Rechte Mythen, NS Verharmlosung und antifaschistischer Protest*, edited by Arbeitskreis gegen den kärntner Konsens, 77–120. Vienna: Mandelbaum, 2011.

Arens, Katherine. "Why Austrian Studies Isn't German Studies: Germanophone Culture(s) – A Once and Future Tale." *Modern Austrian Literature* 36, no. 1/2 (2003): 53–68.

Arnold-de Simine, Silke. *Mediating Memory in the Museum: Trauma, Empathy, Nostalgia.* New York: Palgrave MacMillan, 2013.

Assmann, Aleida. "Limits of Understanding: Generational Identities in Recent German Memory Literature." In *Victims and Perpetrators: 1933–1945: (Re)Presenting the Past in Post-Unification Culture*, edited by Laurel Cohen-Pfister and Dagmar Wienroeder-Skinner, 29–48. Berlin: De Gruyter, 2006.

Assmann, Aleida. "From Collective Violence to a Common Future: Four Models for Dealing With a Traumatic Past." In *Justice and Memory: Confronting Traumatic Pasts: An International Comparison*, edited by Ruth Wodak, 31–48. Vienna: Passagen Verlag, 2009.

Assmann, Aleida. "Transnational Memories." *European Review* 22, no. 4 (2014): 546–56.

Assmann, Aleida. "Transnational Memory and the Construction of History Through Mass Media." In *Memory Unbound. Tracing the Dynamics of Memory Studies*, edited by Lucy Bond, Stef Craps, and Pieter Vermeulen, 65–80. New York: Berghahn Books, 2017.

Assmann, Jan. "Communicative and Cultural Memory." In *Cultural Memory Studies: An International and Interdisciplinary Handbook*, edited by Astrid Erll and Ansgar Nünning, 109–19. Berlin: Walter de Gruyter, 2008.

Azoulay, Ariella. *The Civil Contract of Photography.* Translated by Rela Mazali and Ruvik Danieli. New York: Zone Books, 2008.

Bahovec, Tina. "Der Zweite Weltkrieg im Alpen-Adria-Raum." In *Alpen-Adria. Zur Geschichte einer Region*, edited by Andreas Moritsch, 453–69. Klagenfurt/Celovec: Hermagoras/Mohorjeva, 2011.

Bailer-Galanda, Brigitte, and Wolfgang Neugebauer. "Right-Wing Extremism: History, Organisations, Ideology." In *Incorrigibly Right: Right-Wing Extremists, "Revisionists" and Anti-Semites in Austrian Politics Today*, edited by Brigitte Bailer-Galanda and Wolfgang Neugebauer, 5–21. Vienna: Stiftung Dokumentationsarchiv des österreichischen Widerstandes and the Anti-Defamation League, 1996.

Bal, Mieke. "Guest Column: Exhibition Practices." *PMLA* 125, no. 1 (2010): 9–23. https://doi.org/10.1632/pmla.2010.125.1.9.

Ballinger, Pamela. *History in Exile: Memory and Identity at the Borders of the Balkans* Princeton: Princeton University Press, 2003.

Banoun, Bernard. "Schmalspur-Bahn der Erinnerung: Aspekte des kommunikativen Gedächtnisses in Werner Koflers 'Tanzcafe Treblinka' und Maja Haderlaps 'Engel des Vergessens'." In *Literatur-Politik-Kritik. Beiträge zur Österreichischen Literatur des 20. Jahrhunderts*, edited by Harald Jele and Elmar Lenhart, 17–24. Göttingen: Wallstein, 2014.

Barker, Thomas. *The Slovene Minority of Carinthia*. New York: Columbia University Press, 1984.

Barker, Thomas. "Partisan Warfare in the Bilingual Region of Carinthia." *Slovene Studies* 11, nos. 1–2 (1989): 193–210. https://doi.org/10.7152/ssj .v11i1.3782.

Barth-Scalmani, Gunda. "Memory-Landscapes of the First World War: The Southwestern Front in Present-Day Italy, Austria and Slovenia." In *From Empire to Republic*, edited by Günter Bischof, Fritz Plasser, and Peter Berger, 222–53. New Orleans: University of New Orleans Press, 2010.

Bartov, Omer. *Erased: Vanishing Traces of Jewish Galicia in Present-Day Ukraine*. Princeton: Princeton University Press, 2007.

Bartov, Omer. "Conclusion." In *Bringing the Dark to Light. The Reception of the Holocaust in Postcommunist Europe*, edited by John-Paul Himka and Joanna Beata Michlic, 663–94. Lincoln: University of Nebraska Press, 2013.

Bauer, Kurt. *Die dunklen Jahre. Politik und Alltag im nationalsozialistischen Österreich. 1938 bis 1945*. Frankfurt am Main: Fischer, 2017.

Bauer, Yehuda. *Rethinking the Holocaust*. New Haven: Yale University Press, 2001.

Baum, Wilhelm. *Peršmanhof 1945. Protokolle eines NS-Kriegsverbrechens*. Klagenfurt/Celovec: Kitab Verlag, 2013.

Becker, Cynthia J. "Confederate Soldiers, Voodoo Queens, and Black Indians: Monuments and Counter-Monuments in New Orleans." *de arte* 54 (2019): 1–24.

Bellentani, Federico, and Mario Panico. "The Meanings of Monuments and Memorials: Toward a Semiotic Approach." *Punctum. International Journal of Semiotics* 2, no. 1 (2016): 28–46. http://doi.org/10.18680/hss.2016.0004.

Bengtsson, Mariette. "How to Plan and Perform a Qualitative Study Using Content Analysis." *NursingPlus* 2 (2016): 8–14. https://doi.org/10.1016/j .npls.2016.01.001.

Beniston, Judith. "'Hitler's First Victim'? – Memory and Representation in Post-War Austria: Introduction." *Austrian Studies* 11 (2003): 1–13. https://doi .org/10.1353/aus.2003.0018.

Berchtold-Ogris, Martina, Brigitte Entner, and Helena Verdel. *Die Drau ist eine eigene Frau: ein Fluss und seine Kulturgeschichte. Drava je svoja frava: h kulturi in zgodovini Drave*. Edited by Slowenischer Kulturverband/Slovenska prosvetna zveza. Translated by Vida Obid. Klagenfurt/Celovec: Drava Verlag, 2001.

Berg, Bruce. *Qualitative Research: Methods for the Social Sciences*. Boston: Allyn and Bacon, 2001.

Berger, Karin, Elisabeth Holzinger, and Lotte Podgornik, eds. *Ich geb Dir einen Mantel, daß Du ihn noch in Freiheit tragen kannst. Widerstehen im KZ. Österreichische Frauen erzählen*. Vienna: Promedia, 1987.

Berger, Karin, Elisabeth Holzinger, Lotte Podgornik, and Lisbeth N. Trallori, eds. *Der Himmel ist blau. Kann sein. Frauen im Widerstand. Österreich 1983–1945*. Vienna: Promedia, 1985.

Berger, Stefan, and Caner Tekin. "Conclusion." In *History and Belonging: Representations of the Past in Contemporary European Politics*, edited by Stefan Berger and Caner Tekin, 193–200. New York: Berghahn Books, 2018a.

Berger, Stefan, and Caner Tekin, eds. *History and Belonging: Representations of the Past in Contemporary European Politics*. New York: Berghahn Books, 2018b.

Bertov, Omer, and Eric D. Weitz. "Introduction: Coexistence and Violence in the German, Habsburg, Russian, and Ottoman Borderlands." In *Shatterzone of Empire: Coexistence and Violence in the German, Habsburg, Russian, and Ottoman Borderlands*, edited by Omer Bertov and Eric D. Weitz, 1–20. Bloomington: University of Indiana Press, 2013.

Bietti, Lucas M. *Discursive Remembering: Individual and Collective Remembering as a Discursive, Cognitive and Historical Process*. Berlin: De Gruyter, 2014.

Biondich, Mark. "Representations of the Holocaust and Historical Debates in Croatia Since 1989." In *Bringing the Dark to Light. The Reception of the Holocaust in Postcommunist Europe*, edited by John-Paul Himka and Joanna Beata Michlic, 131–65. Lincoln: University of Nebraska Press, 2013.

Bischof, Günter. "Founding Myths and Compartmentalized Past: New Literature on the Construction, Hibernation, and Deconstruction of World War II Memory in Postwar Austria." In *Austrian Historical Memory and National Identity*, edited by Günter Bischof and Anton Pelinka, 302–41. New Brunswick: Transaction, 1997.

Bischof, Günter. "Victims? Perpetrators? 'Punching Bags' of European Historical Memory? The Austrians and Their World War II Legacies." *German Studies Review* 27, no. 1 (2004): 17–32. https://doi.org/10.2307/1433546.

Bischof, Günter, and Michael S. Maier. "Reinventing Tradition and the Politics of History: Schüssel's Restitution and Commemoration Policies." In *The*

Schüssel Era in Austria, edited by Günter Bischof and Fritz Plasser, 206–34. New Orleans: University of New Orleans Press, 2010.

Björkdahl, Annika, and Stefanie Kappler. "The Creation of Transnational Memory Spaces: Professionalization and Commercialization." *International Journal of Politics, Culture, and Society* 32, no. 4 (2019): 383–401. https://doi.org/10.1007/s10767-019-09334-7.

Black, Graham. *The Engaging Museum: Developing Museums for Visitor Involvement* London: Routledge, 2005.

Blohberger, Gudrun. "Ausstellungsimpressionen. Ein Museumsrundgang in Wort und Bild. Mit Fotos von Zdravko Haderlap." In *Peršman*, edited by Lisa Rettl, Gudrun Blohberger, Zveza koroških partizanov/Verband der Kärntner Partisanen, Društvo/Verein Peršman, 79–93. Göttingen; Wallstein, 2014.

Boast, Robin. "Neocolonial Collaboration: Museum as Contact Zone Revisited." *Museum Anthropology* 34, no. 1 (2011): 56–70. https://doi.org/10.1111/j.1548-1379.2010.01107.x.

Bodnar, John. *Remaking America: Public Memory, Commemoration, and Patriotism in the Twentieth Century*. Princeton: Princeton University Press, 1992.

Bogataj, Mirko. *Ein Volk am Rand der Mitte. Die Kärntner Slowenen*. Klagenfurt/Celovec: Kitab Verlag, 2008.

Bogner, Alexander, and Wolfgang Menz. "The Theory-Generating Expert Interview: Epistemological Interest, Forms of Knowledge, Interaction." In *Interviewing Experts*, edited by Alexander Bogner, Beate Littig, and Wolfgang Menz, 43–80. Basingstoke: Palgrave Macmillan, 2009.

Böhm, Johann. *Die deutsche Volksgruppe in Jugoslawien 1918–1941. Innen- und Außenpolitik als Symptome des Verhältnisses zwischen deutscher Minderheit und jugoslawischer Regierung*. Frankfurt am Main: Peter Lang, 2009.

Bond, Lucy, Stef Craps, and Pieter Vermeulen. "Introduction: Memory on the Move." In *Memory Unbound*, edited by Lucy Bond, Stef Craps, and Pieter Vermeulen, 1–26. New York: Berghahn Books, 2017.

Bond, Lucy, and Jessica Rapson, eds. *The Transcultural Turn: Interrogating Memory Between and Beyond Borders*. Berlin: De Gruyter, 2014.

Božić, Gordana. "Diversity in Ethnicization: War Memory Landscape in Bosnia and Herzegovina." *Memory Studies* 12, no. 4 (2019): 412–32. https://doi.org/10.1177/1750698017714834.

Bracher, Nathan. "History, Memory, and Humanism in the Recent Writings of Tzvetan Todorov." *South Central Review* 15, no. 3/4 (1998): 38–46. https://doi.org/10.2307/3189832.

Broda, Anja, Anja Bieber, Gabriele Meyer, Louise Hopper, Rachael Joyce, Kate Irving, Orazio `Zanetti, et al. "Perspectives of Policy and Political Decision Makers on Access to Formal Dementia Care: Expert Interviews in Eight

European Countries." *BMC Health Services Research* 17, no. 1 (2017): 1–14.
https://doi.org/10.1186/s12913-017-2456-0.

Brunner, Karl-Michael. "Zweisprachigkeit und Identität: Probleme sprachlicher Identität von ethnischen Minderheiten am Beispiel der Kärntner Slowenen." *Psychologie und Gesellschaftskritik* 11, no. 4 (1987): 57–75.

Buchacher, Robert. "Tod dem Faschismus." In *Materialien zu Karel Prušnik-Gašper. Gämsen auf der Lawine,* edited by Lojze Wieser, 19–24. Klagenfurt/Celovec: Wieser Verlag, 2015.

Bulloch, Jamie. *Karl Renner: Austria.* London: Haus, 2009.

Bunzl, Matti. "On the Politics and Semantics of Austrian Memory: Vienna's Monument Against War and Fascism." *History and Memory* 7, no. 2 (1995): 7–40.

Burns, Andrea A. *From Storefront to Monument: Tracing the Public History of the Black Museum Movement.* Amherst: University of Massachusetts Press, 2013.

Busch, Brigitta. "Shifting Political and Cultural Borders: Language and Identity in the Border Region of Austria and Slovenia." In *Culture and Cooperation in Europe's Borderlands,* edited by James Anderson, Liam O'Dowd, and Thomas M. Wilson, 125–44. Amsterdam: Rodopi, 2003.

Byford, Jovan. *Picturing Genocide in the Independent State of Croatia: Atrocity Images and the Contested Memory of the Second World War in the Balkans.* London: Bloomsbury Academic, 2020.

Certeau, Michel de. *The Practice of Everyday Life.* Translated by Steven Rendall. Berkeley: University of California Press, 1984.

Clarke, Katerina. "Socialist Realism in Soviet Literature." In *From Symbolism to Socialist Realism: A Reader,* edited by Irene Masing-Delic, 419–32. Boston: Academic Studies Press, 2012.

Cohen-Pfister, Laurel, and Susanne Vees-Gulani, eds. *Generational Shifts in Contemporary German Culture.* Rochester: Camden House, 2010.

Confino, Alon. "Remembering the Second World War, 1945–1965: Narratives of Victimhood and Genocide." *Cultural Analysis* 4 (2005): 46–75.

Connerton, Paul. "Seven Types of Forgetting." *Memory Studies* 1, no. 1 (2017): 59–71. https://doi.org/10.1177/1750698007083889.

Council of Carinthian Slovenes. "Stellungnahme zum 6. Bereicht des Landes Kärnten/Koroška zur Lage der slowenischen Volksgruppe 2023." 1–21. Accessed 31 July 2023. https://www.nsks.at/aktualno_aktuell/detail /de/porochilo-o-polozhaju-slovenske-narodne-skupnosti-na-avstrijskem -koroshkem-2023.

Crampton, Andrew. "The Voortrekker Monument, the Birth of Apartheid, and Beyond." *Political Geography* 20, no. 2 (2001): 221–46. https://doi .org/10.1016/S0962-6298(00)00062-7.

Čubrilo, Jasmina. "Two Monuments by Stretan Stojanović. Continuity and Discontinuity." *Znanstvena revija za umetnostno zgodovino* 18, no. 2 (2013): 59–72.

Danglmaier, Nadja, Andreas Hudelist, Samo Wakounig, and Daniel Wutti. "Fazit und Ausblick." In *Erinnerungsgemeinschaften in Kärnten/Koroška. Eine Empirische Studie über gegenwärtige Auseinandersetzungen mit dem Nationalsozialismus in Schule und Gesellschaft*, edited by Nadja Danglmaier, Andreas Hudelist, Samo Wakounig, and Daniel Wutti, 241–4. Klagenfurt/Celovec: Hermagoras/Mohorjeva, 2017.

Danglmaier, Nadja, and Werner Koroschitz. *Nationalsozialismus in Kärnten: Opfer. Täter. Gegner.* Innsbruck: Studienverlag, 2015.

Danglmaier, Nadja, and Samo Wakounig. "Rahmenbedingungen für LehrerInnen in Hinblick auf Unterricht und Projekte zum Thema Nationalsozialismus." In *Erinnerungsgemeinschaften in Kärnten/Koroška. Eine Empirische Studie über gegenwärtige Auseinandersetzungen mit dem Nationalsozialismus in Schule und Gesellschaft*, edited by Nadja Danglmaier, Andreas Hudelist, Samo Wakounig, and Daniel Wutti, 77–91. Klagenfurt/Celovec: Hermagoras/Mohorjeva, 2017a.

Danglmaier, Nadja, and Samo Wakounig. "Zur Methodik und Didaktik in Unterricht und bei Projekten." In *Erinnerungsgemeinschaften in Kärnten/Koroška. Eine Empirische Studie über gegenwärtige Auseinandersetzungen mit dem Nationalsozialismus in Schule und Gesellschaft*, edited by Nadja Danglmaier, Andreas Hudelist, Samo Wakounig, and Daniel Wutti, 102–4. Klagenfurt/Celovec: Hermagoras/Mohorjeva, 2017b.

Danto, Arthur C. "The Vietnam Veterans Memorial." *The Nation*, 31 August 1985, 152–5.

Die Presse. "Maja Haderlap erhielt Rauriser Literaturpreis." *Die Presse*, 22 March 2012. Accessed 4 September 2020. https://www.diepresse.com/742535/maja-haderlap-erhielt-rauriser-literaturpreis.

Dillane, Fionnuala, and Gunnþórunn Guðmundsdóttir. "Iceland – Ireland Memory, Literature, Culture on the Atlantic Periphery." In *Iceland – Ireland Memory, Literature, Culture on the Atlantic Periphery*, edited by Fionnuala Dillane and Gunnþórunn Guðmundsdóttir, 1–14. Leiden: Brill, 2022.

Dokumentationsarchiv des österreichischen Widerstandes; Klub Prežihov Voranc, Institut za proučevanje prostora Alpe-Jadran, eds. *Spurensuche. Erzählte Geschichte der Kärntner Slowenen.* Vienna: Österreichischer Bundesverlag, 1990.

Doleschal, Ursula. "Multilingualism in Carinthia: The Case of Slovene and the Slovene Minority." In *The Polyphony of English Studies. A Festschrift for Allan James*, edited by Alexander Onysko, Eva-Maria Graf, Werner Delanoy, Nikola Dobric, and Günther Sigott, 145–62. Tübingen: Narr Francke Attempto Verlag, 2017.

Dreiack, Stefanie, and Marlen Niederberger. "Qualitative Experteninterviews in internationalen Organisationen." *Politische Vierteljahresschrift* 59, no. 2 (June 2018): 293–318.

Đureinović, Jelena. *The Politics of Memory of the Second World War in Contemporary Serbia: Collaboration, Resistance and Retribution*. London: Routledge, 2019.

Đureinović, Jelena. "Marching the Victorious March: Populism and Memory Appropriation of the Yugoslav Partisans in Today's Serbia." *Nationalities Papers* 51, no. 6 (2023): 1250–62. https://doi.org/10.1017/nps.2022.50.

Eigler, Friederike. *Gedächtnis und Geschichte in Generationenromanen seit der Wende*. Berlin: Erich Schmidt, 2005.

Eigler, Friederike. "Writing in the New Germany: Cultural Memory and Family Narratives." *German Politics & Society* 23, no. 3 (2005): 16–41.

Entner, Brigitte. "Zwischen Integration und Ausgrenzung. Kärntner SlowenInnen und britische Besatzungspolitik bis zu den Novemberwahlen 1945." In *Von Neuem. Die Kärntner Slowenen unter der britischen Besatzungsmacht nach dem Jahr 1945. Zeitzeugen, Beiträge und Berichte*, 9–42. Klagenfurt/Celovec: Drava, 2008.

Entner, Brigitte. "Vergessene Opfer? Die 'Verschleppten' vom Mai 1945 im Spiegel regionaler Geschichtspolitik." In *Kärnten liegt am Meer. Konfliktgeschichte/n über Trauma, Macht und Identität*, edited by Wolfgang Petritsch, Wilfried Graf, and Gudrun Kramer, 423–34. Klagenfurt/Celovec: Drava, 2012.

Entner, Brigitte. "Komm, miß dich mit uns, in die Wälder dich trau! Kärntner Sloweninnen im Widerstand." In *Krieg, Widerstand, Befreiung. Ihr Nachhall in den Kulturen und Literaturen des Alpen-Adria-Raums*, edited by Fabjan Hafner and Johann Strutz, 31–48. Klagenfurt/Celovec: Drava, 2013.

Entner, Brigitte. *Wer war Klara aus Šentlipš/St. Philippen? Kärntner Slowenen und Sloweninnen als Opfer der NS-Verfolgung. Ein Gedenkbuch*. Klagenfurt/Celovec: Drava Verlag, 2014.

Entner, Brigitte. "Kärntner Slowenen und Sloweninnen – unbekannte / ungeliebte Minderheit im süden Österreichs." *Psychologie & Gesellschaftskritik* 39, no. 4 (2016): 7–31.

Entner, Brigitte. "Kaj človek vse doživi! Was der Mensch alles erlebt!" In *Odpor in preganjanje v občini Sele 1938–1945. Widerstand und Verfolgung in der Gemeinde Zell: 1938–1945*. Klagenfurt/Celovec: Mohorjeva/Hermagoras, 2018.

Entner, Brigitte, Valentin Sima, and Avguštin Malle, eds. *Widerstand gegen Faschismus und Nationalsozialismus im Alpen-Adria-Raum. Odpor proti fašizmu in nacizmu v alpsko-jadranskem prostoru*. Klagenfurt/Celovec: Drava Verlag, 2011.

Eriksson, Päivi, and Anne Kovalainen. *Qualitative Methods in Business Research*. Los Angeles: Sage, 2013.

Erll, Astrid. "Traveling Memory." *Parallax* 17, no. 4 (2011): 4–18. https://doi.org /10.1080/13534645.2011.605570.

Erll, Astrid. "Transcultural Memory." *Témoigner. Entre histoire et mémoire* 119 (2014): 178.

Erll, Astrid, and Ansgar Nünning. "Literaturkonzepte von Gedächtnis: Ein einführender Überblick." In *Gedächtniskonzepte der Literaturwissenschaft: Theoretische Grundlegung und Anwendungsperspektiven*, edited by Astrid Erll and Ansgar Nünning, 1–9. Berlin: De Gruyter, 2010.

Eschenbach, Insa. "Soil, Ashes, Commemoration: Processes of Sacralization at the Former Ravensbrück Concentration Camp." *History and Memory* 23, no. 1 (2011): 131–56. https://doi.org/10.2979/histmemo.23.1.131.

Fackenheim, Emil. *To Mend the World: Foundations of Post-Holocaust Jewish Thought*. New York: Schocken Books, 1982.

Fanta, Walter, and Valentin Sima. *Stehst mitten drin im Land. Das europäische Ka- meradentreffen auf dem Kärntner Ulrichsberg von den Anfängen bis heute*. Klagenfurt/Celovec: Drava, 2003.

Fedor, Julie, Simon Lewis, and Tatiana Zhurzhenko. "Introduction: War and Memory in Russia, Ukraine, and Belarus." In *War and Memory in Russia, Ukraine and Belarus*, edited by Julie Fedor, Markku Kangaspuro, Jussi Lassila, and Tatiana Zhurzhenko, 1–40. Cham: Palgrave Macmillan, 2017.

Ferenc, Tone, Ferdo Fischer, Davorin Jeršek, Rozalija Lukman, Miroslav Luštek, Marija Oblak-Čarni, and Terzija Traven, eds. *Marec 1941–Marec 1942. Vol. 1 of Dokumenti ljudske revolucije v sloveniji*. Ljubljana: Inštitut za zgodovino delavskega gibanja, 1962.

Fiddler, Allyson. "Carinthia, Interculturalism, and Austrian National Identity: Cultural Reflections on 10 October 1920." *German Life and Letters* 58, no. 2 (April 2005): 195–210. https://doi.org/10.1111/j.0016 -8777.2005.00314.x.

Fischer, Norbert. "Maritime Death, Memory and Landscape: Examples From the North Sea Coast and the Islands." In *Waddenland Outstanding. History, Landscape, and Cultural Heritage of the Wadden Sea Region*, edited by Linde Egberts and Meindert Schroor, 169–80. Amsterdam: Amsterdam University Press, 2018.

Foucalt, Michael. *Language, Counter-Memory, Practice. Selected Essays and Interviews*. Edited by Donald F. Bouchard. Translated by Donald F. Bouchard and Sherry Simon. Ithaca: Cornell University Press, 1977.

Fuchs, Anne, Mary Cosgrove, and Georg Grote, eds. *German Memory Contests: The Quest for Identity in Literature, Film, and Discourse since 1990*. Rochester: Camden House, 2006.

Galli, Matteo, and Simone Costagli, eds. *Deutsche Familienromane: Literarische Genealogien und Internationaler Kontext*. Munich: Wilhelm Fink, 2010.

Gatrell, Peter. "War After the War: Conflicts, 1919–1923." In *A Companion to World War 1*, edited by John Horne, 558–75. London: Blackwell, 2010.

Gauß, Karl-Markus. *Die Vernichtung Mitteleuropas. Essays*. Klagenfurt/Celovec: Wiesler Verlag, 1991.

Gillman, Abigail. "Cultural Awakening and Historical Forgetting: The Architecture of Memory in the Jewish Museum of Vienna and in Rachel Whitehead's 'Nameless Library'." *New German Critique* 93, Special Issue: Austrian Writers Confront the Past (2004): 145–73.

Gould, Mary Rachel, and Rachel E. Silverman. "Stumbling Upon History: Collective Memory and the Urban Landscape." *GeoJournal* 78, no. 5 (2013): 791–801.

Graneheim, U. H., and B. Lundman. "Qualitative Concent Analysis in Nursing Research: Concepts, Procedures, and Measures to Achieve Trustworthiness." *Nurse Education Today* 24, no. 2 (1 February 2004): 105–12. https://doi.org/10.1016/j.nedt.2003.10.001. Medline:14769454.

Greiner, Ulrich. "Gerechtigkeit für die Slowenen." *Die Zeit*, 21 July 2011. Accessed 4 September 2020. https://www.zeit.de/2011/30/L-Haderlap?print.

Grote, Georg. *The South Tyrol Question, 1866–2010*. Bern: Peter Lang, 2012.

Groth, Paul, and Chris Wilson. "The Polyphony of Cultural Landscape Study: An Introduction." In *Everyday America: Cultural Landscape Studies After J. B. Jackson*, edited by Paul Groth and Chris Wilson, 1–22. Berkeley: University of California Press, 2003.

Gstettner, Peter. "… 'wo alle Macht vom Volk ausgeht': eine nachhaltige Verhinderung; zur Mikropolitik rund um den 'Ortstafelsturm' in Kärnten." *Österreichische Zeitschrift für Politikwissenschaft* 33, no. 1 (2004): 81–94. https://doi.org/10.15203/ozp.852.vol33iss1.

Gstettner, Peter. "Die Legende von der Selbstbefreiung Kärntens. Alte Töne und neue Varianten am Rande des 'Gedenkjahres 2005.'" In *Jahrbuch 2006. Schwerpunkt Erinnerungskultur*, edited by Dokumentationsarchiv des Österreichischen Widerstandes, 80–105. Vienna: Lit Verlag, 2006.

Guenther, Christina. "The Poetics of Ritual in Diaspora: Anna Mitgutsch's 'Familienfest' and Vladimir Vertlib's 'Letzter Wunsch'." *Journal of Austrian Studies* 45, no. 1 (2012): 93–118.

Gullberg, Tom. *State, Territory and Identity. The Principle of National Self-Determination, the Question of Territorial Sovereignty in Carinthia and the Post-Habsburg Territories After the First World War*. Åbo: Åbo Akademi University Press, 2000.

Gully, Jennifer M. "Bilingual Signs in Carinthia: International Treaties, the Ortstafelstreit, and the Spaces of German." *Transit* 7, no. 1 (2011). https://doi.org/10.5070/T771009755.

Haderlap, Maja. *Angel of Oblivion*. Translated by Tess Lewis. New York: Archipelago Books, 2016.

Haderlap, Maja. *Im langen Atem der Geschichte. Rede beim Staatsakt anlässlich der 100. Wiederkehr des Jahrestages der Gründung der Republik Österreich*. Göttingen: Wallstein Verlag, 2018.

Haderlap, Valentin. "Die Buben werden nicht durchkommen." In, Spurensuche. Erzählte Geschichte der Kärntner Slowenen, edited by Dokumentationsarchiv des österreichischen Widerstandes, Klub Prežihov Voranc, Institut za proučevanje prostora Alpe-Jadran, 291–5. Vienna: Österrichischer Bundesverlag, 1990.

Hafner, Fabjan. "Es ist die Muttersprache, aber die Mutter ist lange tot … Slowenisches im Werk von Peter Handke." In *Peter Handke*, edited by Klaus Amann, Fabjan Hafner, and Karl Wagner, 47–63. Vienna: Böhlau, 2006.

Hafner, Fabjan. "Slowenien, die Slowenen, das Slowenische im Werk Peter Handkes." *Manuskripte* 46, no. 172 (June 2006): 111–7.

Hafner, Fabjan. "Der „exemplarische Epiker" der Kärntner SlowenInnen: Florjan Lipuš." In *Und (k)ein Wort Deutsch … Literaturen der Minderheiten und MigrantInnen in Österreich*, edited by Nicola Mitterer and Werner Wintersteiner, 133–49. Innsbruck: Studienverlag, 2009.

Handke, Peter. "Wut und Geheimnis. Rede zur Verleihung des Ehrendoktorats der Universität Klagenfurt am 8. November 2002." In *Peter Handke*, edited by by Klaus Amann, Fabjan Hafner, and Karl Wagner, 253–8. Vienna: Böhlau, 2006.

Handke, Peter. *Wunschloses Unglück*. Berlin: Suhrkamp, 2001.

Handke, Peter. *Immer noch Sturm*. Berlin: Suhrkamp, 2010.

Harris, Cecily. "German Memory of the Holocaust: The Emergence of Counter-Memorials." *Penn History Review* 17, no. 2 (2010): 34–59.

Hay, Iain, Andrew Hughes, and Mark Tutton. "Monuments, Memory and Marginalisation in Adelaide's Prince Henry Gardens." *Geografiska Annaler. Series B, Human Geography* 86, no. 3 (2004): 201–16.

Heiß, Franz. *Methodik der Volkszählungen*. Jena: G. Fischer, 1931.

Hemon, Alexsander. "The Bob Dylan of Genocide Apologists." *The New York Times*, 15 October 2019. Accessed 2 June 2022. https://www.nytimes.com/2019/10/15/opinion/peter-handke-nobel-bosnia-genocide.html.

Henneberg, Krystyna von. "Monuments, Public Space, and the Memory of Empire in Modern Italy." *History and Memory* 16, no. 1 (2004): 37–85. https://doi.org/10.2979/his.2004.16.1.37.

Hershkovitz, Linda. "Tiananmen Square and the Politics of Place." *Political Geography* 12, no. 5 (1993): 395–420. https://doi.org/10.1016/0962-6298(93)90010-5.

Himka, John-Paul, and Joanna Beata Michlic. "Introduction." In *Bringing the Dark Past to Light: The Reception of the Holocaust in Postcommunist Europe*, edited by John-Paul Himka and Joanna Beata Michlic, 1–24. Lincoln: University of Nebraska Press, 2013.

Himka, John-Paul, and Joanna Beata Michlic. "The History Behind the Regional Conflict in Ukraine." *Kritika: Explorations in Russian and Eurasian History* 16, no. 1 (2015): 129–36. https://doi.org/10.1353/kri.2015.0008.

Hirsch, Marianne. "Family Pictures: Maus, Mourning, and Post-Memory."
    Discourse 15, no. 2 (1992): 3–29.
Hirsch, Marianne. "Surviving Images: Holocaust Photographs and the Work
    of Postmemory." *The Yale Journal of Criticism* 14, no. 1 (2001): 5–37. https://
    doi.org/10.1353/yale.2001.0008.
Hirsch, Marianne. *The Generation of Postmemory: Writing and Visual Culture
    After the Holocaust*. New York: Columbia University Press, 2012.
Hom, Sharon K., and Eric K. Yamamoto. "Collective Memory, History, and
    Social Justice." *UCLA Law Review* 47 (1999): 1747–802.
Horvat, Marjan. "Maja Haderlap im Gespräch mit Marjan Horvat." In
    Literatur/a. Jahrbuch. 2010/2011, edited by Fabjan Hafner, Klaus Amann,
    and Doris Moser, 130–41. Klagenfurt/Celovec: Robert Musil-Institut der
    Universität Klagenfurt and Kärntner Literaturarchiv, 2012.
Horvatinčić, Sanja. "From Storytelling to Re-Enactment: Strategies of
    Monument-Making in Socialist Yugoslavia." In *Shaping Revolutionary
    Memory – The Production of Monuments in Socialist Yugoslavia*, edited by
    Sanja Horvatinčić and Beti Žerovc, 114–47. Ljubljana and Berlin: Igor Zabel
    Association for Culture and Theory and Archive Books, 2023.
Ignatieff, Michael. "Soviet War Memorials." *History Workshop* 17 (1984):
    157–63.
Jahn, Bernhard. "Familienkonstruktionen 2005. Zum Problem des
    Zusammenhangs der Generationen im aktuellen Familienroman."
    Zeitschrift für Germanistik 16, no. 3 (2006): 581–96.
Jandl, Paul. "Katharsis in Kärnten." *Die Welt*, 23 December 2011. Accessed
    4 September 2020. https://www.welt.de/print/diewelt/kultur/article13781723
    /Katharsis-in-Kaernten.html.
Jeleč, Marijana. "Formen der Vergangenheitsbewältigung in ausgewählten
    zeitgenössischen österreichischen Generationenromanen." In *Familie und
    Identitä in der Gegenwartsliteratur*, edited by Goran Lovrić and Marijana
    Jeleč, 147–62.Frankfurt am Main: Peter Lang, 2016.
Jelin, Elizabeth. *State Repression and the Labors of Memory*. Minneapolis:
    University of Minnesota Press, 2003.
Jesih, Boris. "Political Participation of the Slovene Ethnic Minority in
    Carinthia." *Slovene Studies* 30, no. 2 (2008): 229–33.
Judson, Pieter M. *Guardians of the Nation: Activists on the Language Frontiers of
    Imperial Austria*. Cambridge: Harvard University Press, 2006.
Judson, Pieter M. *The Habsburg Empire: A New History*. Cambridge: Harvard
    University Press, 2016.
Kabalek, Kobi. "Memory and Periphery: An Introduction." *HAGAR Studies in
    Culture, Polity and Identities* 12 (2014): 8–22.
Kacandes, Irene. "Second-Generation Holocaust Literature: Legacies of
    Survival and Perpetration." *The Germanic Review* 83, no. 4 (Fall 2008): 392–6.

Kämmerlings, Richard. "Bachmann-Preis für Haderlap – eine Fehlentscheidung." *Die Welt*, 10 July 2011. Accessed 4 September 2020. https://www.welt.de/kultur/literarischewelt/article13479283/Bachmann -Preis-fuer-Haderlap-eine-Fehlentscheidung.html.

Kansteiner, Wulf. "Finding Meaning in Memory: A Methodological Critique of Collective Memory Studies." *History and Theory* 41, no. 2 (2002): 179–97. https://doi.org/10.1111/0018-2656.00198.

Karge, Heike. "Local Practices and 'Memory From Above': On the Building of War Monuments in Yugoslavia." In *Shaping Revolutionary Memory: The Production of Monuments in Socialist Yugoslavia*, edited by Sanja Horvatinčić and Beti Žerovc, 92–113. Ljubljana and Berlin: Igor Zabel Association for Culture and Theory and Archive Books, 2023.

Karner, Stefan, and Susanne Hartl. "Die Verschleppungen von Kärntnern 1945 durch jugoslawische Partisanen." In *Aussiedlung – Verschleppung – nationaler Kampf*, edited by Stefan Karner and Andreas Moritsch, 53–78. Klagenfurt/Celovec and Ljubljana: Johannes Heyn and Hermagoras/ Mohorjeva založba, 2005.

Karner, Stefan, and Andreas Moritsch. "Zur Einleitung: der nationale Konflikt." In *Aussiedlung -Verschleppung – nationaler Kampf*, edited by Stefan Karner and Andreas Moritsch, 8–14. Klagenfurt/Celovec and Ljubljana: Johannes Heyn and Hermagoras/Mohorjeva založba, 2005.

Karner, Stefan, and Andreas Moritsch, eds. *Kärnten und die nationale Frage. Aussiedlung – Verschleppung – nationaler Kampf*. Vol. 1 of *Kärnten und die nationale Frage*. Klagenfurt/Celovec: Johannes Heyn and Hermagoras/ Mohorjeva, 2005.

Kärntner Abwehrkämpferbund. "Gedenkfeier für die verschleppten und ermordeten Kärntner durch Tito Partisanen." *Kärntner Abwehrkämpferbund*, 10 May 2014. Accessed 4 September 2020. https://www.kab-or.at/82.html.

Kärntner Abwehrkämpferbund. "Organisation." *Kärntner Abwehrkämpferbund*. Accessed 21 August 2020. https://www.kab.or.at/organisation.html.

Kärntner Abwehrkämpferbund. "Partisanenverherrlichung in Klagenfurt." *Kärntner Abwehrkämpferbund*, 20 January 2019. Accessed 4 September 2020. https://www.kab-or.at/253.html.

Kazeem, Belinda, Nicola Lauré al-Samarai, and Peggy Piesche. "Museum. Space. History: New Sites of Political Tectonics. A Virtual Exchange Between Belinda Kazeem, Nicola Lauré al-Samarai, and Peggy Piesche." In *European Institute for Progressive Cultural Policies*, translated by Tim Scharp, June 2008. Accessed 4 September 2020. https://transversal.at /transversal/0708/kazeem-piesche/en.

Kirk, Tim. "Limits of Germandom: Resistance to the Nazi Annexation of Slovenia." *The Slavonic and East European Review* 69, no. 4 (1991): 646–67.

Kirn, Gal. "Transformation of Memorial Sites in the Post-Yugoslav Context." In *Retracing Images. Visual Culture after Yugoslavia*, edited by Daniel Šuber and Slobodan Karamanic, 251–81. Leiden: Brill, 2012.

Kirn, Gal. *The Partisan Counter-Archive: Retracing the Ruptures of Art and Memory in the Yugoslav People's Liberation Struggle*. Berlin: De Gruyter, 2020.

Klabjan, Borut. "'Our Victims Define Our Borders': Commemorating Yugoslav Partisans in the Italo-Yugoslav Borderland." *East European Politics and Societies* 31, no. 2 (1 May 2017): 290–310. https://doi .org/10.1177/0888325416678041.

Klabjan, Borut. "Memory, Revision, Resistance: Reviving the Monuments Along the Slovenian-Italian Border." In *Borderlands of Memory*, edited by Borut Klabjan, 235–51. Oxford: Peter Lang, 2019.

Klemenčič, Matjaž. "German-Slovene Relations in the Slovene Lands From the Mid-19th Century Until Today." *Onomàstica. Anuari de la Societat d'Onomàstica* 3 (2017): 127–60.

Knight, Robert. "Ethnicity and Identity in the Cold War: The Carinthian Border Dispute, 1945–1949." *The International History Review* 22, no. 2 (June 2000): 274–303.

Knight, Robert. "Denazification and Integration in the Austrian Province of Carinthia." *The Journal of Modern History* 79, no. 3 (September 2007): 572–612. https://doi.org/10.1086/517982.

Knight, Robert. "A No-Win Situation? Gerald Sharp and British Policy Towards the Carinthian Slovenes 1945–1960." In *Widerstand gegen Faschismus und Nationalsozialismus im Alpen-Adria-Raum. Odpor proti fašizmu in nacizmu v alpsko-jadranskem prostoru*, edited by Brigitte Entner and the Slowenisches Wissenschaftliches Institut, 84–96. Klagenfurt/Celovec: Drava, 2011.

Knight, Robert. "Kosaken und Kroaten in Kärnten: vernachlässigte Perspektiven." In *Zweiter Weltkrieg und ethnische Homogenisierungsversuche im Alpen-Adria-Raum/Druga svetovna vojna in poizkusi etnične homogenizacije v alpsko-jadranskem prostoru*, edited by Brigitte Entner and Valentin Sima, 127–46. Klagenfurt/Celovec: Drava Verlag, 2012.

Knight, Robert. *Slavs in Post-Nazi Austria: Carinthian Slovenes and the Politics of Assimilation, 1945–1960*. London: Bloomsbury Academic, 2017.

Knipphals, Dirk. "Bedächtige Nachkriegsliteratur." *taz*, 10 July 2011. Accessed 4 September 2020. https://taz.de/!5116688/.

Kohl, Felix Oliver. "Nemški prevodi Lipuševih del ob in po Tjažu v luči konsekracije." *Primerjalna književnost* 41, no. 3 (2018): 17–35.

Kokot, Andrej. *Ko zori spomin. Otroška doživetja v pregnanstvu*. Klagenfurt/ Celovec: Drava Verlag, 1996.

Kokot, Andrej. *Das Kind, das ich war. Erinnerungen an die Vertreibung der Slowenen aus Kärnten*. Translated by Andre Kokot. Klagenfurt/Celovec: Drava Verlag, 1999.

Kolenik, Lipej. *Mali ljudje na veliki poti. Spomini na predvojni, vojni in povojni čas na Koroškem*. Klagenfurt/Celovec: Drava Verlag, 1997.

Kolenik, Lipej. *Für das Leben, gegen den Tod. Mein Weg in den Widerstand*. Translated by Erwin Köstler. Klagenfurt/Celovec: Drava Verlag, 2001.

Koller, Christian. ".. der Wiener Judenstaat, von dem wir uns unter allen Umständen trennen wollen": die Vorarlberger Anschlussbewegung an die Schweiz." In *... der Rest ist Österreich: das Werden der Ersten Republik*, edited by Helmut Konrad and Wolfgang Maderthaner, 83–102. Vienna: Gerold Verlag, 2008.

Konrad, Helmut. "Identität(en) und Erinnerungskulturen in Kärnten." In *CarinthiaJA. Einführung. Überblick. Reflektionen zum neuen Landesausstellungsformat*, edited by Amt der Kärntner Landesregierung, Abeilung 6 – Bildung, Wissenschaft, Kultur und Sport, 79–89. Klagenfurt/Celovec: Amt der Kärntner Landesregierung.

Koshar, Rudy. *From Monuments to Traces: Artifacts of German Memory, 1870–1990*. Berkeley: University of California Press, 2000.

Köstler, Erwin. "Institutionen, Akteure, Modelle: das Kärntner zweisprachige literarische Feld als Anziehungspunkt für deutschsprachige Autor_innen." In *Literarische Mehrsprachigkeit im österreichischen und slowenischen Kontext*, edited by Andreas Leben and Alenka Koron, 79–96. Tübingen: Narr Francke Attempo, 2019.

Kranjc, Gregor. "On the Periphery Jews, Slovenes, and the Memory of the Holocaust." In *Bringing the Dark Past to Light: The Reception of the Holocaust in Postcommunist Europe*, edited by John-Paul Himka and Joanna Beata Michlic, 591–625. Lincoln: University of Nebraska Press, 2013.

Kranjc, Gregor. "Fight or Flight: Desertion, Defection, and Draft-Dodging in Occupied Slovenia, 1941–1945." *Journal of Military History* 81, no. 1 (2017): 133–62.

Kranjc, Gregor. "Talking Past Each Other: Language and Post-World War II Killings in Slovenia." *Journal of Genocide Research* 20, no. 4 (2018): 565–86. https://doi.org/10.1080/14623528.2018.1527080.

Kuchar, Helene. *Jelka: Aus dem Leben einer Kärntner Partisanin*, edited by Thomas Busch and Brigitte Windhab. Basel: Verlag API, 1984.

Kucia, Marek. "The Europeanization of Holocaust Memory and Eastern Europe." *East European Politics and Societies* 30 (2016): 107–19. https://doi.org/10.1177/0888325415599195.

Kuretsisdis-Haider, Claudia. "Strafsache wegen Verbrechen an der Familie Sadovnik. Das Verfahren des Volksgerichts Klagenfurt und der Umgang der österreichischen Justiz mit den Ereignissen auf dem Peršmanhof." In *Peršman*, edited by Lisa Rettl, Gudrun Blohberger, Zveza koroških partizanov/Verband der Kärntner Partisanen, Društvo/Verein Peršman,, 49–89. Göttingen; Wallstein, 2014.

Kuttenberg, Eva. "Austria's Topography of Memory: Heldenplatz, Albertinaplatz, Judenplatz, and Beyond." *The German Quarterly* 80, no. 4 (2007): 468–91. https://doi.org/10.1111/j.1756-1183.2007.tb00086.x.

Kužnar, Andriana Benčić, and Vjeran Pavlaković. "Exhibiting Jasenovac: Controversies, Manipulations and Politics of Memory." *Heritage, Memory and Conflict* 3 (2023): 65–9. https://doi.org/10.3897/ijhmc.3.71583.

LaCapra, Dominick. *History and Memory After Auschwitz*. Ithaca: Cornell University Press, 1998.

Land Kärnten. "Grenzenlose Erinnerungskultur gegen das Vergessen." 15 May 2023. Accessed 26 February 2024. https://www.ktn.gv.at/Service /News?nid=35872.

Landsberg, Alison. *Prosthetic Memory: The Ethics and Politics of Memory in an Age of Mass Culture*. New York: Columbia University Press, 2004.

Langenbacher, Eric. "Memory Regimes in Contemporary Germany." PhD diss., Georgetown University, 2002.

Langenbacher, Eric. "Changing Memory Regimes in Contemporary Germany?" *German Politics & Society* 21, no. 2 (67) (2003): 46–68.

Langenbacher, Eric. "A Plea for an 'Intergovernmental' European Memory." In *Dynamics of Memory and Identity in Contemporary Europe*, edited by Eric Langenbacher, Bill Niven, and Ruth Wittlinger, 209–21. New York: Berghahn Books, 2012.

Langer, Lawrence. *Holocaust Testimonies: The Ruins of Memory*. New Haven: Yale University Press, 1991.

Lantis, Margaret. "Vernacular Culture." *American Anthropologist* 62, no. 2 (1960): 202–16.

Leben, Andreas, and Erwin Köstler. "Von den primären Quellen zum publizistischen Diskurs. Über den bewaffneten Widerstand der Partisanen in Kärnten." *Zeitgeschichte* 34, no. 4 (2007): 226–42.

Leben, Andrej. "Koroške (slovenske) vojne pripovedi med reprezentacijo in diskurzom." *Primerjalna književnost* 38, no. 3 (2015): 121–38.

Lee, Philip, and Prapid Ninan Thomas. "Introduction: Public Media and the Right to Memory: Towards an Encounter With Justice." In *Public Memory, Public Media and the Politics of Justice*, edited by Philip Lee and Prapid Ninan Thomas, 1–22. Basingstoke: Palgrave Macmillan, 2012.

Lehnguth, Cornelius. *Waldheim und die Folgen: Der parteipolitische Umgang mit dem Nationalsozialismus in Österreich*. Frankfurt: Campus Verlag, 2013.

Lenček, Rado L. "Carantania." *Slovene Studies* 15, nos. 1–2 (1993): 191–6.

Levine, Michael P. "Mediated Memories." *Angelaki* 11, no. 2 (1 August 2006): 117–36.

Levy, Daniel, and Natan Sznaider. *The Holocaust and Memory in the Global Age*. Philadelphia: Temple University Press, 2006.

Lewis, Peirce F. "Axioms of the Landscape: Some Guides to the American Scene." *JAE* 30, no. 1 (1976): 6–9. https://doi.org/10.1080/10464883.1976.1075 8067.

Linasi, Marjan. *Koroški partizani. Protinacistični odpor na dvojezičnem koroškem v okviru slovenske Osvobodilne fronte.* Klagenfurt/Celovec: Hermagoras/ Mohorjeva, 2010.

Linasi, Marjan. *Die Kärntner Partisanen: der antifaschistische Widerstand im zweisprachigen Kärnten unter Berücksichtigung des slowenischen und jugoslawischen Widerstandes.* Klagenfurt/Celovec: Hermagoras/Mohorjeva, 2013.

Lindauer, Margaret. "The Critical Museum Visitor." In *New Museum Theory and Practice: An Introduction,* edited by Janet Marstine, 203–25. Hoboken: Wiley-Blackwell, 2005.

Loentz, Elizabeth, Carl Niekerk, Katherine Arens, Helga Schreckenberger, Imke Meyer, Heidi Schlipphacke, Robert Dassanowsky, Allyson Fiddler, Susanne Hochreiter, Hillary Hope Herzog, and Todd Herzog,. "Forum: Austrian Studies." *The German Quarterly* 89, no. 2 (2016): 221–39.

Lonetree, Amy. *Decolonizing Museums. Representing Native America in National and Tribal Museums.* Chapel Hill: The University of North Carolina Press, 2012.

Lorenz, Dagmar C.G. "Intersection Vienna: Crime and Transnationalism in Post-Shoah Austrian Fiction and Films." *Journal of Austrian Studies* 47, no. 4 (2014): 65–87. https://doi.org/10.1353/oas.2014.0052.

Lovrić, Goran, and Marijana Jeleč, eds. *Familie und Identität in der Gegenwartsliteratur.* Frankfurt am Main: Peter Lang, 2016.

Lupu, Noam. "Memory Vanished, Absent, and Confined: The Countermemorial Project in 1980s and 1990s Germany." *History and Memory* 15, no. 2 (2003): 130–64. https://doi.org/10.1353/ham.2003.0010.

Luthar, Oto. "Forgetting Does (Not) Hurt. Historical Revisionism in Post-Socialist Slovenia." *Nationalities Papers* 41, no. 6 (November 2013): 882–92. https://doi.org/10.1080/00905992.2012.743510.

Lyon, Philip W. "After Empire: Ethnic Germans and Minority Nationalism in Interwar Yugoslavia." PhD diss., University of Maryland, 2008.

Maier, Barbara, Franz V. Spechtler, and Peter Handke, eds. *Lojze Wieser. Die Zunge reicht weiter als die Hand. Anmerkungen eines Grenzverlegers.* Vienna: Czernin, 2004.

Maier, Charles S. *The Unmasterable Past: History, Holocaust, and German National Identity.* Cambridge: Harvard University Press, 1997.

Malle, Avguštin. "Der Widerstand der Kärntner Slowenen im Historischen Gedächtnis." In *Widerstand gegen Faschismus und Nationalsozialismus im Alpen-Adria-Raum - Odpor proti fašizmu in nacizmu v alpsko-jadranskem prostoru. Internationale Tagung - Mednarodni posvet,* edited by Brigitte Entner,

Valentin Sima, and Avguštin Malle, 66–83. Klagenfurt/Celovec and Vienna: Drava, 2011.

Malle, Avguštin. "Erinnerung an Vertreibung und Widerstand." In *Pregon koroskih Slovencev 1942-2002 = Die Vertreibung der Kärntner Slowenen 1942-2002*, edited by Avguštin Malle, 213–47. Klagenfurt/Celovec; Drava, 2002.

Malle, Avguštin., ed. *Die Slovenen in Kärnten. Slovenci na Koroškem. Gegenwärtige Probleme der Kärntner Slovenen. Sodobni probleme koroških Slovencev.* Ferlach/Borovlje: Drava Verlag, 1975.

Malle, Avguštin., ed. *Pregon koroških slovencev 1942–2002 = Die Vertreibung der Kärntner Slowenen 1942–2002.* Klagenfurt/Celovec: Drava Verlag, 2002.

Malle, Avguštin. "Konfrontation mit den ehemaligen Verbündeten. Betrachtungen zur Haltung der britischen Besatzungsmächte gegenüber den Kärntner Slowenen in den ersten Jahren nach dem Zweiten Weltkrieg." In *Von Neuem. Die Kärntner Slowenen unter der britischen Besatzungsmacht nach dem Jahr 1945. Zeitzeugen, Beiträge und Berichte*, 44–88. Klagenfurt/Celovec: Drava Verlag, 2008.

Manoschek, Walter. "Kärntner Slowenen als Opfer der NS-Militärjustiz." In *Opfer der NS-Militärjustiz. Urteilspraxis – Strafvollzug – Entschädigungspolitik in Österreich*, edited by Walter Manoschek, 358–87. Vienna: Mandelbaum, 2003.

Marschall, Sabine. *Landscape of Memory: Commemorative Monuments, Memorials and Public Statuary in Post-Apartheid South Africa.* Brill: Leiden, 2009.

Marschall, Sabine. "Collective Memory and Cultural Difference: Official Vs. Vernacular Forms of Commemorating the Past." *Safundi* 14, no. 1 (2013): 77–92. https://doi.org/10.1080/17533171.2012.760832.

McKnight, Douglas Carlton. "Writing Through Crisis: Two Diaries From the Second World War in Carinthia." *Journal of Austrian Studies* 53, no. 1 (Spring 2020): 1–19. https://doi.org/10.1353/oas.2020.0000.

McLaughlin, Eithne. "Cultural Memory and Regional Identities in Northern Ireland and Southern Carinthia." In *Towards a Dialogic Anglistics*, edited by Werner Delanoy, Jörg Helbig, and Allan James, 29–46. Münster: Lit, 2007.

Merriam Webster Dictionary. "landscape (n.)." Accessed 10 November 2019. https://www.merriamwebster.com/dictionary/landscape.

Michalski, Sergiusz. *Public Monuments: Art in Political Bondage 1870–1997.* London: Reaktion Books, 1998.

Mihelj, Sabina. "Between Official and Vernacular Memory." In *Research Methods for Memory Studies*, edited by Emily Keightley and Michael Pickering, 60–75. Edinburgh: Edinburgh University Press, 2013.

Milosević, Anna, and Tamara Trošt, eds. *Europeanisation and Memory Politics in the Western Balkans.* Cham: Palgrave Macmillan, 2020.

Mirnik, Ivan. "Marijan Matijević: A Century Tribute." *The Medal* 51 (2007): 23–31.

Misztal, Barbara A. *Theories of Social Remembering*. Maidenhead: McGraw-Hill International, 2003.

Mitcham, Carl. "Thinking Re-Vernacular Building." *Design Issues* 21, no. 1 (2005): 32–40. https://doi.org/10.1162/0747936053103039.

Mohar, Andrej. *Otoki Spomina/Gedenkinseln. Partizanska spominska obeležja na južnem Koroškem/Gedenkstätten für die Partisanen in Südkärnten*. Klagenfurt/Celovec: Drava Verlag, 2018.

Moritsch, Andreas. "German Nationalism and the Slovenes in Austria Between the Two World Wars." *Slovene Studies* 8, no. 1 (1986): 15–20. https://doi.org/10.7152/ssj.v8i1.3613.

Moshenska, Gabriel. "Memory: Towards the Reclamation of a Vital Concept." In *Heritage Keywords*, edited by Kathryn Lafrenz Samuels and Trinidad Rico, 197–206. Boulder: University Press of Colorado, 2015.

Mračnikar, Andrina, dir. *Verschwinden/Izginjanje*. Vienna: Soleil Film GmbH, 2022.

Müllender, Yannick. "Generationenkonzepte in zeitgenössischen österreichisch-jüdischen Romanen." *Journal of Austrian Studies* 46, no. 2 (2013): 23–47. https://doi.org/10.1353/oas.2013.0030.

Mumford, Lewis. *The Culture of Cities*. New York: Harcourt, Brace, and Co., 1938.

Mutton, Alice F.A. "Carinthia: A Province of Austria's Southern Frontier." *Geography* 38, no. 2 (1953): 83–93.

Narvselius, Eleonora. "The "Bandera Debate": The Contentious Legacy of World War II and Liberalization of Collective Memory in Western Ukraine." *Canadian Slavonic Papers* 54, nos. 3–4 (2012): 469–90. https://doi.org/10.1080/00085006.2012.11092718.

Neugebauer, Wolfgang. *Der österreichische Widerstand 1938–1945*. Vienna: Steinbauer, 2008.

Neuhäuser, Stephan. "Coming to Terms With the Past: The Case of the 'House of Austrian History' (Haus der Geschichte Österreich) in the Wake of the Rise of Populist Nationalism in Austria." *Modern Languages Open*, no. 1 (2020): 1–18. https://doi.org/10.3828/mlo.v0i0.326.

Nora, Pierre. *Realms of Memory: Rethinking the French Past*. Translated by Lawrence D. Kritzman. New York: Columbia University Press, 1996.

Olick, Jeffrey K. "What Does It Mean to Normalize the Past?: Official Memory in German Politics Since 1989." *Social Science History* 22, no. 4 (1998): 547–71. https://doi.org/10.2307/1171575.

Olick, Jeffrey K. "Memory: The Two Cultures." *Sociological Theory* 17, no. 3 (1999): 333–48.

ORF. "Denkmal für NS-Justizopfer." *Kärnten ORF*, 22 April 2013. Accessed 4 September 2020. https://kaernten.orf.at/v2/news/stories/2581088/.

ORF. "Upreti se načrtom Heimatdiensta." *Volksgruppen ORF*, 28 October 2019. Accessed 4 September 2020. https://volksgruppen.orf.at/slovenci /stories/3019231/.

ORF. "Heimatdienst gedenkt Hans Steinacher." *ORF Kärnten*, 30 September 2020. Accessed 4 February 2024. https://kaernten.orf.at/stories/3069163/.

ORF. "Land fördert Schulbesuche in Mauthausen." *ORF Kärnten*, 21 February 2020. Accessed 4 September 2020. https://kaernten.orf.at/stories/3035665/.

ORF. "Van der Bellen entschuldigt sich." *ORF*, 10 October 2020. Accessed 10 October 2020. https://orf.at/stories/3184660/.

ORF. "Erinnern gegen das Vergessen." *ORF Volksgruppen*, 19 April 2022. Accessed 26 February 2024. https://volksgruppen.orf.at/diversitaet/stories /3152654/.

ORF. "Ehrenzeichen für Opfer des Peršmanhofs." *ORF Kärnten*, 27 February 2023. Accessed 26 February 2024. https://kaernten.orf.at/stories/3196425/.

Osborne, Dora. *What Remains: The Post-Holocaust Archive in German Memory Culture*. Rochester: Camden House, 2020.

Otorepec, Božo. "Triglav: ein Symbolberg." *Histoire des Alpes = Storia delle Alpi = Geschichte der Alpen* 2 (1997): 137–41.

Pages, Neil Christian . "Architectures of Memory: Rachel Whiteread's 'Memorial to the 65,000 Murdered Austrian Jews'." *Austrian Studies* 11 (2003): 102–21. https://doi.org/10.1353/aus.2003.0039.

Pakier, Małgorzata, and Bo Stråth, eds. *A European Memory? Contested Histories and Politics of Remembrance*. New York: Berghahn Books, 2010.

Petek, Franc, ed. *Koroška v borbi. Spomini na osvobodilno borbo v Slovenski Koroški*. Klagenfurt/Celovec: Zveza bivših partizanov Slovenske Koroške, 1951.

Phillips, Kendall R., and G. Mitchell Reyes, "Introduction. Surveying Global Memoryscapes: The Shifting Terrain of Public Memory Studies." In *Global Memoryscapes: Contesting Remembrance in a Transnational Age*, edited by Kendall R. Phillips and G. Mitchell Reyes, 1–26. Tuscaloosa: University of Alabama Press, 2011.

Pirker, Peter. "Partisanen und Agenten: Mythen um die SOE-Mission Clowder." *Zeitgeschichte* 38, no. 1 (2011): 21–38.

Pirker, Peter. "British Subversive Politics Towards Austria and Partisan Resistance in the Austrian-Slovene Borderland, 1938–45." *Journal of Contemporary History* 52, no. 2 (1 April 2017): 319–51.

Pirker, Peter. "The Victim Myth Revisited: The Politics of History in Austria Up Until the Waldheim Affair." *Contemporary Austrian Studies* 29 (2020): 151–72.

Pirker, Peter, Johannes Kramer, and Mathias Lichtenwagner. "Transnational Memory Spaces in the Making: World War II and Holocaust Remembrance in Vienna." *International Journal of Politics, Culture, and Society* 32, no. 4 (2019): 439–58.

Plut-Pregelj, Leopoldina, and Carole Rogel. *The A to Z of Slovenia*. Plymouth: Scarecrow Press, 2010.

Pollerhof, Thorben. "Mit Akkubohrer und Cif-Reiniger gegen das Vergessen." *Der Standard*, 9 November 2019. https://www.derstandard.at/story /2000110853940/mit-akkubohrer-und-cif-gegen-das-vergessen.

Polzer-Srienz, Mirjam. "The Slovene Community in Austria." In *The Ethnopolitical Encyclopaedia of Europe*, edited by Karl Cordell and Stefan Wolff, 35–40. New York: Palgrave Macmillan, 2004.

Priestley, Tom. "Denial of Ethnic Identity: The Political Manipulation of Beliefs About Language in Slovene Minority Areas of Austria and Hungary." *Slavic Review* 55, no. 2 (1996): 364–98. https://doi.org/10.2307 /2501916.

Priestley, Tom. "Maintenance of Slovene in Carinthia (Austria): Grounds for Guarded Optimism?" *Canadian Slavonic Papers/Revue Canadienne des Slavistes* 45, no. 1/2 (2003): 95–117.

Priestley, Tom. *From Phonological Analysis at My Desk to Linguistic Activism with Slovene in the Austrian Alps*. Oxford: The University of Mississippi Printing Services for the Southeast European Studies Association, 2014.

Priestly, Tom, and Ruxandra Comanaru. "'Identity' Among the Minority Slovenes of Carinthia, Austria." *Razprave in Gradivo, Revija za narodnostna vprašanja* 58 (2009): 6–23.

Priestly, Tom, Meghan McKinnie, and Kate Hunter. "The Contribution of Language Use, Language Attitudes, and Language Competence to Minority Language Maintenance: A Report from Austrian Carinthia." *Journal of Slavic Linguistics* 17, nos. 1–2 (2009): 275–315.

Primiano, Leonard Norman. "Vernacular Religion and the Search for Method in Religious Folklife." *Western Folklore* 54, no. 1, Reflexivity and the Study of Belief (1995): 37–56. https://doi.org/10.2307/1499910.

Prochazka, Katharina. "Minderheitensprachen zählen! Über Sprachzählungen und Minderheiten(-sprachen)." *Wiener Linguistische Gazette* 83 (2018): 1–26.

Prochazka, Katharina. "Diffusion Modeling of Language Shift in Austria(-Hungary)." PhD diss., University of Vienna, 2019.

Prušnik-Gašper, Karel. *Gamsi na plazu. Zapiski in spomini*. Ljubljana: Glavni odbor zveze borcev NOV Slovenije, založba Borec, 1958.

Prutti, Brigitte. "'Ist es nicht ein finsterer Wald, in den wir gerieten?' Waldgänge und Waldgänger in Maja Haderlaps Roman 'Engel des Vergessens'." *Studia Theodisca* 21, no. 85 (2014): 85–137. https://doi .org/10.13130/1593-2478/4399.

Pušnik, Maruša. "Common History, Divided Memories: Slovenian and Austrian Struggle for the Carinthian Past." *Anthropological Notebooks* 14, no. 1 (2008): 49–61.

Pušnik, Maruša. "Media Memorial Discourses and Memory Struggles in Slovenia: Transforming Memories of the Second World War and Yugoslavia." *Memory Studies* 12, no. 4 (2019): 433–50. https://doi .org/10.1177/1750698017720254.

Putnik, Vladana. "Second World War Monuments in Yugoslavia as Witness of the Past and the Future." *Journal of Tourism and Cultural Change* 14, no. 3 (2016): 206–21. https://doi.org/10.1080/14766825.2016.1169344.

Randall, Richard R. "Political Geography of the Klagenfurt Basin." *Geographical Review* 47, no. 3 (1957): 406–11. https://doi.org/10.2307/212014.

Rausch, Josef. *Der Partisanenkampf in Kärnten im Zweiten Weltkrieg.* Vienna: Österreichischer Bundesverlag, 1979.

Reading, Anna. "Identity, Memory and Cosmopolitanism: The Otherness of the Past and a Right to Memory." *European Journal of Cultural Studies* 14, no. 4 (2011): 379–94. https://doi.org/10.1177/1367549411411607.

Reindl, Donald F. *Language Contact: German and Slovene.* Bochum: Universitätsverlag Dr. N. Brockmeyer, 2008.

Rettl, Lisa. "Die Ermordung der Familie Sadovnik am 25. April 1945. Ein Humanitätsverbrechen im zeitgeschichtlichen Kontext. Einleitende Vorbemerkungen." In *Peršman*, edited by Lisa Rettl, Gudrun Blohberger, Zveza koroških partizanov/Verband der Kärntner Partisanen, and Društvo/Verein Peršman, et al., 29–37. Göttingen: Wallstein, 2014.

Rettl, Lisa. "Vom Tatort zum musealen Erinnerungsort. Zur Geschichte der Gedenkstätte." In *Peršman*, edted by Lisa Rettl, Gudrun Blohberger, Zveza koroških partizanov/Verband der Kärntner Partisanen, and Društvo/ Verein Peršman, 191–208. Göttingen: Wallstein, 2014.

Rettl, Lisa. "Kampf um die Erinnerung – Partisanendenkmäler und antifaschistisches Gedächtnis in Kärnten." Lecture at the Alfred Klahr Gesellschaft. Lecture held 29 October 2005. Accessed 5 March 2024. https:// www.klahrgesellschaft.at/Mitteilungen/Rettl_1_06.html.

Rettl, Lisa. *PartisanInnendenkmäler.* Innsbruck: Studienverlag, 2006.

Rettl, Lisa. "'… Dass wir für immer aufgehört haben, Sklaven zu sein …' Erinnerungskultur der Kärntner SlowenInnen am Beispiel des Peršmandenkmals." *Zeitgeschichte* 38, no. 1 (2011): 5–20.

Rettl, Lisa. "Museum Peršmanhof. Tatort-Erinnerungsort-Lernort." *Neues Museum. Die österreichische Museumszeitschrift* 3, no. 4 (2013): 76–80.

Rettl, Lisa, Gudrun Blohberger, Zveza koroških partizanov/Verband der Kärntner Partisanen, and Društvo/Verein Peršman, eds. *Peršman.* Göttingen: Wallstein, 2014.

Révész, Tamás. "The Land of Peace? The 1921 Borderland Conflict of Burgenland in the International Context." *Südost-Forschungen* 79, no. 1 (2020): 124–50. https://doi.org/10.1515/sofo-2020-790109.

Rigney, Ann. "Portable Monuments: Literature, Cultural Memory, and the Case of Jeanie Deans." *Poetics Today* 25, no. 2 (2004): 361–96. https://doi.org/10.1215/03335372-25-2-361.

Rigney, Ann. "The Dynamics of Remembrance: Texts Between Monumentality and Morphing." In *Cultural Memory Studies: An International and Interdisciplinary Handbook*, edited by Astrid Erll, Ansgar Nünning, and Sara B. Young, 345–53. Berlin: De Gruyter, 2008.

Rigney, Ann. "Fiction as a Mediator in National Remembrance." In *Narrating the Nation: The Representation of National Narratives in Different Genres*, edited by Stefan Berger, Linas Eriksonas, and Andrew Mycock, 79–96. Oxford: Berghahn Books, 2009.

Rothberg, Michael. *Multidirectional Memory. Remembering the Holocaust in the Age of Decolonization*. Palo Alto: Stanford University Press, 2009.

Rothberg, Michael, and Neil Levi. "Memory Studies in a Moment of Danger: Fascism, Postfascism, and the Contemporary Political Imaginary." *Memory Studies* 11, no. 3 (2018): 355–67. https://doi.org/10.1177/1750698018771868.

Saldaña, Johnny. *Fundamentals of Qualitative Research*. Oxford: Oxford University Press, 2011.

Sanford, William E. "Government-Minority Dialogue in Austria: The Ethnic Advisory Councils." *International Journal on Group Rights* 3, no. 4 (1995): 261–82.

Sauer, Carl. "The Morphology of Landscape." *University of California Publications in Geography* 2, no. 2 (1925): 19–54.

Schein, Richard H. "Normative Dimensions of Landscape." In *Everyday America: Cultural Landscape Studies After J.B. Jackson*, edited by Chris Wilson and Paul Groth, 199–218. Berkeley: University of California Press, 2003.

Schein, Richard H. "A Methodological Framework for Interpreting Ordinary Landscapes: Lexington, Kentucky's Courthouse Square." *Geographical Review* 99, no. 3 (2009): 377–402. https://doi.org/10.1111/j.1931-0846.2009.tb00438.x.

Schein, Richard H. "Belonging through Land/Scape." *Environment and Planning A: Economy and Space* 41, no. 4 (April 2009): 811–26. https://doi.org/10.1068/a41125.

Schein, Richard H. "Cultural Landscapes." In *Research Methods in Geography*, edited by John Paul Jones III and Basil Gomez, 222–40. Chichester: Blackwell Publishing, 2010.

Schmutz, Wolfgang. "Wo die Republik beginnt und endet. Zum errinnerungspolitischen Rahmen für Vermittlung und Gestaltung an der KZ-Gedenkstätte Mauthausen." In *Erinnerungsorte in Bewegung. Zur*

Neugestaltung des Gedenkens an Orten nationalsozialistischer Verbrechen, edited by Daniela Allmeier, Inge Manka, Peter Mörtenböck, and Rudolf Scheuvens, 343–64. Bielefeld: Transcript, 2016.

Schneider, Peter. "Saving Konrad Latte." *New York Times Magazine*, 13 February 2000, 13, 52–7, 72–3, 90, 95.

Schoiswohl, Michael. "Austrian Measures for Victims of National Socialism – An Overview." *Austrian Review of International and European Law Online* 8, no. 1 (2005): 327–41.

Schwartz, Barry. *Abraham Lincoln and the Forge of National Memory*. Chicago: University of Chicago Press, 2000.

S.E. "Vorwort." In *Das Tagebuch des Thomas Olip. Wie ein im Käfig eingesperrter Vogel*, edited by Wilhelm Baum, 13–16. Vienna: Kitab, 2010.

Segal, Jose. *Art and Politics: Between Purity and Propaganda*. Amsterdam: Amsterdam University Press, 2016.

Shepherd, Ben. *Terror in the Balkans: German Armies and Partisan Warfare*. Cambridge: Harvard University Press, 2012.

Sierp, Aline. *History, Memory, and Trans-European Identity*. New York: Routledge, 2014.

Sima, Valentin. "Das Peršman-Massaker in der Erinnerungspolitik und seine justizielle Untersuchung." In *Widerstand gegen Faschismus und Nationalsozialismus im Alpen-Adria-Raum. Odpor proti fašizmu in nacizmu v alpsko-jadranskem prostoru*, edited by Briggte Entner, Valentin Sima, and Avguštin Malle, 117–27. Klagenfurt/Celovec and Vienna: Drava, 2011.

Sima, Valentin. "Die Vertreibung slowenischer Familien als Höhepunkt deutschnationaler Politik in Kärnten." In *Pregon koroskih Slovencev 1942-2002 = Die Vertreibung der Kärntner Slowenen 1942-2002*, edited by Avguštin Malle, 133–72. Klagenfurt/Celovec: Drava, 2002.

Sima, Valentin. "Gewalt und Widerstand 1941–1945." In *Die Kärntner Slovenen. 1900–2000. Bilanz des 20. Jahrhunderts*, edited by Andreas Moritsch, 263–80. Klagenfurt/Celovec: Hermagoras/Mohorjeva, 2000.

Snyder, Timothy. "European Mass Killing and European Commemoration." In *Remembrance, History, and Justice: Coming to Terms with Traumatic Pasts in Democratic Societies*, edited by Vladimir Tismaneanu and Bogdan C. Iacob, 23–44. Vienna: Central European University Press, 2015.

Sodaro, Amy. *Exhibiting Atrocity: Memorial Museums and the Politics of Past Violence*. New Brunswick: Rutgers University Press, 2018.

Spreicer, Jelena. "Geschichte Aus Dem Slowenischen Blickwinkel – Maja Haderlaps 'Engel Des Vergessens'." In *Narrative im (post)imperialen Kontext. Literarische Identitätsbildung als Potential im regionalen Spannungsfeld zwischen Habsburg und Hoher Pforte in Zentral-und Südosteuropa*, edited by Matthias Schmidt, Daniela Finzi, Milka Car, Wolfgang Müller-Funk, and Marijan Bobinac, 251–9. Tübingen: Narr Francke Attempto Verlag, 2015.

Stangl, Paul. "The Soviet War Memorial in Treptow, Berlin." *Geographical Review* 93, no. 2 (2003): 213–36.

Statistik Austria. *Volkszählung. Hauptergebnisse. Kärnten.* Vienna: Verlag Österreich, 2003.

Steger, Jožica Čeh. "Die zerstörte Dorfidylle an der österreichischslowenischen Grenze: Maja Haderlaps Engel des Vergessens." In *Imaginäre Dörfer: zur Wiederkehr des Dörflichen in Literatur, Film und Lebenswelt,* edited by Nell Werner and March Weiland, 339–56. Bielefeld: Transcript, 2014.

Stevens, Quentin, Karen A. Franck, and Ruth Fazakerley. "Counter-Monuments: The Anti-Monumental and the Dialogic." *The Journal of Architecture* 17, no. 6 (2012): 951–72. https://doi.org/10.1080/13602365.2012.746035.

Stump, R.W. "Toponymic Commemoration of National Figures: The Cases of Kennedy and King." *Names* 36 (1988): 203–16. https://doi.org/10.1179/nam.1988.36.3-4.203.

Sturken, Marita. "The Wall, the Screen, and the Image: The Vietnam Veterans Memorial." *Representations*, no. 35 (1991): 118–42. https://doi.org/10.2307/2928719.

Sturm, Marjan Borut, and Črtomir Zorec, eds. *Padlim za svobodo: pomniki protifašističnega boja na Koroškem = Den Gefallenen für die Freiheit: Gedenkstätten des antifaschistischen Kampfes in Kärnten.* Klagenfurt/Celovec: Drava, 1987.

Sturm-Schnabl, Katja. "Tito, mein Retter." In *Spurensuche. Erzählte Geschichte der Kärntner Slowenen,* edited by Dokumentationsarchiv des österreichischen Widerstandes, Klub Prežihov Voranc, Institut za proučevanje prostora Alpe-Jadran, 153–8.Vienna: Österrichischer Bundesverlag, 1990.

Suppan, Arnold. "Zur Lage der Deutschen in Slowenien zwischen 1918 und 1938. Demographie – Recht – Gesellschaft – Politik." In *Geschichte der Deutschen im Bereich des heutigen Slowenien 1848–1941. Zgodovina nemcev na območju današnje Slovenije 1848–1941,* edited by Helmut Rumpler and Arnold Suppan, 171–240. Vienna: Verlag für Geschichte und Politik, 1988.

Suppan, Arnold. "Kärnten und Slowenien: Die Geschichte einer schwierigen Nachbarschaft im 20. Jahrhundert." In*Kärnten und Slowenien – "Dickicht und Pfade,"* vol. 5 of *Kärnten und die Nationale Frage,* edited by Stefan Karner and Janez Stergar, 9–69. Klagenfurt/Celovec: Johannes Heyn and Hermagoras/Mohorjeva, 2005.

Suppan, Arnold. *The Imperialist Peace Order in Central Europe:Saint-German and Trianon, 1919–1920.* Vienna: Austrian Academy of Sciences, 2019.

Swanson, John C. "The Sopron Plebiscite of 1921: A Success Story." *East European Quarterly* 34, no. 1 (2000): 81–94.

Switzer, Catherine, and Sara McDowell. "Redrawing Cognitive Maps of Conflict: Lost Spaces and Forgetting in the Centre of Belfast." *Memory Studies* 2, no. 3 (2009): 337–53. https://doi.org/10.1177/1750698008337562.

Tamm, Marek. "In Search of Lost Time: Memory Politics in Estonia, 1991–2011." *Nationalities Papers* 41, no. 4 (2013): 651–74. http://doi.org/10.1080/00905992.2012.747504.

Teeb, Claudia. *The Politics of Repressed Guilt. The Tragedy of Austrian Silence.* Edinburgh: Edinburgh University Press, 2018.

Thaler, Peter. *The Ambivalence of Identity: The Austrian Experience of Nation-Building in a Modern Society.* West Lafayette: Purdue University Press, 2001.

Tiemann, Guido. "'Kärnten' = Austria, 'Koroška' = Yugoslavia? A Novel Perspective on the 1920 Carinthian Plebiscite." *Historical Social Research* 45, no. 4 (2020): 309–46. https://doi.org/10.12759/hsr.45.2020.4.309-346.

Till, Karen E. *The New Berlin: Memory, Politics, Place.* Minneapolis: University of Minnesota Press, 2005.

Todorov, Tzvetan. "The Uses and Abuses of Memory." *Common Knowledge* 5, no. 1 (1996): 6–26.

Tomasevich, Jozo. *War and Revolution in Yugoslavia, 1941–1945: Occupation and Collaboration.* Palo Alto: Stanford University Press, 2001.

Troha, Nevenka. "Slovenia. Occupation, Repression, Partisan Movement, Collaboration, and Civil War in Historical Research." *Südosteuropa* 65, no. 2 (2017): 334–63. https://doi.org/10.1515/soeu-2017-0021.

Trommler, Frank. "Austria Past, Austria Present: Stages of Scholarship in the American University." *Monatshefte* 111, no. 1 (2019): 1–18.

Uhl, Heidemarie. "Of Heroes and Victims: World War II in Austrian Memory." *Austrian History Yearbook* 42 (April 2011): 185–200. https://doi.org/10.1017/S0067237811000117.

Uhl, Heidemarie. "Culture, Politics, Palimpsest. These on Memory and Society." In *A European Memory?: Contested Histories and Politics of Remembrance*, edited by Małgorzata Pakier and Bo Stråth, 79–86. New York: Berghahn Books, 2012.

Uhl, Heidemarie. "From the Periphery to the Center of Memory: Holocaust Memorials in Vienna." *Dapim: Studies on the Holocaust* 30, no. 3 (2016): 221–42. https://doi.org/10.1080/23256249.2016.1257217.

Vedder, Ulrike. "Erblasten und Totengespräche. Zum Nachleben der Toten in Texten von Marlene Streeruwitz, Arno Geiger und Sibylle Lewitscharoff." In *Literatur im Krebsgang: Totenbeschwörung und memoria in der deutschsprachigen Literatur nach 1989*, edited by Arne de Winde and Anke Gilleir, 227–41. Amsterdam: Rodopi, 2008.

Vergès, Françoise. "A Museum Without Objects." In *The Postcolonial Museum: The Arts of Memory and the Pressure of History*, edited by Ian Chambers,

Alessandra de Angelis, Celeste Ianniciello, Mariangela Orabona, and Michaela Quadraro, 25–37. London: Routledge, 2017.

Virloget, Katja Hrobat, and Neža Čebron Lipovec. "Heroes we Love? Monuments to the National Liberation Movement in Istria Between Memories, Care, and Collective Silence." *Studia ethnologica Croatica* 29, no. 1 (2017): 45–71.

Wakounig, Metka. "Oj, mladost ti moja ali Slovenščina kdo bo tebe ljubil?" *Literatura* 24/251–2 (Summer 2012): 1–7.

Weinmann, Ute. "Die südslawische Frage und Jugoslawien. Grenzziehungen im süden Österreichs unter besonderer Berücksichtigung der Kärntenproblematik." In *Das werden der ersten Republik … Der Rest ist Österreich*, edited by Helmut Konrad and Wolfgang Maderthaner, 119–38. Vienna: Carl Gerolds Sohn, 2008.

Wertsch, James V. *Voices of Collective Remembering*. Cambridge: Cambridge University Press, 2002.

Widrich, Mechtild. "The Willed and the Unwilled Monument: Judenplatz Vienna and Riegl's Denkmalpflege." *Journal of the Society of Architectural Historians* 72, no. 3 (2013): 382–98. https://doi.org/10.1525/jsah.2013.72.3.382.

Widrich, Mechtild. "After the Counter-Monument: Commemoration in the Expanded Field." In *The Routledge Companion to Critical Approaches to Contemporary Architecture*, edited by Swati Chattopadhyay and Jeremy White, 57–67. New York: Routledge, 2019.

Wikimedia Commons Contributors. "File: Locator Map of Kärnten in Austria.png." *Wikimedia Commons, the Free Media Repository*, 1 March 2011. Accessed 4 September 2020. https://commons.wikimedia.org/w/index .php?title=File:K%C3%A4rnten_in_Austria.svg&oldid=454017102.

Williams, Maurice. "Another Final Solution: Friedrich Rainer, Carinthian Slovenes, and the Carinthian Question." *Slovene Studies* 19, nos. 1–2 (1997): 43–60. https://doi.org/10.7152/ssj.v19i1.14315.

Winkels, Hubert, ed. *Klagenfurter Texte. Die besten 2011. Die 25. Tage der deutschsprachigen Literatur in Klagenfurt*. Munich: Piper, 2011.

Winter, Jay. *Sites of Memory, Sites of Mourning: The Great War in European Cultural History*. Cambridge: Cambridge University Press, 2014.

Wulz, Janine, and Jonas Kolb. "Der Gedenkort Peršmanhof. Ein Stachel in der kärntner Erinnerungslandschaft." In *Friede, Freude, deutscher Eintopf. Rechte Mythen, NS-Verharmlosung und antifaschistischer Protest*, edited by Arbeitskreis gegen den Kärntner Konsens, 315–32. Vienna: Mandelbaum kritik & utopie, 2011.

Wüstenberg, Jenny. *Civil Society and Memory in Postwar Germany*. Cambridge: Cambridge University Press, 2017.

Wüstenberg, Jenny, and David Art. "Using the Past in the Nazi Successor States From 1945 to the Present." *The Annals of the American Academy of*

Political and Social Science 617 (2008): 72–87. https://doi.org/10.1177
/0002716207312762.

Wutti, Daniel. *Drei Familien, drei Generationen das Trauma des
Nationalsozialismus im Leben dreier Generationen von Kärntner SlowenInnen.*
Klagenfurt/Celovec: Drava, 2013.

Wutti, Daniel. "Identität, Gewalt und 'Brückenfunktionen.' Die Analyse
qualitativer Gruppeninterviews mit jungen SlowenInnen." In *Kärnten und
Slowenien: getrennte Wege – gemeinsame Zukunft. Koroška in Slovenija: Ločene
poti – skupna prihodnost Jugend zwischen Heimat, Nation und Europa. Mladi o
domovini, narodu in Evropi,* edited by Jürgen Pirker, 311–25. Baden-Baden:
Nomos, 2015.

Wutti, Daniel. "Between Self-Governance and Political Participation: The
Slovene Minority in Carinthia, Austria." *Razprave in gradivo: revija za
narodnostna vprašanja,* no. 78 (2017): 59–71.

Yellow Horse Brave Heart, Maria. "Historical Trauma Response Among
Natives and Its Relationship with Substance Abuse." *Journal of Psychoactive
Drugs* 35, no. 1 (2003): 7–13. https://doi.org/10.1080/02791072.2003.10399988.
Medline:12733753.

Young, James E. "The Biography of a Memorial Icon: Nathan Rapoport's
Warsaw Ghetto Monument." *Representations,* no. 26 (1989): 69–106.

Young, James E. "The Counter-Monument: Memory Against Itself in
Germany Today." *Critical Inquiry* 18, no. 2 (1992): 267–96.

Young, James E. *The Texture of Memory: Holocaust Memorials and Meanings.*
New Haven: Yale University Press, 1993.

Young, James E. "Berlin's Holocaust Memorial: A Report to the Bundestag
Committee on Media and Culture 3 March 1999." *German Politics & Society*
17, no. 3 (52) (1999a): 54–70.

Young, James E. "Memory and Counter-Memory." *Harvard Design Magazine* 9
(1999b). Accessed 4 September 2020. http://www.harvarddesignmagazine
.org/issues/9/memory-and-counter-memory.

Young, James E. "The Memorial's Arc: Between Berlin's *Denkmal* and New
York City's 9/11 Memorial." *Memory Studies* 9, no. 3 (2016): 325–31. https://
doi.org/10.1177/1750698016645266.

Young, Marilyn B. *The Vietnam Wars, 1943–1990.* New York, 1991.

Zadravec, Franc. "Die slowenische Gegenwartsliteratur." In *Die slowenische
Literatur in Kärnten. Ein Lexikon,* edited by the Verband slowenischer
Schriftsteller/innen, Übersetzer/innen und Publizist/inn/en in Österreich,
137–51. Klagenfurt/Celovec, Austria: Drava, 1991.

Zeyringer, Klaus. "Austrian Literature: A Concept." In *Shadows of the Past.
Austrian Literature of the Twentieth Century,* edited by Hans Schulte and
Gerald Chapple, 1–33. New York: Peter Lang, 2009.

Archival Material

United States Holocaust Memorial Museum Photo Archives. Photograph
Number 78594A. Courtesy of National Archives and Records
Administration, College Park, MD.

Interviews Conducted by Author

Blohberger, Gudrun. Interview by author. 15 January 2020. Mauthausen,
Austria.
Haderlap, Zdravko. Interview by author. 21 January 2020. Lepen/Lepena,
Austria.
Haider, Hans and Alexandra Schmidt. Interview by author. 22 January 2020.
Villach/Beljak, Austria.
Mohar, Andrej. Interview by author. 20 January 2020. Klagenfurt/Celovec,
Austria.

Index

German and European Studies

General Editor: James Retallack